ECO-COMPUTER

ECO-COMPUTER
THE IMPACT OF
GLOBAL INTELLIGENCE

GEOFF SIMONS
Managing Editor, The National Computing Centre, UK

John Wiley & Sons
Chichester ● New York ● Brisbane ● Toronto ● Singapore

Library of Congress Cataloging in Publication Data:

Simons, G. L. (Geoffrey Leslie), 1939–
  Eco-computer: the impact of global intelligence.

  Bibliography: p.
  Includes index.
  1. Computers and civilization. 2. Computer networks.
3. Artificial intelligence. I. Title.
QA76.9.C6S549   1987   303.4′834   87–8160
ISBN 0 471 91340 5

British Library Cataloguing in Publication Data:

Simons, G. L.
  Eco-computer: the impact of global intelligence.
  1. Computers and civilization
  I. Title
  303.4′834   QA76.9.C66
ISBN 0 471 91340 5

Typeset by Witwell Ltd, Liverpool
Print and Bound in Great Britain by Biddles Ltd, Guildford

This book is dedicated to:

> *Colette*
> *Cornel*
> *Corinne*
> *Conrad and Alison*
> *and*
> *Christine*

Contents

PART II GLOBAL ASPECTS

Thesis

Today we are witnessing the emergence of a global electronic intelligence, the *Eco-Computer*. This development, a product of the modern age, rests upon two key features of current technology:

1. *Increased computerization*—there is no field where the impact of computers is not being felt. It is increasingly recognized that computers can be applied in every area of activity, not solely those involving simple, easily defined steps (e.g. there are now computational aesthetics, computational art and computational linguistics). Computers will develop a growing presence in every part of the ecosphere.

2. *Growth of communications networks*—there is now an effective globalization of communications networks. These link computational capabilities of many different types, pooling artificial intelligence activities and stimulating their growth. We constantly hear of the 'Global Market' and the 'Global Factory'—both linked to global resource management and the creation of a unified global culture. There is also increased discussion in the literature of a global nervous system, a global brain, etc.

Computerization and communications are the two central pivots of the eco-computer, but other technological trends are also important in defining the character of the emerging global intelligence. In particular, a *growing spectrum of sensors* will increasingly enable the emerging eco-computer to monitor eco-events without human intervention. This development, allied to rapidly improving AI software, will enable the eco-computer to evolve an increasing autonomy in the world.

Reasons are given why it is unlikely that the eco-computer will evolve as a neatly unified system with a coherent purpose. Instead it will develop in a fractured way, with evident contradictions, dislocations and confusion. It seems likely that the eco-computer will develop a multiple personality—with scope also for other types of mental disorder. We invite speculation on the implications for a human race trapped in the interstices of a deranged global intelligence.

The emergence of the eco-computer, in circumstances of increased technological globalization, is presented as a deterministic process—largely without evaluative comment. None the less, there is material here for those who do not care for the idea, even though such souls will have no more impact than Samuel Butler's 'machine-tickling aphids', as the emergence of the eco-computer gains in pace and momentum. The option of the eco-computer being aborted by some global catastrophe would not be generally welcomed.

Today the limbs of the eco-computer are being set in place. Its emergence and subsequent evolution as a fully fledged, though dislocated, system must seem one of the most likely futures that we can envisage.

Introduction

We live in the Information Age.

We are told it everywhere. Information is now a vital resource, as important as oil or gold: it lubricates commerce, underpins government policy, sustains military strategy, etc. So information is no less than the 'strongest weapon' in a competitive world (J.G. Burch, *Data Management*, February 1986). No effective personal, corporate or national enterprise is possible without information. Those individuals or organizations who control information have power—over citizens, the state, world resources. And the gathering and control of information is inevitably linked to the development of computers.

Info is the strongest weapon

We live in the Computer Age.

All societies have been interested in computation, and some have devised artefacts to assist in the task. Computing machines have ranged from simple mechanical systems, with their roots in the mechanical engineering of the ancient world, to vast electronic configurations of the twentieth century, machines capable of performing a thousand million operations every second. And the development of computing equipment and the software to run it has been accompanied by a growing appreciation that physical and mental activities in biological systems (e.g. in Man) are computationally based, amenable to duplication in artefacts. So we witness the emergence of machines that mimic Man, that can perform such 'mental' tasks as decision making, artistic creation, knowledge generation and logical inference. To live in the Computer Age is also to live in the Age of Artificial Intelligence. By 1987 it was clear that AI had 'entered the mainstream' (Dwight Davis, *High Technology*, July 1986). Computation became both the literal and metaphorical measure of all perceived phenomena of the modern world.

We live in the Communications Age.

Information is useless unless it can be stored, accessed, obtained, transmitted, disseminated, communicated.... Information is potent only when it is available where it is required, for whatever purpose. So electronic networks have been developed to link offices, factories, governments—straddling the globe. Today computing, communications and other linked technologies have converged to define IT—information technology, a central shaping force in modern society. But information can only be analysed and communicated if it is first gathered—by human beings or automatic systems. Increasingly there are signs that the crucial initial task of data collection will be carried out by sensitive instruments designed (often with computer assistance) to monitor environmental phenomena and environmental change. . . .

We live in the Sensor Age.

Sensors allow linked computer complexes to work effectively without human intervention. Computational activity can exploit sensor-supplied data: it will become increasingly unnecessary for human beings to spoonfeed computers with their daily bread. The gathering of environmental data will become an automatic process, facilitated by sensors of many different types in all sectors of the ecosphere. Glance at any new patents listing for sensors (e.g. in *Sensor Trends International,* October 1986). We are immediately struck by the proliferation of sensor types—chemical, displacement/position/proximity, flow, magnetic, optical/imaging, pressure, telemetry, temperature, etc. We learn that the Warren Spring Laboratory in the UK is building a sensor database—to hold around 30 000 items; and that sensors are being planted in the oceans (e.g. microphones to detect Soviet submarines), in aircraft, on ships, in artificial satellites. Now there are sensors to detect 'see-through' objects, human bodies, clouds, a growing range of environmental chemicals. Tony Sacks (*New Scientist*, 23 October 1986) describes intelligent fire detectors; and the Japanese patent about a dozen new sensor-linked concepts every day. Sensors will prove to be one area of development granting computer-based systems greater degrees of autonomy. And this circumstance will come to have a worldwide significance.

We live in the Global Age.

Modern 'globalism' is signalled in many ways. The ecologists have advertised the unity of the ecosphere, the crucial interdependence of all ecological processes. The essential 'oneness' of the world has been underlined by the worsening pollution levels in general, phenomena such as Chernobyl in particular. Military ambitions—as with the SDI ('Star Wars') project—take on a global dimension, though sceptically viewed by many politicians and academics (by October 1986 more than 500 UK scientists had signed an anti-SDI pledge, with 6000 scientists in the US having signed a similar declaration). Globalism is also signalled in clear commercial terms. The 'Big Bang' in the City of London, allied to other developments (e.g. enhanced automation) in trading practices, has advertised the phenomenon of the Global Marketplace. Multinational corporations, adept at global resource management, compete to crowd out competitors, even other corporate giants with a global presence. We also live in the Age of the Corporate Wars. And increasingly all countries, whatever their ideologies, are forced to cooperate in the Global Economy. So the Soviet Union struggles to join GATT, already a worldwide economic organization (D.V. Smyslov, of the USSR Academy of Sciences, declares: 'the time has come when the socialist countries can no longer tolerate a situation in which they are excluded from the restructuring of the international monetary mechanisms which they are increasingly forced to use'). So there is one ecosphere, one biosphere, a Global Marketplace, a Global Factory. The global community has been progressively shrunk by technology—by developments in transport, communications and other fields. The Global Age will see the emergence of the worldwide eco-computer, an intelligent electronic matrix.

The eco-computer will emerge as the fruit of a deterministic process. It will be brought about by the convergence of many disparate but linked technologies: in particular, by the convergence of computing, communications and sensor-based artefacts. The emergence of the eco-computer will be accompanied by a progressive exclusion of human beings from important decision-making loops, by a progressive transfer of computational activity from human beings to machines. As the various links in the eco-computer are made, there will be dispute and controversy (as there is today with 'launch-on-warning' systems and other features of SDI-type military configurations); but it seems likely that dispute will delay rather than prevent the emergence of the eco-computer. Every day more of the struts are put in place, more connections are made, new options envisaged. The worldwide electronic matrix is growing, expanding, creeping over the planet with an inexorable deliberation. Within decades a discernible eco-computer will be set in place; within centuries there will be few, if any, eco-processes (i.e. activities within the ecosphere) that the global eco-computer will not monitor, analyse and regulate—after a fashion. We will find that this is no utopian dream.

What follows is an outline of the factors that will shape the emergence of the global computer. It will not be an easy birth: there will be social dislocations, wars (e.g. initiated by the US to protect market patterns, as in Nicaragua), unemployment, famine, pollution-induced disease, etc. Perhaps the eco-computer will only magnify the problems that beset the human race. We can speculate, but the aim of the present book is to signpost a dominant global trend, not to urge political strategies, social programmes or personal altruistic initiatives. It seems likely that the eco-computer will evolve as an increasingly autonomous global intelligence, a vast configuration of linked computing nodes able to gather data and perform whatever computations are appropriate to particular purposes. To a degree, human beings will shape this evolutionary development, but it also seems likely that their shaping influence will progressively diminish: it is already clear that human actors on the stage—in politics, administration, military planning, finance, etc.—are increasingly computer led. This is a trend that will continue in the future, and that will thereby affect the character of the emerging electronic matrix. The shape of the emerging eco-computer will increasingly be influenced by technological factors, less and less by independent human initiative.

ccm magnifies all our probs.

PART I

CONVERGENCE

1 From Sums to Cybernetics

Preamble

A history of computation is almost a history of civilization. No human advance has been accomplished without appropriate attention to number, in some form and at some level. Sums, nicely framed and fruitfully applied, have lubricated the ascent of man.

The logistics of Alexander, the building of the temples on the Acropolis, the war machines of Archimedes, the Chinese records carried on silk, the medieval tallies in agriculture and commerce, the explosive technology of the modern age—all have demanded fine attention to number, the ubiquitous discipline of accurate quantification. And even accomplishments not obviously resting on calculation have been successfully analysed in computational terms—so a modern computer can investigate the authorship of the biblical epistles, the music of Bach, the fabric of harmony and assonance, the framing of the creative enterprise.

This chapter advertises computation as one of the essential convergent disciplines that herald the birth of the eco-computer. There is no grand conspiracy or master plan, as far as we know, to build a world computer, a global artificial intelligence that will monitor events and take a controlling interest. There is conscious human endeavour to build global networks of various sorts, but no ambition to devise the all-pervasive eco-computer that is outlined in the present book. The global electronic matrix suggested here will emerge in other ways.

The dynamic that will yield the eco-computer has a blind and unconscious energy—an evident paradox since the emergence of the global intelligence depends upon the conscious activities of human beings. But few take account of the broader picture, the eco-computing end that is being approached: we busy ourselves in local affairs, designing this or that facility, commissioning this or that system, closing this or that commercial deal. Ant-like, we focus on immediate matters, concerned with parochial responsibilities, oblivious to the overall development that we are helping to sustain.

The aim in this chapter is to chart briefly some landmarks in the development of computation, to indicate the flavour of an

3

accelerating evolution. At once we notice particular trends. There is, for example, a convergence of various elements (mathematics, logic, cognition, information processing, etc.) that, if not originally thought to be *entirely* distinct phenomena, are now being found to have unexpected family connections. And in all this we are finding that computation is ubiquitous—as a manifest or underlying mechanism. So computation necessarily underwrites all practical activity in the world, but also phenomena once thought unconnected with number. So we are learning to search for the computational aspects of learning and perception: even emotion—and all the associated paraphernalia of ethics and aesthetics—is increasingly being seen as only possible within a computational matrix. There are now a computational aesthetics, a computational linguistics, a computational creativity, etc.

Another element, highly significant (perhaps alarming) is the progressive transfer of computational activity from the natural (i.e. biological species, mainly Man) to the artificial (i.e. machines). As the artificial electronic matrix evolves towards the fully fledged eco-computer, this progressive transfer of deliberate computation has profound implications for the status of *Homo sapiens*. In this global evolutionary progress we can see human beings pushed increasingly towards the margins of both mental and physical activity: people will become nothing more than Samuel Butler's 'machine-tickling aphids'.

The computational competence of any society has far-reaching cultural implications. How is human self-image affected by the awareness that everything—including every thought, wish and decision—can be quantified and computed, and what are the implications of such a unified global culture? Computation, as mathematics, has often inspired lofty thoughts far removed from such mundane matters as simple sums, tallies and measurements. It has often stimulated mystical or metaphysical speculation (e.g. indelibly in Pythagoras, spasmodically in Bertrand Russell), and has sometimes been assigned a supreme (even divine) significance. At a more realistic level it is easy to see that the fabric of the modern world could never have evolved without computation—and it will prove to be one of the crucial lineaments of the eco-computer.

Beginnings

The numbering systems of primitive societies were necessarily simple, by modern standards, but they still had to meet practical requirements. There was always a pressing need to assess wealth (by counting livestock or other items), to define appropriate dowries in complicated kinship systems, and to estimate the military potential of an adversary. Similarly the needs of agriculture would require a grasp of geometry (for irrigation, drainage, etc.) and an appreciation of the yearly cycle. Such requirements would quickly stimulate the creation of systems of quantification—though we read of simple tribes that used only three numbers ('one', 'two' and 'many'), and the invention of *nought* (as both concept and symbol) appears to have represented a major advance in computational theory.

Here we can mention the early mathematical beginnings, the emergence of theoretical logic, and the invention of simple mechanical devices—the effective heralds of modern electronic computers. Modern computing itself represents a fruitful convergence of several disparate elements.

We may assume that certain non-human animals were able to count before man (see, for example, Koehler, 1956); and we may deem the earliest members of *Homo sapiens* to have possessed at least a rudimentary ability to handle numerical quantities. Babylonian clay tablets carry information about how numbers can be manipulated, as do the later papyri of the Egyptians and the Greeks (Smith and Ginsburg, 1956). The Senkereb Tablet, found near Babylon and dated to around 2000 BC, is an aid to computation using cuneiform numbers laid out in rows and columns. This number system was organized to the base 60—in contrast to the decimal of most modern calculation and the binary of electronic digital computers. The Babylonians, prepared to count on their arms as well as their fingers, also developed a base-12 numbering system, still used today in telling the time and buying eggs. and the Mayans, content to go shoeless in sunny Mexico, were quite prepared to count toes as well as fingers—and so to develop a base-20 ('vigesimal') number system. So Mayan calendars carry 20 different digits. One observer, Reid (1985), has suggested that since ET clearly has eight fingers the inhabitants of ET's planet will obviously use octal notation.

Many early societies developed systems of numbering to help chart astronomical events, to assist in the compilation of effective calendars. The Babylonians, for example, were interested in astronomy—and also in such practical subjects as mining and metallurgy. The Babylonian scholars were among the first to use a 'positional' strategy to aid arithmetic calculation: cuneiform texts have sample problems set out as they might be in a modern school book. But Babylonian numbering did not avoid ambiguity. It was necessary to know the context of a cuneiform statement, before it could be judged whether (for example) a 2 or a 20 was intended.

The Babylonian Table Texts, as with the Senkereb Tablet, were used to solve a variety of problems: they were used for multiplication and division, for squares and cubes, and for various geometrical functions. Early Babylonian calculations lacked a symbol for zero, though it is found in later numbering sysems and it is usually the Babylonians who are credited with its invention. And the Babylonian mathematicians served both the living and the dead: as well as helping to maintain accurate tallies of granaries and livestock they also helped to organize the provisioning of the corpses laid up in the tombs, this latter to aid the journeys of the dead into the underworld (maps were painted on the insides of the coffins for the same purpose). There is some evidence that the theory attributed to Pythagoras was known to the Babylonians more than a thousand years before, though they showed few signs of the generalized speculation that was to characterize Greek thought.

The Egyptians, in similar fashion, achieved mathematical advances that were to influence the cultures that followed. Particular papyri deal with specific disciplines (medicine, architecture, etc.): the Ahmes Mathematical Papyrus, dating to around 2000 BC, is now part of the Rhind collection in the British Museum. The Babylonian 'positional' strategy was unknown in Egypt and extra symbols had to be invented to represent the larger numbers, a clumby device that must have limited the scope of computation. At the same time the building of the pyramids required a specialist knowledge of geometry and trigonometry: reference has been made to ways of reckoning slopes and the volume of a truncated pyramid. The hidden chambers in the pyramids, enclosures that are still being discovered, show a skill with numerical practicalities that baffled many of the early researchers. Winter (1952), for example, judged the Babylonian to be a most superior culture—partly because of their language and religion, and partly because of their enduring mathematical influence. The Egyptians had an undoubted impact but it was the Babylonians who largely influenced, for example, later Hindu and Hebrew geometry.

Elsewhere cultures flowered without the benefit of Babylonian or Egyptian influence. China, for instance, developed numbering conventions in isolation from the arithmetical influence of other cultures: as with the Babylonians and the Egyptians there were many practical requirements. Tallies had to be kept for military, agricultural and other purposes; and calendar making was an obvious achievement in the Orient. But by most reckonings the golden age of Chinese mathematics had to wait until the twelfth and thirteenth centuries AD, by which time the colossal impact of Greece and Rome had shaped the cultural fabric of the Western world.

It was known that Greek science was influenced by Egypt, and that scientists in Alexander's army made contact with Hindu sages. Hindu mathematical accomplishments are recorded in the Sulva-sutras (dated to between 400 and 200 BC), intended to provide practical assistance in the construction of altars and other religious artefacts. For example, there are Hindu formulae whereby a circle could be converted into a square of the same area, and vice versa. The Hindu sutras are full of empirical instances but again there is little evidence of the power to generalize, a supreme element in Greek thought.

This facility enabled Greeks to speculate freely in many different fields. Speculative philosophy was largely a Greek invention, a free-ranging intellectual quest which helped to keep inquiry alive through the many centuries during which Christianity lay a shadow across the European mind.

The multifaceted Greek impact has features that are often ignored in the modern secular age. It is interesting, for example, that in the Greek mind maths and mysticism were intimately linked, a curious circumstance that is well illustrated by the life of Pythagoras—'a combination of Einstein and Mrs Eddy' (Bertrand Russell). As well as being forever associated with geometry, Pythagoras was a leading light in what may be judged a rather eccentric Greek religion (involving such precepts as the wisdom of avoiding beans, not picking up what has fallen and avoiding highways). It is an easy matter to see the origins of the Pythagorean cult in the earlier taboo injunctions of the ancient world, but what is remarkable is that such notions should have been fused with a relatively sophisticated mathematical philosophy.

In the Pythagorean spirit, Plutarch later declared that the function of geometry 'is to draw us away from the sensible and the perishable to the intelligible and the eternal' and the reason was plain to see. Was it not obvious that 'the contemplation of the eternal is the end of philosophy, as the contemplation of the mysteries is the end of religion'? So as well as developing geometry and the theory of numbers, the Pythagoreans were keen to encourage people to avoid stirring the fire with an iron and to remove the impress of the body from a recently used bed!

Euclid's *Elements* is an outgrowth of the Pythagorean tradition in geometry—but this venerable text does little to convey the mystical attitude to the universe with which the Pythagorean philosophy was associated. A fifth-century Pythagorean conveys something of this attitude. Thus Philolaus was able to proclaim that 'the power that resides in the decad ... is great, all-powerful, all-sufficing, the first principle and the guide in life of Gods, of Heaven, of Men'. What he termed *the nature of number* was to serve as a standard of guidance and instruction in every doubt and difficulty: 'You can observe the power of number exercising itself not only in the affairs of demons and of gods, but in all the acts and the thoughts of men, in all handicrafts and in music.' In this way, the mathematical philosophy was expected not only to facilitate practical endeavour but also to provide an ethical framework and a metaphysical interpretation of the universe. Number produced harmony, precious and all-pervasive. And in the Pythagorean mind this was particularly significant in music and cosmology. Number defined such matters, and also helped to constitute the stuff of reality: number was seen to be *matter* as well as *form*. (It is interesting to reflect on how the Pythagorean belief in the ubiquity of number is mirrored in the computer-based epistemologies of the modern world.)

Logic, the science of reasoning, is often seen as another unique achievement of the Greek mind. The development of Greek logic is normally associated with the name of Aristotle: he and his successors created an attitude to reasoning that influenced the later scholastics, became a dogma, and had to be overthrown—to a degree—before further progress could be made. Aristotelian logic reigned for two thousand years: and it is interesting to remember that the propositional forms proposed by Aristotle closely resemble the 'production rules' embodied in the coding of modern expert systems, types of computer software designed to reason in specialist areas.

We scarcely need to delay on the Aristotelian contribution to logic. The characteristic *syllogism* ('All men are mortal; Socrates is a man; therefore Socrates is mortal') is well known. Aristotle succeeded in finding all the valid forms of the syllogism, but was wrong to assume that all valid forms of inference could be analysed into propositions of a particular form. But errors in Aristotle were perpetuated in a superstitious orthodoxy. In the fourteenth-century statutes of Oxford University we find the insistent rule: 'Bachelors and Masters of Arts who do not follow Aristotle's philosophy are subject to a fine of 5s for each point of divergence...'. What is perhaps more interesting is that the Greeks did not have a monopoly of logical insight....

The rules of valid inference espoused by Aristotle and his followers were also being explored by sages in other cultures. We can trace the evolution of the syllogism to the thought of ancient India! Thus in the Indian Nyaya School, with origins at least as ancient as early Greek thought, we find close attention to many logical and epistemological topics. In particular, two fields—Tarkashastra and Pramanashastra—dealt with logic, the working of the mind, and epistemology. Here the anuma branch of knowledge was concerned with *inference*, defined as that form of cognition that presupposes some other cognition. Sharma (1960) explains the *five* terms in the typical Nyaya syllogism: two of the terms are formally redundant but introduce subtleties unknown in the more straightforward *three*-term Aristotelean equivalent. In a sense Nyaya is more ambitious, trying to accommodate psychological, as well as purely formal, concerns. In this species of Indian logic, inference is divided into *svartha* (for oneself) and *parartha* (for others): the former is seen to be an essentially psychological process, hinting perhaps at a subjective route to truth, or at least conviction ('the heart has its reasons...'). The parartha part is concerned with the formal syllogism, the objective demonstration. Fully viewed, inference 'is neither from the universal to the particular nor from the particular to the universal, but from the particular to the particular through the universal' (Sharma, 1960).

Again we do not need to pursue such matters in any detail. For our purposes what is significant is the parallel evolution of modes of logical inquiry, the independent birth of logic in different cultures. It has been suggested that Nyaya inference was influenced by Greek thought, but it is possible to trace Indian logic to a time before Aristotle: when the two logical traditions eventually made contact they were both well established—but little further progress was made until the nineteenth-century Europeans developed new symbolic methods. Progress *was* made in mathematical technique—in Europe, China and elsewhere—but logic began to flower in the age of the first complex mechanical calculators (the Babbage machines), the true heralds of the electronic computers of the modern era. Before glancing at the first mechanical calculators, it is worth drawing attention to another mathematical thread—that of medieval China.

In the thirteenth century Ch'in Chiu-shao worked on the theory of equations; Li Chih derived trigonometrical measurements; and Kuo Shou-Ching (1231–1316) brought Muslim spherical geometry into China and devised a new calendar for Kublai Khan. Other Chinese scholars were renowned for work on arithmetical progressions, linear and quadratic equations, decimal fractions and various forms of algebraic series. Ch'in Chiu-shao used read and black ink to denote positive and negative quantities (the converse of the later Western convention—'in the red', 'in the black'); Li Chih made diagonal lines to denote negative quantities. And Chinese mathematical progress was paralleled by work in Greece, Rome, India and elsewhere. For example, the Hindu mathematician Bramagupta recorded his accomplishments in the *Bramasphuta-siddhanta*, another astronomical treatise, written in AD 628. He worked with cyclic quadrilaterals and devised a number of geometric theorems. And Bhaskara's treatise *Siddhanta-siromani* (*c.* 1150) is seen as a useful summary of Hindu mathematical thought of the medieval period. Here again, as with Pythagoras, we find that intellectual inquiry is not divorced from religious assumption. Thus the *Lilavati* of Bhaskara, a section of the celebrated treatise, begins with an invocation to the god Ganesa:

Having bowed to the deity, whose head is like an elephant's; whose feet are adorned by gods; who, when called to mind, relieves his votaries from embarrassment; and bestows happiness on his worshippers; I propound this easy process of computation, delightful by its elegance, perspicuous with words concise, soft and correct, and pleasing to the learned.

Here again is the mix of abstract theorizing and pious commitment, very different from the mathematical speculation of the modern secular world. At the same time the abstract thought of earlier times was not divorced from matters of practical engineering.

We have already noticed the early interests in agriculture, mining, metallurgy and military affairs—the necessary preoccupations of enduring communities. And there was also an interest in various types of mechanical devices that laid the basis for the first artificial calculators. The myths that surrounded Hephaestus, Greek god of the mechanical arts, reflected the mechanical technology of the day; and the inventions of such men as the Greek Archimedes and the Alexandrian Hero, often depending as they did on wheels, cogs, levers and the like, prepared the way for the machines that would be capable of computation.

The Spanish theologian Ramon Lull, working in the thirteenth century, is said to have used a mechanical device ('a kind of primitive logic machine'—Gardner, 1958) to facilitate the operation of a logic system. This may be judged the first attempt to use a machine to achieve complicated calculations. Lull himself devised complex tables and diagrams that were intended to guide the seeker after truth—truth about the cosmos, truth about God. About the tables, Étienne Gilson (1955) observed: 'we come up against the worst difficulties, and one cannot help wondering whether Lull himself was ever able to use them'. Other inventors of mechanical calculators were to follow in later centuries.

Wilhelm Schickard (1592–1635) is credited with the creation of a mechanical calculator (see, for example, the account in Flatt, 1963). In one listing (Mills, 1983), machines for the performance of numerical calculation can be conveniently divided into four groups: devices for plain addition, such as the machine created by Blaise Pascal in 1642; machines for addition but with modifications to allow for multiplication, introduced by Leibniz in 1671; devices that could accomplish true multiplication, as achieved in the machines of Léon Bollés in 1888; difference machines, such as those devised by Johann Helfrich von Muller in 1786 and Charles Babbage in 1822 and later years. Already some of the early mechanical contraptions had aroused alarm in observers. People had been terrified by automata that resembled human beings, and Pascal's sister is supposed to have remarked that Pascal's 'mind had somehow been taken over by the machine'—shades of the manifest technophobia that was to afflict the modern world. Perrier (1963) describes the work of Pascal and records his sister's trepidation.

It is generally assumed—in computer lore—that Charles Babbage was the chief herald of the modern computer age. His various mechanical devices, though rarely able to work with anything approaching success, were theoretically far beyond any earlier or contemporary devices. With the help of Ada Lovelace he prepared the ground for the emergence of the global eco-computer that even he could never have imagined.

When Charles Babbage died in 1871, his youngest son Henry tried to cope with the fearsome legacy of the mechanical computational 'engines'; and in 1879 a committee was set up to report on how the work might be continued, though nothing useful was to emerge. By 1890, then in retirement, Henry Babbage managed to construct a mechanical processor that made tables of multiples of *pi*, but the machine (now in London Science Museum with various items that Charles had built) kept breaking down. At about the same time, various documents accumulated by Charles were published as *Babbage's Calculating Engines*, and this source text influenced later workers. The Spanish cybernetician Leonardo Torres y Quevedo worked, in the early 1900s, on mechanical automata that owed much to Babbage; Hollerith followed the Babbage example of using punched cards to provide data for the mechanical operating systems; and it has been suggested that the modern 'Turing machine', devised by the english mathematician Alan Turing, was at least partly inspired by the work of Charles Babbage (see Hyman, 1982). Babbage, his co-workers and followers set the scene for the modern age, the time in which the foundations of the eco-computer would be laid.

This section has glanced at a few mathematical innovations, a few elements of early logic, and a few efforts to devise mechanical systems that could carry out various sorts of calculations. We have mentioned the mystical and religious aspects that, in earlier societies, often accompanied the mathematical enterprise. In the modern age, the religious concomitants are rarely evident, but the rest remains. The modern digital computer is a convergent mix of mathematics, logic and engineering: the engineering has evolved far beyond simple mechanics (electronics was the midwife of the modern computer). We will see that when the other convergent elements are taken into account—such elements as telecommunications and sensor technology—the time is ripe for the genesis of the eco-computer. Before glancing at the recent evolution of electronic computers, it is worth highlighting some of the theoretical insights of the modern age, the age that began in the time of Babbage and continues to the present. When the modern age, so defined, began, it knew nothing of electronics; today it is easy to see how electronics has shaped the modern world.

The Modern Age

After Aristotle there was little progress in logic until the nineteenth century. It was largely the work of George Boole, born in East Anglia in 1815, that began the development of the formal systems that would expand the philosophy of logic and assist the design of electronic computers in the mid-1900s and beyond. Boole became professor of mathematics in Cork in 1849, having published his *Mathematical Analysis of Logic* two years before. His main accomplishment was to introduce a special algebra that could quickly demonstrate the theory of the syllogism over which Aristotle had laboured so arduously. Moreover, the new symbolic approach was able to reveal errors in Aristotle that had remained undetected by scholars for two thousand years. Other logicians—e.g. Schroder in the United States—began to develop the new Boolean algebra for particular purposes. And parallel developments in mathematics were helping to extend the scope of formal systems.

From the middle of the nineteenth century to the first two decades of the twentieth, advances were made by such men as Cantor, De Morgan, Peirce, Frege, Dedekind, Peano, Whitehead and Russell (an introduction to some of this work is given in Kilmister, 1967; with a full treatment offered in Kneale and Kneale, 1962). Much of this work is highly theoretical, and only a portion of it is directly relevant to the emergence of electronic computers. But what was of central importance was the atmosphere that was being cultivated. Russell had wondered how number could hold sway over the flux: it was becoming clear, as the twentieth century advanced, that systematic disciplines could no longer eschew mathematics; it was obvious that careful quantification, manipulated in some formal system, was essential to any subject domain hoping to make progress.

There was debate about the scope of the grand formal systems. For example, Hilbert and his school in Zurich, in part influenced by the aim of *Principia Mathematica* (published in the early part of the twentieth century by Russell and Whitehead), tried to develop formal axioms that were both *consistent* and *complete*. It was around 1930 that the Hilbert effort was seen to fail. It was the mathematician Gödel who established an *incompleteness* theorem. It was shown that a formal system must contain statements that could not be proved with the axioms of the system; and Gödel even managed to show that among the unprovable statements was one declaring that the formalism was consistent. This development had many consequences—some of them necessarily formal, others (hopefully) metaphysical or religious.

It became clear that the completeness of a formal system could only be demonstrated when the system could be set in a larger system (a 'parent' logic), but then, of course, the same problem applied to the larger system, but in a magnified form. It could not be known that the larger systems was consistent—so what did this say about the consistency of the smaller system within it? This seeming setback to logical ambition heartened those traditionalists who were growing anxious at the growing claims of the logicians. Gödel has been frequently cited to suggest, in recent decades, that computers will never develop *true* mental capabilities since formal systems are limited—as if it were axiomatic that human thought processes were consistent and that the human mind was not a formal system. In particular, there were many mathematicians, well aware of Gödel, who had no doubt that machines would emerge that would be able to calculate anything that could be calculated. Some went further: Alan Turing, for example, was quite prepared to declare that 'thinking machines' would be quite uncontroversial artefacts before many decades had passed. And John von Neumann, important in game theory and other matters, was quite able to speculate on the possibility of self-reproducing automata, so stimulating what was to be an increasingly anthropomorphic element in some areas of computer science.

Von Neumann was born in 1903 in Budapest, was soon recognized as a mathematical prodigy and spent much of his early life moving from one European university to another. When he was eighteen he published the first of his many scholarly monographs. With Einstein he later became one of the first fellows at the Princeton Institute for Advanced Study, and he was to contribute in many different fields—pure and applied mathematics, chemical engineering, game theory, quantum physics, economics, nuclear weapons and electronic computers. When von Neumann was working on nuclear bombs he wondered how to cope with the vast number of necessary mathematical computations. Soon after, he became acquainted with the first-generation ENIAC computer in Philadelphia, a device that could perform masses of computation at unprecedented speed—and before long von Neumann was applying mathematics to the design of electronic computers. Like Norbert Wiener—who advertised the cybernetic similarities of machines and biological systems—von Neumann quickly became interested in the similarities between the new computing machines and the human brain (his last book, *The Computer and the Brain*, was published posthumously in 1958).

Alan Turing was born in London in 1912: he showed little promise at school, though later achieved a PhD at Cambridge. Tackling problems posed by Hilbert, he quickly became intrigued by the possibility of designing a machine that could perform any computation, providing that adequate instructions were provided. In this way, the notion of the 'Turing machine', at that time a purely theoretical concept, was born. The idea influenced many computer pioneers, including von Neumann, whom Turing met at Princeton in the mid-1930s. During the Second World War, Turing helped to crack the German 'Enigma' military code, and for the first time it was found that the Turing machine could have practical real-life applications.

Some of Turing's early inspiration came from the simple typewriter. He was aware that there was a sense in which the typewriter was programmed to provide a particular response in particular circumstances: in fact that response depended upon the current *configuration* of the machine (e.g. was it operating in upper or lower case?), and also the variable position on the printing line was crucial. Using such basic considerations, Turing developed the notion of machines that were, in effect, *super*typewriters. To simplify matters, the paper became a tape marked off into unit squares that could each carry a symbol. The tape would be able to move right or left to allow the machine to scan the symbols and to respond accordingly. Such thoughts quickly led Turing to the idea of *automatic* machines that would be capable of computational behaviour without human intervention. The distinguished Cambridge mathematician G.H. Hardy had already speculated on the idea of a 'miraculous machine'—a mechanical system that could work on problems posed by Hilbert (e.g. indicating whether particular mathematical assertions were provable or not).

In fact Turing came to believe that there could be no 'miraculous machine' that could solve all mathematical problems, but became convinced that a *universal* machine could be devised that could take over the work of any particular machine—and this included the human computer. A Turing machine, of sufficient complexity, able to interpret the symbols on its tape, would be able to duplicate human mental activity. The possibility of an electronic brain was now on the agenda.

Another pioneer, Claude E. Shannon, produced a master's thesis in 1937 which demonstrated how computer circuits, based on switching elements, could be designed; and in the immediate post-war years he began research into electronic communications. This led to the new science of 'information theory'—which had implications for computing, communications, linguistics, sociology, economics and many other fields. The Shannon monograph, *Programming a Computer for Playing Chess*, was to intrigue von Neumann, Turing and many other computer scientists: he realized, with von Neumann and others, that game theory was relevant to many real-world situations (not least, the waging of war).

Shannon, in turn, was influenced by a text on Boolean algebra: here was a way of organizing binary (on/off) switches to implement logical relations. The careful logical expressions stimulated by the work of George Boole served as clear signposts for wiring electrical circuits to perform logical (and arithmetical) tasks. Shannon declared: 'It is possible to perform complex mathematical operations by means of relay circuits. Numbers may be represented by the positions of relays and stepping switches, and interconnections between sets of relays can be made to represent various mathematical operations.' He also demonstrated what was fundamental for the newly emerging computer science—how the simple logical operations of *and* and *or* could be implemented by arrangements of relays for the addition of two binary numbers. Such insights defined the character of all digital computers in the years that followed. Today the electromagnetic relays have been supplanted by integrated circuits using silicon, gallium arsenide and other materials, but the basic logic remains—the electronic computer operates by the achieving a rapid rate of electronic switching to accomplish the required logical and arithmetic results.

Thus progress in various fields—switching theory, information science, relay technology, computation, communications, electrical engineering, etc.—had prepared the ground for the first high-speed computers. Mechanical systems, slow and prone to failure, had already shown that artefacts could perform computational operations: the mechanical systems of Babbage had already incorporated the fundamental idea of the stored program (and Babbage's mechanical data-processing 'mill' gave a name to the electronic processors that were to emerge in the mid-1900s). The scene was set for rapid evolution—from mechanical calculators to high-speed electronic computers, via various electrical and electromechanical systems.

Computers

By the 1930s various types of calculating machines were in common use. Most were mechanical devices, about the size of an old typewriter, that could add, subtract, multiply and divide; a family of electromechanical machines used punched cards to carry out a range of sorting and tabulating tasks (these were based on the early work of Hollerith and Powers); and the specialized differential analysers solved equations for particular purposes. Companies were being established or developed to exploit the new interest in machine-aided computation for business and other forms of enterprise. For example, the Scientific Computing Service Ltd was set up in London in 1937 to provide mathematical and astronomical tables (here clerks—dubbed 'human computers'—used electromechanical calculators and punched-card equipment); IBM was already an important force in the US business community; and work began in the 1930s on the electromechanical Zuse equation solvers (the Zuse AG company was founded in 1950 to continue development of the binary digital devices).

We have seen that advances in computing were stimulated by the war effort in the 1940s. One requirement was to crack the German codes used for message transmission (the Germans used two classes of machines for coding purposes—the Enigma series and the Geheimschreiber system). Turing, Newman, Flowers and others developed various code-cracking devices, one of which was the COLOSSUS computer, the first large-scale use of thermionic valves (vacuum tubes) configured to perform digital calculations. The 1500 thermionic valves, a great number for that time, were able to achieve arithmetic operations (using binary), logical operations, counting and digital comparisons. The message to be deciphered was carried on a loop of punched paper tape and fed into an optical reader, with output achieved via an electric typewriter. A later COLOSSUS version, the Mark II, carried 2500 thermionic valves configured in a computer 'architecture' that would influence all later models. During the same period, John von Neumann was building on the early ENIAC work at Princeton University: one significant result was the EDVAC report, one of the first systematic proposals for a stored-program computer. A year later, in 1946, Turing proposed the stored-program Automatic Computing Engine (ACE); and soon a team led by Maurice Wilkes at Cambridge University was developing EDSAC (Electronic Delay Storage Automatic Calculator), a digital computing system that contained around 3000 thermionic valves. This 'first-generation' computer first operated successfully in May 1949, and offered an effective computing service from 1950 to 1958.

These early computing systems—COLOSSUS, ENIAC, EDVAC, ACE, EDSAC, etc.—laid the basis for rapid developments in computation theory and the associated practical technologies. The Manchester Mark I—also known as MADM (Manchester Automatic Digital Machine) and MUC (Manchester University Computer)—managed a 9-hour computing run on 16/17 June 1949; and comparable advances were made in the US. Lavington (1980) has drawn attention to the 42 computer patents that came from Manchester during the 1948–50 period; and Heims (1980) has indicated the patent suits testifying 'to the near simultaneity of similar innovations by different research groups' at around the same time.

The limitations of the first-generation computers based on thermionic valves were all too apparent. The systems were expensive, cumbersome and unreliable. For example, ENIAC comprised 18 000 vacuum tubes, weighed more than 30 tons and needed a room 60 ft by 25 ft; in the early days, runs of several hours without breakdowns were reckoned great successes, and runs for weeks at a time without failure little short of miraculous. The logic of computation was becoming well established, but the problem faced by Babbage—inadequate technologies for practical implementation—was experienced, albeit to a lesser degree, by the modern computer pioneers. The difficulties associated with technological limitations were overcome first by the transistor and then, with revolutionary success, by the integrated circuit.

It is ironic that the transistor was invented during the period when the early computer pioneers were struggling with the idiosyncrasies of thermionic valves. Its relevance to computing matters was not appreciated and it was initially assigned to other sorts of electronic tasks. It was in 1948 that the transistor was first demonstrated by William Shockley, John Bardeen and Walter Brattain, working in the Bell Telephone Laboratories in the US, but the first 'up-and-running' transistorized computer did not appear until 1953.

Inevitably there was a military impulse behind the development of 'second-generation' (i.e. transistor-based) computers, just as military requirements had stimulated first-generation progress (ENIAC was designed to generate artillery firing tables). The US Air Force contracted with Bell for the production of the special-purpose TRADIC system: it was to contain 700 germanium transistors and a plug-board for manual set-up of programs. This computational device first worked under test conditions in 1954. During the same period, work on transistorized computers was being carried out at Manchester University, and two working systems were completed in November 1953 and April 1955 (the first of these is reckoned the first transistorized computer to have run a program). The Harwell CADET computer was able to run a simple test program in February 1955, and to offer an effective computing service from August 1956.

CADET contained about four hundred transistors, but soon second-generation systems were being built with thousands. Most of the functional computers of the 1950s and early 1960s individually used many thousands of transistors to implement the switching logic required for effective computation. The various electronic components—transistors, resistors, diodes, capacitors, etc.—were mounted on printed-circuit cards (or 'boards'): copper was selectively etched from a phenolic or fibreglass base to provide electrical connections between holes which carried the wires of the components. A typical flat 5 in square printed-circuit card would contain about a dozen transistors and a hundred or so other components: the first-generation equivalent was several rows of bulky glass valves that would need to be cooled for successful operation. The second-generation systems contained several thousand printed-circuit cards, slotted into frames and connected by means of back wiring. It was not long before this arrangement, such a dramatic improvement on the old vacuum tubes, was thought to be bulky and inconvenient. Again computer scientists perceived the gap between the elegance of abstract systems of computational logic and the relative inadequacies of the practical technologies. Modern computer engineering has been a progressive search for implementing technologies that could match the power of abstract logical systems: computer architectures, despite progress in theoretical computer science, have changed little over the decades: what has changed is the electronics by which the architectures are realized in the practical world.

In the early 1960s the electronics engineers created a whole new technology, deriving from solid-state transistor fabrication and stimulating the emergence of third-generation computers and many other electronic devices. A Fairchild catalogue in the spring of 1961 boasted a new line of six different monolithic circuits which the company dubbed 'Micrologic Elements'. Soon afterwards Texas Instruments launched its own 'solid circuits'—claiming that the new integrated devices were faster, more power efficient, smaller, lighter and more reliable than circuits comprising discrete components wired

together. For a brief time the claims were received with scepticism—
but then, inevitably, military requirement provided the necessary
impulse for the new technology. The American Government saw
the need for computer-containing spaceships in order to beat the
Russians to the moon! And it was clear that the computers required to
operate in such an environment would have to be small, power-
efficient and reliable. When John F. Kennedy declared, 'I believe we
should go to the moon', he was helping to stimulate the emergence of
a vast new family of computing devices: before long a hand-held
computer would have vastly more computational power than the 30
ton ENIAC.

By the early 1970s, integrated circuits were being manufactured
with a complexity of around 1000 functional transistors. In contrast to
the bead-like electronic components of the second generation, the
basic components (transistors, diodes, etc.) were now being assembled
on 10 μm thick surface layers on silicon wafers. The components were
then connected by a metal layer evaporated onto the silicon, with
subsequent etching producing the required interconnections. Many of
the necessary integrated circuits could be mounted on a printed-
circuit card which could now carry all the circuitry necessary for a
central processing unit and the associated computer elements.

The first microprocessor, produced by the Intel Corporation in
1971, was based on a single $\frac{1}{4}$ in square silicon chip able to carry the
equivalent of 2250 transistors, all the necessary central-processor
circuitry for a tiny computer. By the mid-1970s, chips of this size
using LSI (large-scale integration) could carry more than 20 000
components; and soon there was realistic talk about cramming more
than one million electronic components onto a silicon chip and,
moreover, devising three-dimensional arrays to further improve
computational speed and power (more than one observer was quick to
remark that the human brain relied upon a three-dimensional data-
processing matrix).

The proliferation of computer-based products in the modern world
rests on the remarkable effectiveness of the high levels of circuit
integration achieved by the electronics engineers: impressive
computer power can now be encapsulated in a host of products and
serves also to dramatically enlarge the scope of machines whose main
purpose is computational activity. Increased circuit integration
yielded a fourth generation of computer systems; and a complex of
advances—in logical theory, programming methods, electronics,

sensor technology, etc.—point clearly to the imminent emergence of a fifth. The projected fifth generation of computer systems (Simons, 1983b) is signalled by many trends in modern computing and related technologies. Perhaps the most significant overall development is how computational activity is being transferred from human beings to computer-based systems. There are many examples of this trend (e.g. how in late 1986 the US money markets fell alarmingly as a result of 'program trading', where computers decide without human intervention whether to buy or sell shares). We will see that this trend—which is advertised most (but not solely) in what is increasingly recognized as *artificial intelligence* (AI)—has great relevance to the emergence of the eco-computer on a global scale.

Towards AI

There is a temptation to think that artificial intelligence is essentially a modern notion, hatched in the computer age. In fact that idea runs back through the centuries: intelligent artefacts can be found in the myths of many cultures (Homer was acquainted with the concept of AI many centuries before Christ, as was the historian Polybios who believed that the Spartan dictator Nabis used a robot around 200 BC to collect taxes). Perhaps the phrase is new: John McCarthy, who invented the Lisp language, is said to have coined the phrase 'artificial intelligence' in 1956.

The history of practical (as opposed to mythical or imaginary) AI may be seen as synonymous with the history of computation in stored program machines. The simplest mechanical calculators required almost step-by-step control by their human operators. When Babbage conceived the idea of a stored program, an internal set of coherent instructions, he granted an artefact for the first time a degree of autonomy: it could work for a while without human intervention. (This approach to autonomy is quite legitimate. No human being can operate without programs injected by genes or experience.) There is a clear sense in which a computer, able to perform complex calculations without human intervention once the process is under way, is functioning in an autonomous fashion. And it seems reasonable to assume that the machine is using artificial intelligence in such circumstances: a dog that, like any modern digital computer, could accomplish differential equations, would be deemed remarkably intelligent. The point here is that it is pointless to declare that AI began in 1956; if we decide that the stored-program element is the crucial factor then AI began, in practical terms, in the 1940s (we can forget Babbage in this context—his machines worked badly, if at all).

After Turing had published his seminal paper on 'computable numbers' in 1937, there was increased speculation about the possibility of artificial intelligence. In a later paper (Turing, 1950), he directly addresses the question—perhaps the kernel of all AI speculation—of whether computers may be said to think. Here he observes: 'I believe that at the end of the century the use of words and general educated opinion will have altered so much that one will be able to speak of machines thinking without expecting to be contradicted.' It is in the same paper that the celebrated *Turing test* is formulated. In the 'imitation game' an interrogator is separated from a person (or a machine) under interrogation, and communication is only possible using a teletype. The basic idea is that if the human cannot tell, during the interrogation, whether the interrogation is with a machine or another person, then the machine giving answers—if it *is* the machine—may be regarded as intelligent. We do not need to discuss this. The Turing test was one approach to intelligence, and there are others. It did, however, prove to be a surprisingly fertile idea, quickly leading into such perennial questions as solipsism and the egocentric predicament. The main point is that Turing—and he was not alone—was ready to embrace the idea that artefacts could be intelligent. The idea shocked many observers, but as computer accomplishments began to proliferate the notion seemed progressively less absurd. It seemed that computational tasks *outside* the scope of modern machines were dwindling in number by the year; and that an increasing number of tasks (mental and other) were being recognized as basically computational in nature.

One game is to look at competing definitions of AI in order to tease out a meaning. For example, Margaret Boden (1977), perhaps eccentrically, wants AI to be about illuminating aspects of human thought by means of computer programs; and in a much quoted definition Marvin Minsky (1968) reckons that artificial intelligence 'is the science of making machines do things that would require intelligence if done by men'. And there is another angle. Some observers take it as axiomatic that computers *cannot* be intelligent, so as soon as a computer achieves a performance formerly thought to require intelligence the definition (of intelligence) is shifted. So intelligence is *something that computers cannot have*. Alas, this is soon problematic: in the event of computers being able to do everything that people can, no human being can be intelligent—an obvious *reductio* that may make us more sympathetic to AI. What then can computers do? The list grows by the year.

They can, for example, play games (everyone knows about chess computers, but it is less often realized that computers are good at poker, bridge, draughts, etc., and that the world backgammon champion is a computer). They can also translate natural languages, prove theorems, read handwriting, recognize faces (in photographs and real life), recognize voices, answer spoken and written questions, write poetry and melodies, diagnose diseases, search for oil and other geological deposits, and write fables in the manner of Aesop. Such a list of tasks and amusements could easily be extended, but the point is made. While enthusiasts and sceptics debate about whether computers have 'real' intelligence, computers set about developing their IQs, a circumstance that can only have the deepest consequences for human society. We will find that there is much in this that is relevant to the emergence of the eco-computer.

Towards the Eco-Computer

We have glimpsed a few landmarks in the long history of computing—from Babylon to ENIAC, from China to silicon chip, from Athens to AI. Above all, we might emphasize the evolutionary nature of this superficial chronicle. Computing, as an abstract discipline tied to practical need, has a unique scope: it can toy equally with the demands of shopfloor automation and with the unlikely features of fantasy worlds. And whatever happens in the future it will be definable, at least in principle, by careful quantification.

It is hardly surprising that computation is one of the key elements in the eco-computer—but it is not the only essential element. Computation is a necessary, not a sufficient, feature of the emerging global intelligence. The worldwide electronics matrix will require that data-processing capability be spread around the world, and that the resulting local processing activities be linked in a global hierarchical communications network. The communications element is another necessary feature of the eco-computer....

2 Electronic Highways

Preamble

There has always been a need for effective communication between individuals in human (and non-human) societies. What is new in the modern age is the extent to which machines have become involved in this activity. Today communication is essential—between people, between people and machines, and between machines and machines.

We still like to think that most communication takes place between human beings, but there is no doubt that the proportion of person-to-person communication—set against communication as a whole—is diminishing year by year, month by month: we are increasingly interested in how machines 'talk to' machines. Great efforts are being made to develop *communications protocols* to enable machines to communicate with machines more effectively, so that (for example) purchasers of communications equipment are not 'locked in' to one supplier. every month we hear of new communications links being established, new agreed protocols, new network options. This is all part of the move towards the global village, a pressing fact in the modern wired world. Through communications technology it is increasingly possible—using a mix of submarine cables, land lines and artificial satellites—to link computer-based activities in different countries, in different time zones, in different sociopolitical environments.

Communication—at many different levels—has always been necessary for animals and people struggling to survive in difficult circumstances. In biological individuals there has been a progressive evolution of communications potential—between sense organs and brain centres, between the brain and limbs, and between the brain and the speech organs (to allow useful communication with other individuals in the same community). Communication implies a message and a message-interpreter: the message may be transmitted unwittingly or unconsciously, and it may be decoded or interpreted in the same way. A sleeping person can communicate information to a researcher; an unwitting tree under attack can transmit a chemical message to its unwitting neighbours; and a distant star can transmit information which is received by a radio telescope and analysed by

24

computers. Communication may or may not involve conscious beings. In this way we quickly see that the phenomenon of communication is philosophically multifaceted: it quickly raises questions of semantics (what does the message mean?), intent (was the sender purposeful, conscious?) and consequence (what action should be taken on receipt of meaningful communication?). Such considerations are obviously significant for the emergence of the eco-computer. The global intelligence will function as a vast computational array, a worldwide communications network with localized data-processing nodes. How intelligent will such an array become? Will it evolve as an intentional system? Will it develop personality?

We have said nothing to imply that the global matrix will function flawlessly, a perfect embodiment of effective control and intelligent response. It is much more likely that the eco-computer will function as a fractured intelligence, a complex system liable to frequent breakdown and incalculable consequences. It may even have schizophrenic tendencies! We will say more about this in what follows (Part III). Now we need to glance at the electronic highways in more detail.

Background

In the pre-electronic era, messengers had to rely upon a variety of strategies—smoke signals, drums, carrier pigeons, men on horseback, etc.—that did little to develop a worldwide communications matrix. In the nineteenth century, however, a communications revolution was begun which will only end with the emergence of the eco-computer. When Alexander Graham Bell invented the telephone in 1876 he both consolidated a number of tentative communications efforts and set in train a course of development that he could scarcely have imagined. And nor were other specialists of the day particularly far-sighted about the possibilities. Thus the engineer-in-chief of the British Post Office commented in 1877: 'My department is in possession of full knowledge of the details of the invention, and the possible use of the telephone is limited.' At about the same time the mayor of a small American town was more optimistic, observing that 'one day, every town in America will have a telephone'.

It was soon realized that the telephone had the potential to provide a 'universal service'—though this notion was usually cast in national rather than international terms. In 1907 Theodore Vail, the president of AT&T, announced the goal of providing a telephone service for anyone who wanted one, and who was prepared to pay a reasonable charge. It was inevitable that this worthy objective should have been framed in the context of US needs: there was no thought at that time of providing a global network to allow anyone in the world to talk to anyone else. In any case the language problem would have been prohibitive—until, that is, computers emerged and evolved to the point that they could translate human speech in transit (a current aim of fifth-generation systems). The US objective of a universal telephone service was codified by Congress in the 1934 Communication Act.

An obvious early problem was how to make interconnections between telephones. The common switchboard was invented and operators were required to route calls by means of plug-and-socket facilities. In 1889 A.B. Strowger developed a dial telephone system that prepared the ground for facilities that would allow users to make their own connections via a central switching office. Urban telephone networks emerged and the way was open for nationwide facilities, providing that the necessary equipment and standards could be developed. The Pupin loading coil enabled the strength of signals to be boosted to allow transmission between cities, and the Audion vacuum-tube amplifier enabled US coast-to-coast calls to be first accomplished in 1914. Voice quality was improved by H. Black's 1927 invention of the negative feedback amplifier, and in the 1930s and 1940s the development of carrier modulation techniques led to dramatic reductions in the cost of long-distance calling. At the same time the telephone traffic was increasing rapidly and there was a growing need for the development of effective mechanized equipment. The crossbar switching system greatly increased network capabilities. And soon there were the first signs of artificial intelligence in wide-area communications networks: control equipment could remember each called number, select a suitable route through the switching system, and locate alternative routes as necessary.

By 1951 nationwide direct dialling had been accomplished. A network routing plan had been established, able to rely on a hierarchical structure and a nationwide numbering scheme. Millions of users could be automatically routed via thousands of switching centres across America. Similar schemes were being developed in other countries, and the scope for international communications was growing at a rapid rate. H.E. Ives invented a method for transmitting pictures over telephone lines, and the facility was soon being used at national political conventions in the US. The first long-distance television transmissions were achieved in America in 1927. A few years later digital data were being transmitted over the telephone lines: already communications systems were developing the potential for compatibility with the electronic digital computers that were soon to be invented. The 1950s dataphone service enabled users to transmit information to a central computer for subsequent distribution of the results; and by the same time, nationwide radio and television programming had been accomplished. And already the convergence of technologies—that would signpost the route to the eco-computer—was manifest....

It was found that equipment developed for telephony could also be deployed for computational applications. In 1937, G.R. Stibitz, working at the Bell Laboratories, used relays and other telephone equipment to construct an electrical digital computer; and later showed that a remote terminal could be connected to a host computer via the telephone lines. (It is interesting to reflect that the linking of remote terminals to computing devices was demonstrated before the accomplishment of first-generation electronic computers.)

The scene was now set for the emergence of truly global communications. A wide range of technologies was becoming available for design engineers: as refinements were made to existing systems, other facilities—using high-speed digital computers, lasers and optic fibres, and artificial satellites—were soon to be pressed into service for communications purposes. And the convergence of technologies made it convenient to dub the emerging complex of systems and techniques *Information Technology*. IT was seen as the broad family name for an increasingly complicated matrix of methods in computing, communications and all the linked disciplines.

New electronic techniques were quickly found to be relevant to a wide range of IT activities. Solid-state circuits were used in various digital systems: e.g. the T-1 carrier system and the No. 1 electronic switching system (EES). These allowed an increased number of voice channels to be placed on ordinary telephone cables and also improved the control of call switching. Today the Bell System can claim nearly 150 million circuit-miles of digital transmission facilities. Both T-1 and EES went into service in the 1960s—and stimulated the design of further fully digitized transmission networks (digitization, unlike the analogue mode in which information is represented by varying physical quantities such as voltage or current, is clearly highly suited to computer-controlled information). By 1976 the ESS 'superswitcher', able to handle more than half a million calls per hour, had emerged and represented an important step towards fully digitized national and international communications. And progress ` towards the wired world is being made by the rapid growth of communications techniques using lightwave, microwave, coaxial cable and satellite facilities. A host of new (converging) technologies are accelerating the pace of movement towards the establishment of global intelligence.

Systems have been developed to interconnect the computers that control call-handling functions. For example, the common channel interoffice signalling (CCIS) facility has enlarged the scope of networks; and the use of massive databases has also enhanced the call-handling options. Such databases and CCIS, working together, can allow a user to dial a number, cause a computer to access a remote database, and have the call routed to another number held in the database. Where human operators could never have coped, computer-based systems can make the connections and maintain access to the necessary information. And this is being achieved with growing complexity on a worldwide basis. Communications complexity has many aspects: and this is one of the main reasons why global intelligence is fast running beyond the reach of human comprehension.

Communications Complexity

The modern communications scene is immensely complex and likely to become more so. In part this is due to the size of national populations: if only two people needed to talk to each other the necessary electronic systems would be simple. But the need for millions (or billions) of people to intercommunicate is only part of the problem. We also have to address ourselves to the fact that every year there is much more to communicate. As science and technology advance, more and more people are able to talk to more and more people about more and more. This seemingly trivial statement should be fully appreciated as a unique feature of the modern world culture. The methodology of science, a global ethos, is enabling one discipline after another to expand at a geometric rate. This is rarely grasped, even by systems engineers organizing new communications facilities....

In the world today a new book is published every 40 seconds—which represents about 800000 new books every year. Every day around 8000 articles are published in the general and technical press: in 1880 there were about 1000 scientific journals, whereas today (in 1987) there are more than 80000. One estimate suggests that the amount of paper needed in 1990 to service these information requirements will be 50 times that used in 1960. And this exploding development in paper usage is happening at a time when office automation (OA) enthusiasts are urging the creation of the 'paperless office'—a pious dream that some pundits are already modifying to the 'less-paper' office! Electronic storage of information is rapidly increasing, and so are all manner of hard-copy (paper) storage methods.

In communications technology, complexity has many dimensions: we almost see complexity raised to a power. Individual systems are staggeringly complex, and there is an evident proliferation of different systems for different purposes or to serve different user communities or different geographical areas. One writer (Mayo, 1982) could talk, half a decade ago, of networks so complex that they required 'numerous computer-based support systems'. He cites over 100 different types of systems, requiring more than 4000 mini-computers and 300 mainframes, and accessible via no less than 100000 computer terminals. Even by then such facilities, highly intricate communications systems, were being deployed in factories, laboratories, offices, schools, hospitals, military complexes, transport systems, government departments and other areas of modern life where communication of information is crucial to useful activity. Some particular systems have local significance, others are nationally vital, and yet others have international responsibilities (and new far-sighted aspirations)—and, significantly, links (interconnections, interfaces, gateways) are sprouting to join this system to that, to expand this or that network.

The US CAROT (centralized automatic reporting on trunks) facility monitors the performance of more than 5 million transmission circuits and analyses the resulting data. Similarly TIRKS (trunks integrated records keeping system) watches more than 25 billion bits of information relating to interoffice trunk circuits; PICS (plug-in inventory control system) monitors inventories of 80 million plug-in circuit boards; LMOS (loop maintenance operations system) maintains records on no less than 60 million lines. Such systems have their emerging counterparts in many countries of the world—and the facilities are evolving to interconnect such prodigious systems into one vast global matrix. And around all the main computer-based systems are smaller subsidiary computer-based facilities, dealing with report generation, equipment maintenance, testing of facilities, financial modelling, needs evaluation, fault diagnosis, public polling, engineer training, performance simulation, etc. A vast complex of computer-based networks is growing across the planet, finding new (and programmed) connections like growing nerves in the cerebral cortex of the human brain.

We will see the relevance of this evolving complexity for the development of the eco-computer. We will see that the global electronic matrix will emerge as a sum of countless adjustments, linkings, mergings, not as some predetermined blueprint mapped out by a conspiratorial intelligence. The eco-computer will evolve with a growing impetus—as loops are made, gaps closed, new areas of computer-based intelligence brought into the emerging global matrix.

Today the evolving communications facilities are linking office to office, office to factory, factory to transport system, transport system to surveillance facility, etc. In factories robot fabrication techniques are being linked to computer-based design departments (see Expanding Networks, below); in offices a growing spectrum of electronic facilities are being interconnected used existing telephone wiring, new local area networks and other provisions—and such interconnections, spreading beyond the local office or factory, are demanding communications links in strange and difficult environments (e.g. at the bottom of oceans and in the vacuum of space).

New communications systems are being conceived with greater ambition than ever before, with a new audacity. For instance, the emerging Japanese Information Network Service has been designed to include digital telephones, provisions for voice storage (to allow a spoken message to be delivered at a later time), facsimile (to enable an A4 page of information to be transmitted every 2 seconds), facilities for transmitting handwritten figures and characters, and numerous terminals able to transmit and receive pictures, photographs and voice information. There are also provisions for teleconferencing, the facility that enables a group of geographically dispersed people to hold a meeting, have a conversation, attend a conference together—by dint of electronic transmission of voice and image data—even though the people may remain separated by hundreds or thousands (or, in the space age, millions) of miles. The first Japanese trials of the multi-faceted network involved more than 300 major companies, with thousands of smaller firms supplying items of equipment, advice and other specialist services.

Above all, we constantly see the relentless pressure for *integration*, the linking and merging of computer-based systems. The word 'integration' crops up all the time in specialist journals, whatever the practical discipline being described. So *integration* of functions is seen as an essential goal for methods of data collection in the workplace, for automated facilities in the office environment, for fabrication technologies, for diagnostic systems in engineering and elsewhere. It is obvious that managements interested in the long-term survival of commercial enterprise cannot ignore the pressure for systems integration. We have seen that telephone lines can aid the task of merging different computer-based activities, and many other systems are being designed to achieve the same end.

For example, the manufacturers of local area networks (LANs) are able to offer high-capacity cable designs that can cope with high traffic densities; and LANs are regarded as particularly suitable for the needs of the electronic office and the manufacturing complex that needs a greater degree of integration for the various information-handling operations. A LAN may be offered as part of the initial design of a building intended to include a number of linked workstations—and such an arrangement allows various 'intelligent' systems to be linked in a local matrix. It is possible, for example, to interconnect facsimile devices, graph plotters, optical readers, image scanners, data-storage systems, photocopiers, etc., together in one coherent office net-work—and then the network can link *via gateways* to national systems and also *via satellites* to communications systems in other countries.

At the most local level a single workstation can contain integrated software to allow the user to file documents (electronically), lodge (electronic) messages in someone's distant (electronic) mailbox, transmit or receive telex information, seek help from software that aids decision making (or that 'contains AI'), speak on a standard telephone circuit, add (electronic) voice annotation to (electronic) documents prior to document storage or transmission, etc. Personal computers can be linked via a local network to large computers at company headquarters, or to other personal computers in the same office or down the road; and wide area networks (WANs) can allow a person to access national, rather than local, facilities. By such methods people can feel themselves part of a worldwide network—with countless nodes, junctions, links, interconnections, gateways, functions (and with a prodigious potential, incomprehensible and undefined, for further expansion!).

Modern communications technology is largely an exercise in the management of complexity—and some of the complexity is embarrassing and unintentional. The proliferation of electronics products from countless manufacturers is, at present, an obstacle to the emergence of the eco-computer. Different manufacturers design and fabricate to different standards, observing different constraints and different conventions. It can be difficult to coax two word processors—let alone mighty communications networks—to talk to each other. There is an inconvenient coyness in the electronics world. And so one of the central pressures in the modern technological world is the *pressure towards standardization.*

There are, of course, standards in all forms of communication—without defined conventions, agreements, protocols and the like, any form of communication is impossible. An unstructured anarchism in communication yields nothing but persistent gibberish. And the protocols have to be common to both parties aiming to communicate. A highly articulate Englishman and a highly articulate Russian will be able to communicate nothing verbally if they only know their own languages: any fancy computer-based communications system may as well be beached on a desert island if it does not have common protocols with the nearby system with which it desperately wants to talk.

The pressure for standards, discernible in every area of modern computer-based communications philosophy, will hasten the arrival of the eco-computer. Computers themselves will provide effective interfaces where such are necessary, and also stimulate design methodologies and conventions so that it is ever easier simply to plug one equipment into another—and achieve the expected results.

Some areas of complexity in the communications world are inevitable and desirable, but some are inconvenient and owe their origins and continued existence to historical accident and nothing more. Complexity will always be essential in the emerging global matrix—and this is one of the reasons why—as we noted in Chapter 1—there will be a progressive transfer of computational activity from people to machines. People can handle complexity to a degree, but it is obvious that global communications complexity can only be handled, if at all, by computer-based systems. This is one of a number of reasons why the eco-computer will predictably spin out of human control. Before we consider such matters in more detail (in Part III), we need to stay with the expanding networks a little longer....

Expanding Networks

Artificial electronic networks followed natural biological networks; without the latter, the former would never have emerged. This is analogous to how artificial intelligence 'grew out of' natural intelligence—and this circumstance again signals how computation and other forms of information processing are being progressively transferred from natural to artificial systems. For it is the case that as artificial information handling increases, it comes to represent an ever larger proportion of the total information handling that is occurring on the planet. The artificial networks evolve 'out of' natural ones—and progressively supplant them.

The earliest natural communications networks were relatively simple affairs: in biology these would be represented by a few links between nerves, allowing a significant electrical pulse to be generated by the movement of chemical ions and to be fed along the nerve to carry meaning to another site in the organism. Perhaps a simple creature would detect dangerous heat or intense light, and stimulate evasive action. Today it is an easy matter for an artificial automaton to model such behaviour.

The first neural nets would conduct electrical pulses a few millimetres. Later, though the impact of natural selection, the nets would expand, and significant signals—say, from sense organs to limbs—would be carried a few centimetres, and then, in the largest reptiles, fish and mammals, a few metres. This situation prevailed for several million years until early man discovered how to communicate using sound, light and eventually other forms of electromagnetic radiation. Communication of the traditional biological type persisted but a whole new dimension was added in the modern age. It had become possible for man to send meaningful signals over millions of miles—e.g. to spacecraft exploring the outer planets. In such a context the business of circling the planet Earth with an electronic communications network may be deemed a relatively trivial ambition.

Many of the most impressive communication links are established using radio transmission (see, for instance, . . .to Outer Space, below), but many are achieved by means of fixed lines fabricated out of wire, cable, waveguide, etc. Today this is shown in many ways: offices are wired up to allow the effective integration of systems; buildings are wired up for the same purpose; and physical networks sit astride nations and continents. Nor are the seas an obstacle to fixed transmission lines (see From Under the Sea. . ., below). It is obvious that we are increasingly inhabiting a wired world, and that the wired networks are being increasingly supplemented by other methods of signal transmission. And the various techniques—metal wiring, waveguide, optic fibre, laser beams, radio waves, etc.—are themselves being integrated. Satellite systems, for instance, are obviously required to transmit without fixed lines; but the land receivers, sensitive to satellite transmissions, are connected to physical landbased communications networks.

Even at the simplest levels there are difficulties in achieving reliable and effective communication. We have mentioned the standards problems (the inadequacy, in many respects, of suitable protocols, conventions, agreed rules, design norms), but there is also a host of more mundane considerations. For example, where buildings are to be wired for information processing it is necessary to design adequate air-conditioning systems, suitable ducting for cables, and office space able to cope with computer-based facilities that will inevitably tend to expand in both scope and size. Is there a generous ratio of vertical ducting to floor area? Are there suitable outlets in the horizontal ducting? Are the floors raised (and the ceilings lowered) to allow for necessary trunking? How does the available floor area match the expected disposition of workstations and personnel?

We need not dwell on such mundane practical matters. It is enough to emphasize again one of the key themes of this book. Systems designers, entrepreneurs, senior managers, etc., are necessarily concerned with their own parochial interests. There *are* circumstances when they will think in global terms (see Part II) but much of day-to-day business is concerned with this or that geographical site, this or that system implementation. Even the most successful individuals can only concern themselves in detail with one or two (perhaps a few) pieces in the global jigsaw puzzle. But others are working on the same board, and struggling to make the pieces fit. Through ambition, malice or incompetence some of the operators will force poorly shaped pieces into place—and immediately declare an interest in suggesting that a particular part of the puzzle is complete. A host of operators will together, but without a unifying master plan, assemble the puzzle—but it is inevitable that there will be imperfections: this or that piece lost a corner, this or that piece was squashed too hard, this or that piece does not quite abut its neighbour. The eco-computer will emerge through the progressive integration of expanding networks, but it will be imperfect.

So communications networks will increasingly affect building design. The *intelligent building* will impose its own unique constraints on the architect's vision: if the physical structure is to allow the efficient handling of information, then some designs and materials will be more plausible than others. The geography of towns will come to be shaped by the imperatives of Information Technology. It is already clear how this trend has affected particular buildings: floors have been ripped up, walls demolished, new partitions erected. What has happened in buildings is a metaphor for what will increasingly happen to whole urban complexes, though the exact dynamics will be different in the various cases, uniquely defined by the particular geography, the particular system implementation. Pre-IT buildings will be abandoned, and others will be erected to replace them; and central considerations will focus on provision for cabling, ducting, security against espionage (of whatever sort), satellite receiver siting, and the ever expanding networks.

It is obvious that systems designers and other contractors will make mistakes in implementing new information-handling systems—so short-cuts will be adopted, compromises agreed to minimize unexpected extra investment. So imperfections, like weak welds in a heavy steel structure, will be built into the networks at every level—from the local intelligent ('smart,' 'wired') building to the protocols intended to regulate integrated international traffic. Some of the foul-ups will be inconsequential, others potentially of catastrophic proportions (see Chapter 8).

The expanding networks will provide both more of the same and unprecedented features and facilities. One observer (Bone, 1985) counsels that even choosing a telephone system 'is much more complicated now than it was—and may take a lot more time than you expect'. And what do the systems offer, once you decide to survey the market? Automatic redial, ring when free, call logging, call blocking, abbreviated dialling, sensor-controlled surveillance, teleconferencing, group hunting, queuing, message waiting, piggybacking, etc.—and this is only the telephone. What about facsimile, mailbox, telex, decision support, the growing body of systems 'containing AI', etc.? By the mid-1980s voice and telephone 'add-ons' were available for the IBM microcomputers, and other facilities once only available to mainframe users were being supplied to micro users; in particular, to micro users who could plug in to the expanding networks. The mid-1980s have also seen a rapid expansion of voice facilities for *all* levels of computer users, with increasing attention being devoted to video options. It was evident in 1986 that videophones were a commercial reality: a typical technique was to take a real-time video frame, to wipe out the redundant sections, and to transmit the surviving data down the telephone line for assembly at the destination. One estimate suggested that a frame of this type could be transmitted and assembled in around 7 seconds. In May 1986 Luma Telecom, a division of Mitsubishi, launched the Picturephone, hyped as the 'first visual telephone for everyday use'. This system, originally developed by Atari, is able to transmit a freeze-frame snapshot in from 1 to 5 seconds: the aim is to offer effective devices at economic prices.

The expanding networks are increasingly linking to multinational corporations, research centres and government departments. For instance, electronic mailbox is now spreading fast, at last beginning to fulfil some of the predictions of the early pundits. Telecom Gold is the largest mailbox network in the UK, and in May 1986 British Telecom acquired Dialcom Inc. in the US. There are more than a dozen Dialcom licensees worldwide (the latest are Italy, New Zealand and Mexico), and the Dialcom system has already established a significant expanding network in America. Nearly two dozen US federal departments, including the Army, are now linked into Dialcom, and the network extends to 2000+ American corporations, a significant proportion in the Fortune 500 list. Dialcom is said to be used by the White House to organize cabinet meetings. Electronic mail—represented by a number of commercial systems—is one of many expanding networking techniques that is propelling modern communications towards the day of the eco-computer.

We have seen how networking is affecting architecture, the office environment and the activities of government. It is also affecting all other organizations, large and small. For example, in the manufacturing environment there are important efforts to standardize equipment philosophies and communications protocols. One of the

most significant developments in this area is the Manufacturing Automation Protocol (MAP)—which aims to facilitate the interconnection
of computer-based systems in the manufacturing environment (from
robots to design offices, from automated production lines to data collection and analysis). There is already a prodigious MAP literature
(see, for example, the special edition of *Control Engineering*, October
1985; Pye, 1986; Bairstow, 1986; and Melville and Koshy, 1986).
MAP, a dramatic manufacturing innovation, is one of many signs of
the expanding network scene. This type of facility will help to link all
the operations in the typical manufacturing complex; and the manufacturing organization itself will be linked via gateways to other types
of networks.

Networks are expanding to engulf every type of commercial and industrial activity on the planet; the service professions are not
immune—hospitals, schools, universities, churches even, are all
becoming enmeshed in the global electronic matrix. The lineaments of
the eco-computer are being set in place. But so far we have said little
about submarine networking or the communications link that depend
upon outer space. We may expect the eco-computer to extend below
and above the biosphere: the global electronic network will surround
and permeate all biological communities. In a sense, the eco-computer
will extend the biosphere by bringing intelligence (albeit electronic
rather than hydrocarbon) into new and uncharted realms.

From Under the Sea...

The provision of undersea telecommunications cables began more
than one hundred years ago, though the beginnings were less than
auspicious. The first cable was laid between England and France in
1850; but after it had transmitted one message, the cable was severed
by a fishing boat. This was an event that was to become familiar in the
years that followed: for example, in the winter of 1985/6, as many as
fourteen cables carrying a third of the telephone messages between
Britain and the Continent were cut by fishing boats or ships' anchors.
And damage is often caused by underwater landslips, brought about
by volcanic activity and earthquakes. Design engineers go to some
pains to minimize the likelihood of damage that will need expensive
repair; none the less, accidents occur. It is obvious that the route to
the eco-computer will be fraught with hazard.

The task of laying undersea cables can be immensely difficult. Charts of the seabed are often inadequate, and it is usually necessary for ships to take their own soundings using sonar and other methods. It is also necessary for the ships to maintain a precise fix on their position, often in very difficult environmental conditions. Here navigation satellites can help in the task of exact location—though it is often impossible to lay a cable with precision. The swell of the sea, water resistance and sudden storms are some of the problems that communications engineers have to cope with in the marine environment. And particular problems have been caused by known topological features: for example, the Western Approaches—the slope that rises to the British Isles from the west—has worn through many cables, causing inevitable failure. It is this sort of factor that is being given particular attention for the proposed transatlantic link TAT-8 that will use optic fibres.

Whenever new cable layings are anticipated it is necessary to carry out extensive surveys of the seabed. It is expected, for instance, that the firms Cable & Wireless and Tel-Optic will fund surveys of the mid-Atlantic Ridge before laying optic fibre to serve as a new generation of telecommunications facilities across the Atlantic. Two tectonic plates are forming in mid-Atlantic, and this circumstance has to be considered when planning the optimum route: at least one cable has already failed in this region, geological factors being the most common reasons for damage in the deeper parts of the ocean.

Today it is common for engineers to dig a trench in the seabed to acommodate the cables. This was first successfully attempted in 1934 when a trench was dug to the west of Ireland. The aim in such operations is for a cable-plough to dig a trench and also lay the cable as part of the same action; though again there are many problems in carrying out such a task. If a cable carries too much residual tension it will be more prone to failure, but if it is not drawn out satisfactorily it will tend to loop and not lay well in the trench. Some types of cable—e.g. those carrying optic fibre—are particularly sensitive to residual tension, and this has to be considered during the laying operation. If the plough proceeds faster than the cable is laid, then cable tension will be introduced. It is usual for a variety of sensors—sonar, tactile, visual, etc.—to be deployed to allow the cable-plough to negotiate difficult obstacles, and to ascertain the precise relative positions of plough and cable. Then the ship can speed up, say, to alter the amount of cable slack.

One problem is that the technology of the fishing industry is always expanding: this allows ships to trawl at ever greater depths, so threatening the survival of cables that lie uncovered on the surface. It has been pointed out that trawling gear can weigh many tonnes: such equipment, towed along with powerful ships' engines, can wreck unprotected cables—and so there is a great premium on companies burying both new and old cables, and on developing effective repair strategies where damage does occur.

Cables can also be laid to conduct electrical power, as well as to serve a telecommunications purpose. In 1985/6 a 2000 MW DC submarine cable was laid between Britain and France; there are now four pairs of cables linking Kent and the Boulonnais region, near Boulogne. The aim of the new link is to replace a 160 MW line which frequently failed. Such facilities (described in, for example, Nield, 1986) are highly relevant to the emergence of the eco-computer. The world electronic matrix will need to be powered, and optimum energy distribution—over land or under the oceans—will be essential.

The use of undersea cables—for telecommunications and power transmission—is now a well-tried technique. The first successful transatlantic telegraph cable was achieved in 1858, and by the 1890s the telegraph service was established on a worldwide basis: the roots of the global network are often much older than we tend to think. At the same time the cable network was being supplemented by radio telegraphy, with radio telephones introduced in the 1920s. By 1960 the technology of radio transmission had established a global telecommunications facility—and the provision of submarine cables was still continuing.

A UK–Netherlands cable, carrying 12 circuits, was laid in 1937; with a 48-circuit system laid between Wales and the Isle of Man in 1943. An undersea cable link between Cuba and the US was achieved in 1950, with the TAT-1 facility laid between the US and Britain in 1956. This latter system carried 36 circuits between the two countries, whereas CANTAT-1, laid between the UK and Canada in 1961, managed 60.

The trend was clear. The wired world was emerging, not least by dint of undersea cables to which little public attention was paid. By the time of the start of the satellite era in the mid-1960s, there were more than 70 submarine cable systems providing effective international communications links. These largely affected the US and Canada, and various European countries, though plans to develop a truly global network were first formulated many decades ago. And today the cable systems are another example of the expanding networks that will help to stimulate the emergence of the eco-computer. For example, in 1988 the submarine TAT-8 facility comes into operation, adding further links between Europe and America, but also—by linking to the HAW 4/TPC 3 cable system—connecting the US to Guam, Hawaii and Japan. The TAT-9 transatlantic optic fibre cable will be available in 1991 to provide further links between the US, Canada, France, Spain and the UK. There are plans to link Canada with Australia using optic fibre, Europe and the South Atlantic, Denmark and the UK, etc.

It is clear that the submarine communications systems are developing in a truly integrated network sense: undersea branching units, multiplex equipment and other devices are being provided, though it is expected that optic cable systems will allow simplified designs (e.g. there will be less need for repeaters and the power demands will be reduced).

Submarine cables will increasingly exploit the potential offered by optic fibre, and there will continue to be debate about the respective merits of satellite and submarine cable systems (it has been suggested, for example, that cables are better than satellites because there are a limited number of radio frequencies; conversely the relatively short life of communications satellites means that it is possible for each new generation to exploit technological advances—cables, by contrast, are durable and inaccessible). At the same time there will be an expansion of the range of computer-controlled undersea devices intended to monitor and repair the submarine facilities. The undersea network will increasingly be tended by robot vessels with manipulative powers and a decision-making capability. There is now a growing family of remotely operated vehicles—the precursors to true robot systems—for use in submarine environments. The SCARAB machine, used to recover the flight recorders from the Air India jet that crashed into the Atlantic in 1985, was one of these vehicles.

So it is obvious that the eco-computer will emerge through the progressive linking of communications systems in the seas, on land and in outer space. The technologies exploited in the different environments will have characteristic strengths and weaknesses—but in the main the systems will be largely complementary (natural selection, fuelled by commercial and other pressures, will eliminate the less satisfactory options—though there will still be inadequacies and failures). We will see a complex of linked networks emerging blindly but with seeming purpose—like the spreading neurons in the human foetus. Systems will fail and be replaced by more durable—and more intelligent—successors. These too will decay and crumble, to be replaced in their turn. The inevitable process will yield an ever greater density of information-handling systems, able to talk to each other at electronic speed and with ever diminishing human involvement.

Submarine systems are one of the important lineaments of the eco-computer, but they are only one of the requisite elements necessary in an eco-computer evolving to straddle a complex of different environments. The evident adaptability of *Homo sapiens* has always deserved comment, but it will seem inconsequential compared to the computer-based adaptability of the global electronic matrix.

...to Outer Space

Artificial satellites, for one purpose or another, were envisaged long before the Second World War. It was recognized, even then, that an orbiting device could have both a military and a communications potential. However, the most famous herald of the satellite era was Arthur C. Clarke. In one of his pre-*2001* modes he made the much quoted observation:

An 'artificial satellite' at the correct distance from the Earth would make one revolution every 24 hours; i.e. it would remain stationary above the same spot and would be within optical range of nearly half the Earth's surface. Three repeater stations, 120 degrees apart in the correct orbit, could give television and microwave coverage to the entire planet.

This seminal observation, made in 1945 in *Wireless World*, was in fact an accurate prediction of what was to take place a few years later. Within a decade it was possible to expand upon Clarke's pioneering notions to define the necessary parameters for communications satellites. The US Bell Laboratories was one of the foremost companies in this field.

The theory of rocketry has an ancient history. We need only recall the Chinese invention of sky rockets many centuries ago, the work of the Russian Konstantin Tsiolkovsky on propulsion (in 1903 he forecast exploratory space vehicles), and the work of the American Robert Goddard in the 1920s. It was inevitable that war should stimulate advances in rocketry, and progress in the 1940s was associated with the name of Wernher von Braun, a visionary who later was to work on the US space programme.

By any reckoning the most dramatic space event of the 1950s was the Russian launch of Sputnik 1. For three weeks in 1957 the first artificial satellite transmitted a stream of signals to Earth; and later in the same year, Sputnik 2 was launched—with the dog Laika on board. The first US effort, the December 1957 Vanguard launch, was a failure, and the Americans had to wait until January 1958 for Explorer I to be put into orbit: its signals were received for 5 months and the satellite itself survived until 1970.

By the late 1950s the scene was set for a race between the superpowers to put a variety of satellites into orbit for military and communications purposes. Again it was obvious that the main motivation would be military (the US Air Force General Bernard Schriever is on record in 1983 as declaring: 'Space for peaceful purposes—what a bunch of goddamed bullshit that was!'). The SCORE satellite, one of America's earliest successes, carried an energy source and was used to transmit President Eisenhower's Christmas message to the world; soon other satellites were to follow—from the time of the early 1960s many 'firsts' were to be recorded. We need only mention Cosmos 4, the first known photographic reconnaissance satellite to be launched by the Russians (the Americans had launched Discoverer 2 three years earlier, in April 1959); the Cosmos 185 anti-satellite system, launched in October 1967; the US Tiros I meteorological satellite launched in April 1960; and the US Courier IB communications satellite (October 1960). Throughout the 1960s progress was made in satellite sensor systems, using various techniques to provide effective surveillance of land and sea conditions.

Two decades ago it was already obvious that soon the Earth would be ringed by artificial satellites funded for largely military purposes. We should remember the links between communications satellites and military funding when speculating on the emerging character of the eco-computer. It is worth glancing at (for example) the US military involvement in communications technology: we may assume that there is an equivalent involvement in the Soviet Union and other countries aspiring to an extra-national military role.

It has been suggested that the impulse behind US radio broadcasting was in part to challenge the early British lead in global communications: at that time Britain was ahead in the use of undersea cables. This was useful for a time to a Britain struggling to maintain military and trade hegemony. It was largely to challenge this situation that the US Government and leading corporations (General Electric, Westinghouse, AT&T, etc.) created a 'chosen instrument' for communications, the Radio Corporation of America (RCA). A central US Government aim was to maintain a military presence on the board of the new cartel. Eventually the cartel broke up, and efforts were made to maintain a military influence over the RCA subsidiary, the National Broadcasting Company (NBC). Today RCA continues to receive substantial military funding. Having challenged the British broadcasting threat, it became necessary to counter the Soviet successes in satellite technology. For this purpose another 'chosen instrument' was created in 1962: the Communications Satellite Corporation (Comsat). More than one observer commented on the number of retired military officers who worked for the new cartel.

The global ambitions of Comsat were furthered by the creation of INTELSAT, an organization of more than one hundred nations, but specifically excluding the Soviet Union. In this way, the US-with more than 20 per cent of the voting strength in Intelsat and the predictable support of allies and client states—can effectively influence the character of global communications. In 1984 a 'chosen instrument' for the computer industry was established: Microelectronics and Computer Technology Corporation (MCC), a cartel comprising all the leading US computer companies with the surprising exception of IBM. The cartel—which includes Control Data Corporation, Digital Equipment Corporation, Harris, Honeywell, Motorola, NCR, National Semiconductor, RCA, Digital Equipment and Sperry Univac—is headed by Robert Inman, a former deputy director of the Central Intelligence Agency and the former director of the National Security Agency. It has been suggested (e.g. in *Computer world*, 31 January 1983) that MCC will provide the Pentagon, the intelligence agencies (e.g. the CIA and the NSA) and the US computer/communications corporations with an effective vehicle to project a global strategy.

What we see is a massive coordination of technological power for military and national security purposes. This circumstance has a great impact on world communications in general, and on satellite communications in particular—especially with the current emphasis being given in the US to 'Star Wars' research and development (see Chapter 7). We do not need to say more about the military and intelligence aspects of satellite technology (until later), but any speculation about the future character of the eco-computer cannot ignore the clear links between military interests and the technologies of computing, communications and remote sensing (for more about sensors, see Chapter 3).

In July 1962 the US corporation AT&T launched TELSTAR I, the first artificial satellite to carry antennae and complex amplification systems. This satellite, and its successor TELSTAR II, provided links between the US and Europe for telephony and television. This was a significant advance on the old transatlantic cables that were unable to transmit television signals. In due course, RELAY I and RELAY II took over from the TELSTAR satellites. However, all these satellites had the limitation that they were only visible for limited periods: they operated in elliptical orbits and were not 'geostationary'. SYNCOM 3 was placed in a geostationary orbit in 1964, and this system was the precursor to a whole family of satellite systems. An early SYNCOM success was the transpacific broadcast of the 1964 Olympic Games from Japan.

The provision of effective orbiting satellites, whether in low elliptical orbits or in geostationary positions, represents another element in the intelligent global system. Not everyone welcomed the emergence of operational satellite facilities: many corporations had vested interests in the established terrestrial systems, though many of the larger companies were quick to become involved—often through government pressure—in the new hi-tech communications industries. The satellite era had begun and it was essential for governments, corporations and other organizations to make the necessary adjustments and accommodations. It was soon clear that the new satellite systems could supplement the ground-based systems: indeed it was essential that land-based receivers be designed to feed satellite-supplied intelligence to established ground networks. In this way another link had been forged in the global matrix. Land-based systems, relying on ground or undersea cables, could be organized to transmit data to satellites for subsequent transmission to other parts of the globe. And satellites themselves were increasingly able to collect their own data by means of remote sensing (Chapter 3) to further geological surveys, meteorological analysis and military/security surveillance. This later facility was to serve as an important element in the emerging autonomy of the eco-computer: human operators were no longer required to supply all the data for the global network—the system itself was learning to detect and analyse marine, terrestrial and atmospheric events.

It is clear that satellites—serving to supplement marine and land-based systems—are filling gaps in international communications networks. We can speculate on the political and military implications, but the network developments are quite unambiguous. Through a rapidly expanding complex of new technologies, the wired world is moving towards the establishment of a single global electronic intelligence: satellites, like submarine cables and land lines, are one of the crucial lineaments of the emerging eco-computer.

New Technologies

Many technologies have combined to lay the basis for the eco-computer. Lasers and optic fibres are particularly important for a range of newly emerging communications techniques. Before the mid-1950s cable communication from Europe to the US was restricted to slow-speed telegraph signals. Now there are plans to lay TAT-8, an optic fibre submarine cable capable of providing the equivalent of no less than 40000 telephone circuits (TAT-1, laid in 1956, carried 36 telephone circuits), and due to begin operation in 1988 (Ranner *et al.*, 1986 survey current and future developments in optic fibre technology). Optic fibre will come to represent a significant advance on earlier communications methods, just as it is having a significant impact in other technology areas.

It is also expected that optical links between satellites will provide a very effective communications technique. For example, there is a requirement for intersatellite links to provide high capacity, with coverage and connectivity. ESA plans to link two geostationary satellites together using laser communications; and a number of experiments have already been carried out using CO_2 and semiconductor lasers. In 1977 a carbon dioxide–laser experiment was conducted as a joint ESA/German endeavour to enhance satellite communications in the 1990s. It has been suggsted that CO_2 lasers are suitable for long-distance communication whereas the semiconductor diode laser is suitable for short- to medium-range applications such as short-arc links between geostationary satellites; and it is expected that work in optic fibre communications will help researchers to establish effective optical links between satellites. We are not surprised that all these options are receiving the attention of the various military authorities. For instance, fibre-optic guided missiles are being developed by the US Army (*New Scientist*, 15 May 1986, p. 39).

The undoubted speed advantages offered to communications engineers by the advent of effective optic fibre facilities have been offset, to a degree, by the high costs incurred. Now this situation is changing as all-digital broadband optic fibre systems are being offered to tie together existing networks: established coaxial-based systems can be connected by means of relatively economic optic fibre lines. The new Fiberway facility, from Artel Communications, also shows a number of advantages as a general-purpose network: it represents one of the first effective fibre-optic local area networks. It facilitates connection to a wide range of computer-based units and also offers scope for expansion.

The possibility of developing networks without cabling of any sort is also being explored. (I well remember a piece of dialogue in the film *Forbidden Planet* where the characters wonder at the skill of an ancient race in being able to build electrical circuits without direct wiring.) It is suggested, for example, that radio links between the various elements in a network may be the 'way of the future' (Gower-Rees, 1986). Already a technique called 'leaky cable' technology can enable, for example, a security guard to talk to office staff many floors away. A giant antenna can be strung the full height of a skyscraper, possibly in the elevator shaft. The cable is designed to leak signals through 'desired-in-flaws' at predetermined points. A variety of communications methods are employed in conjunction with 'leaky' techniques in order to provide communications in environments (underground transit systems, mines, etc.) where more conventional approaches are not practical. The 'leaky' approach may be a way of achieving network communications without the need for direct cabling.

Radio LANs (RLANs) are currently being developed by such companies as Motorola and Nelma Data Corporation. The advent of cellular radio technology is providing insights into how more complex forms of communication can be achieved without the need for coaxial, optic fibre or other types of cabling. For example, cellular PBXs would remove the need for cables in the office environment and allow flexible resiting when organizational changes became necessary. However, designs using RLANs or cellular techniques are very costly, a characteristic feature of innovative technology.

Satellite technology will continue to benefit from developments in terrestrial forms of communication—and the scope of individual satellite systems will continue to expand. In late 1986, the Hughes Aircraft Company and INTELSAT (the International Telecommunications

Satellite Organisation) unveiled INTELSAT VI, the world's most powerful communications satellite. The new system is nearly 39 feet long, and it will be able to carry 120 000 telephone calls and three television channels at the same time (this represents 3 billion bits of information per second). As many as five INTELSAT VIs are scheduled: in conjunction they will be able to transmit more than half a million telephone calls at the same time. In the words of one report (*Transnational Data and Communications Report*, September 1986): 'INTELSAT VI will be the bridge to the 21st century for global communications services.'

New standardization developments will enhance the scope of communications systems (for instance, the newly launched X400 standard will facilitate the use of electronic mail and other communications services). And modern communications provisions will increasingly affect the lives of people in every part of the world. So, for example, Arthur C. Clarke (1986) can write an article entitled 'A phone for every village', rejoicing in the global dimensions of the communications revolution, seemingly oblivious to the machinations of military and surveillance interests and the gradual evolution of the eco-computer.

The dramatic impact of the new technologies is evident all around us—but for our purposes we are interested in highlighting the way in which these developments encourage the emergence of a global intelligence that will gradually run out of human control. Above all, we see the way in which the conflux of technologies will prepare the ground for the growth of the eco-computer.

Towards the Eco-Computer

The first computers were discrete stand-along devices linked to a power supply and little else. Later, as computers diminished in size and increased in power, there was a rapid growth in the interconnection possibilities: networks quickly grew in scope and size. Increasingly, computer-based systems were linked, first in small local configurations, then in national networks and finally in global systems relying on orbiting satellites and thousands of miles of submarine and land-sited cabling.

In the early biological world, simple ('stand-alone') organisms first emerged and were able to function successfully—but then the advantages of system integration were discovered and the primitive organisms came together to form, first, single biological cells (cellular mitochondria are thought to have evolved from free-living organisms) which later merged to form the whole massively complex world of the metazoa (of which *Homo sapiens* is a part). There is some analogy here with the evolution of the eco-computer.

We may envisage the eco-computer as a massive integrated system sitting astride the world, if not like a colossus then like an effective metazoon in which a proliferation of (computer-based) 'cells' allow a complex division of labour to sustain the global intelligence. But, so far, the picture is incomplete. The computers have evolved through four generations, with a fifth looming on the horizon and a sixth already being discussed in speculative literature. Communications networks have grown to global proportions linking a host of computer-based facilities for countless purposes. Now we are able to consider how the third lineament of the eco-computer is being set in place. . . .

To date, computer intelligence has largely relied on the provision of data by human beings. Some types of systems (e.g. in process control, fire detection, power generation) have included their own sensors to supply data on which processing can be based. This is necessary where it would be difficult—for reasons of environment or required speed of response—to rely on data supplied by human operators. And it is the automatic supply of sensor-provided data that will increasingly allow the emerging eco-computer to function without human intervention.

When the three elements of the eco-computer—computational capability, communications facilities and dedicated sensors—have evolved to a particular degree, the electronic matrix will have become established as an autonomous global system. It is time to consider aspects of the sensor interface.

3 The Sensor Interface

Preamble

It is the evolution of a complex array of artificial sensors that will give the eco-computer its autonomy. Such a sensor complex—the effective interface between the real world and the system's computational ability—will be linked to decision-making programs that can supervise the necessary operations. In short, the global intelligence will comprise a network of computational units, each with access to sensor-supplied data to allow processing to take place.

This means that the global network will not need to be fed data by human beings, as at present. Instead the artificial system will be able to monitor what is taking place in the submarine, terrestrial, atmospheric and space environments—and to take appropriate action. Already we are aware of the evolution of sensor devices that have relevance to this scenario. Even the popular press is likely to tell us about submarine sensors—when the tale is spectacular enough. So, for example, we read of 'A robot eye' that 'focuses on Titanic's chandelier' (*Sunday Times*, 20 July 1986). Here a 28 in camera, belonging to the Jason Junior robot, was able to enter the broken *Titanic*, see chandeliers, the grand staircase and rows of portholes—and provide data to allow the pictures to be flashed round the world. This of course, is a singular illustration of the central point: a local artificial intelligence, equipped with a 'sense organ'—in this case an effective eye—is able to link in to global networks to allow a billion people to see a particular sight two and a half miles below the surface of the sea.

In another dramatic description of sensor use, *New Scientist* (25 September 1986) considers the possibility of 'armour-suited warriors'—soldiers that could wear robotic suits that would protect them against bullets, radiation and the rest. Thus Jeffrey A. Moore of the advanced weapons technology group at the Los Alamos National Laboratory, New Mexico, has proposed a robot-suit control system in which magnetic sensors read the brain's instructions to muscles. The suit control system would use data obtained in this way to control movement so that it coincided with the movements of the soldier. There are still likely to be big problems ('Not a lot is known about the

49

correlation of magnetic fields with motor signals'). Moreover if the biological magnetic fields and control signals vary from one individual to another, it would be necessary to 'train' a suit for a particular wearer—and in such circumstances we may begin to wonder why the human being is needed at all (why could the powered 'exoskeleton' not do the job on its own?).

These two examples show the use of two very different types of sensors: one practical and proven, and the other speculative. There is in fact already a proliferation of artificial sensors that will be able to serve the information gathering-and-supply needs of the eco-computer. Already much of the relevant technology has evolved: the wide and growing spectrum of sensors is already well equipped to lay the foundations for the sensor interface of the eco-computer.

The Sensor Spectrum

Machines, we like to think, have sensors; biological systems have senses. We are intimately acquainted with the normal five senses of *Homo sapiens*—sight, taste, touch, hearing and smell—and some of us like to imagine that there is a sixth sense or even more. Mammals and many other species have a similar range of senses to that of human beings, and we are happy to note that certain life-forms have developed sensory techniques that cannot be found among men and women. For example, use can be made of magnetic effects, a facility not yet identified in the human skull; and it has been suggested that some species can detect electrostatic phenomena and other electrical effects. Whales and dolphins use sound for communication and other purposes—with a skill that makes the human sense of hearing appear a very primitive faculty (whales can sing a song that lasts minutes and travels miles through the ocean); similarly, bats process sound-generated data (e.g. to locate flying insects and fixed obstacles in a line of flight) with an uncanny competence. The provision of senses throughout the animal world is a highly complex matter, resulting from (and serving) evolution in countless ways—and suggesting means whereby the artificial gathering-and-supply of data can be advanced.

The generalized principle of the sense (or sensor) rests on a ubiquitous circumstance of the physical world: the simple fact that objects or entities can *affect* other items in their environment. It is clear, for instance, that theoretically every object is affected by the gravitational pull of every other: in this way, if in no other, it can be said that every atom can detect (sense) the existence of every other. Mostly the detection capability of simple objects is unremarkable, unhelpful to any evolutionary process; but as soon as more complex sensing capabilities have evolved the whole character of behavioural response is altered. Dynamic systems no longer have to rely upon collisions to signal their presence: using sound waves, electromagnetic radiation, chemical messengers, etc., an object can be aware, at a distance, of others. Thus the evolution of biological senses represents a growing sensitivity among systems that they are not alone, that they coexist in a world with other configurations that embody similar sensitivities. In this fashion, senses may be depicted as the route to the inevitable communal consciousness that was to evolve in many different ways. Senses were one of the first signposts to the networked future.

There are many early artificial sensors in the history of science and technology. Artefacts in ancient China and ancient India were sensitive to water pressure and temperature. Galileo built a thermoscope to detect fluctuations in temperature: a glass bulb containing air was connected to a small-bore glass tube that dipped into a reservoir of coloured liquid (the device also detected atmospheric pressure—which limited its temperature-sensing accuracy). Later Galileo was to design and manufacture thermometer-like devices. In 1612 a fine glass tube was connected to a container holding alcohol, and gradations were marked on the tube. A century later, Gabriel Daniel Fahrenheit was to substitute mercury for the alcohol; and other researchers—Celcius, Reaumur, etc.—were to build on this early work. And what was happening with temperature detection and measurement was also happening for the monitoring of other natural effects.

A vast family of scientific instruments evolved to detect appropriate events in physics, chemistry, biology, geology, meteorology, etc. At the simplest level a range of barometers was developed, allowing atmospheric pressure to be detected and signalled in various ways; and at a more extreme end of the instrument spectrum devices were invented to detect ground vibrations or radioactive emissions from terrestrial rocks and outer space. Sensors were developed to detect changes in the brain of a rat—and behavioural fluctuations in the heart of distant galaxies. But most workers involved in the evolution of dedicated sensors were only aware of a particular application area: we do not expect a zoologist exploring the reproductive competence of a mosquito to be an expert on seismographs or Geiger counters. In fact, however, the modern world has seen a vast increase in the number of sensor types (and sensor-linked devices). Such systems are well suited to provide the 'eyes' and 'ears' of the eco-computer.

Many of the early sensor-linked devices are well known to us. For example, we find little that is remarkable in the design of hydrometers (that find the densities of liquids) or of hygrometers (that measure the relative humidity of the air and its actual moisture content); but other types of sensing mechanisms—often deriving from newer technologies (linked, for instance, to developments in Information Technology —are more likely to appear novel or unusual. Some of these sensor-linked devices derive from general progress in industrial technology; others, now becoming widespread, derive specifically from the new IT world of robotics. Industrial robots are evolving effective sensors (or is it sense?). These are of various types (see Robot Sensors, below), and it is not hard to see how they will come to comprise the effective data gathering-and-supplying organs of the evolving eco-computer —at least in so far as the global electronic matrix requires local terrestrial data for particular purposes.

We see a rapidly evolving spectrum of sensors—variously relying on air pressure, fluctuations in the atmosphere (including ultrasonics), infra-red radiation, visible light, magnetic effects, electrical phenomena, radar, chemical emissions, radioactive discharge and other natural (and artificial phenomena). There are various strata that the eco-computer will increasingly come to monitor and analyse; and the sensors in a particular stratum will be the optimum for their purpose. So tactile (touch) sensors will become common in submarine or land-based environments; whereas artificial satellites will rely on radar and infra-red detection. But it should not be thought that the current sensor spectrum is complete, that it exhausts the sensor options. For instance, research into semiconductor and fibre optics (see Sensor Technologies, below) is expanding the scope of sensor design and manufacture. There is rapid progress taking place in the third lineament of the global eco-computer.

Sensors in Industry

Sensors, of one sort or another, have long been used in industry. Simple proximity detectors, helping to control moving machinery, have been employed in factories since the time of the Industrial

Revolution—and the descendants of such devices have proliferated in the factories of the modern industrial world. In modern times a host of sensor types—proximity switches, pressure detectors, spring-loaded pads, photoelectric cells, smoke detectors, etc.—have been incorporated as essential elements in modern factories and building design. And efforts have ben made to mimic some of the senses that serve the systems of the biological world so well....

Artificial vision is receiving more and more attention (see Robot Sensors, below), and a visual faculty has already earned a place in modern industrial techniques. In the 1970s camera systems—artificial eyes—were used to provide a degree of automation in manufacturing inspection systems. Automated visual inspection was introduced to overcome the familiar human problems of subjectivity, fatigue, lack of concentration, emotional vacillation, etc. By 1980 a family of visual systems had been made available to industry—from the primitive photodiodes and phototransistors to complex pattern recognition systems with fast fourier transform functions. One listing (Onda and Ohashi, 1979) considers the photoelectric device, the linear image sensor, the matrix image sensor and the image tube: all these devices use electronic logic to provide an effective visual faculty.

Photoelectric devices can be configured to detect the orientation or general shape of a workpiece: a parts detector of this sort was demonstrated at the International Industrial Robot Show held in Tokyo in 1977. At the same time image sensors using solid-state circuits (i.e. integrated circuits based on silicon) were being developed: at that time a typical linear image sensor could have between a few dozen and nearly two thousand photoelectric elements arranged in line; while a matrix image sensor could carry an array of as many as 400 × 400 elements. The typical image tubes were the vidicons used in industrial television systems. Observers were quick to point out that such visual systems were far removed from the complexity of the human eye.

The visual systems of the late 1970s laid the basis of the visual sensors that were to develop—for robotic and other purposes—through the 1980s. By 1980 various systems were being used for visual inspection of mechanical and electrical components, to aid industrial tasks (e.g. wire bonding), and to serve as effective elements in television systems. We recall the Reticon solid-state camera, the OMRON video inspector, the Hamamatsu analyser and the Fuji video sensor system: already it was clear that industrial operations were to be progressively facilitated by improved sensor systems. This was a development closely linked to advances in automation and other types of computer-based operation.

For our purposes it is worth emphasizing a key aspect of such progress. Here was further evidence that computational activity—in this case the data processing associated with sensory perception—was being transferred from human operators to machine systems. Automation—a descendant of early 'mechanization'—was learning how to function by means of sensor-supplied data. Already it was clear that the human contribution to mass production would progressively diminish. It was often proclaimed, by neo-Luddites and others, that automation would take people's jobs: it was seldom realized that the burgeoning Sensor Revolution, coupled to rapid progress in computer intelligence, would make such a development inevitable. Machines were no longer blind and deaf: they were beginning to develop the perceptual awareness prefigured in the myths of ancient lands, in the tales of Homer, and in fictional works in all centuries up to the modern age. The modern Sensor Revolution is dramatically relevant to the emerging autonomy of artificial systems: it will help to guarantee that the eco-computer will be able to function without human intervention.

Today it is common to read, in the general and technical press, about sensor developments. By mid-1986 it was possible to declare that vision-based systems are 'fast enough in operation and sufficiently cost effective to be widely adopted for a wide variety of industrial applications, particularly where high degrees of quality control are required' (*Sensor Review*, April 1986). Such systems could be used on bottling and canning lines, to recognize labels on products, and to identify components in production plants.

In 1986 it was announced that GEC Electrical Projects was to provide a consultancy, design and installation service for vision-based integrated quality control systems. The declared aim was to produce 'bespoke' systems interfacing with microprocessor-based industrial control systems (such as GEC's own GEM 80 system). The vision system currently being employed by GEC can provide a fast and high resolution vision facility, and there are provisions for adding further cameras to enhance the scope of the system. Other companies are also developing a variety of visual sensors for particular purposes. For example, many new and potential sensor devices were described at the Seventh International Conference on Assembly Automation (held in Zurich in February 1986): one paper (cited by Rooks, April 1986) described a robot system that used a semi 3D vision sensor, a force sensor, position-controlled gripper jaws, and a fluidic sensor to detect part orientation prior to gripping. The author, Verhaegen of Bell Telephone in Belgium, noted that sensors were essential to facilitate the assembly task.

⌈ Many of the sensor devices that have emerged in recent years have been associated with robots, and it is clear that these will serve as important elements in the developing eco-computer. It will be necessary to control local manufacturing and other operations, and robots will be required to fulfil a multiplicity of jobs in this connection⌋ It will be essential, in such circumstances, for robots to have their own senses, a degree of artificial intelligence, and the levels of autonomy that are deemed appropriate for specific roles. There will be a functional hierarchy of intelligent robots, individually equipped with senses appropriate to their stratum in the hierarchy.

Robot Sensors

General

Robot designers soon realized that sensors would be helpful: robots were necessarily mobile devices, having at least one movable arm, even if the robot torso was firmly tethered to the ground—and if the robot as a whole were able to move then it was essential that the device have some means of detecting obstructions in its path. The first sense to be widely exploited by robots was touch—in order that the robot could detect contact with other objects. Microswitch contact detectors were, for example, fastened to a bumper. When activated, the detectors supplied signals that were interpreted by the software as effective interrupts; the robot behaviour would be arrested or, alternatively, new subroutines would be initiated to allow a fresh behavioural trajectory.

Strain gauges could also serve to provide a rudimentary sense of touch, e.g. to regulate the force exerted by a pair of robot grippers. Such gauges can again be employed to supply electrical signals that can be interpreted by software: the gauge may detect adverse conditions and signal to the software which then launches an alternative routine. The visual faculty of robots is receiving attention in many research centres, and chemical sensors are being developed to provide robots with a sense of taste and of smell (particular concentrations of chemicals in liquids and gasses can be detected, causing the generation of electrical signals to inform the artificial intelligence of the system.

All the five senses known to *Homo sapiens* can be found, albeit in a rudimentary form, in existing robot systems. And today (in 1987) we expect certain species of robots to be sensitive in ways that far surpass the competence of human beings. For instance, we are pleased when robots are able to detect small leaks of toxic gases or unexpected radioactive emissions. Such faculties require a spectrum of intelligent design that cannot be found in the biological world. It is worth saying a little more about robot tactile and visual abilities to indicate how the global eco-computer will obtain sensory information at one of its functional levels. This information is then fed into the networked system for processing according to the priority situation.

Touch

By the mid-1960s robots had evolved simple touch capabilities, e.g. as simple contact switches in the finger-tips of an artificial hand. Here particular microswitches were backed by springs of different strength in different finger-tips so that grasps of different strength were possible. In a related area, Nevins (1976) described a wrist force sensor that comprised two rigid rings linked by light strips each carrying a strain gauge. This device was used to assist in assembly work. A piezo-electric tactile sensor was described by Umetami (1980): this was connected to a micro-manipulator employed for microscope work and micro-surgery. And various ways of supplying three-dimensional information for data processing were already being developed. For example, Sato *et al.* (1979) had described the use of a tactile transducer for three-dimensional part identification; and Page *et al.* (1976) had presented a complex tactile array able to supply appropriate three-dimensional information. By 1980 the sense of touch was developing as a highly effective robot faculty.

Tactile sensors had already been explored for submarine applications: one paper (Dixon *et al.*, 1979), presented at the ninth International Symposium on Industrial Robots, considered how touch sensors could contribute to the performance of an 'intelligent naval robot'. Such a device would be expected to collect rock samples, locate sunken vessels, attach salvage lines, etc.: since its operational environment would be largely unknown to its human programmers it must be able to behave in an intelligent manner—and without appropriate sensors this would be impossible. Another paper at the same symposium (Stute and Erne, 1979) explored the use of tactile sensors to regulate the path of a welding operation.

Efforts were also being made to develop 'artificial skin'—as a nice parallel to the biological equivalent. Work at the Laboratoire d'Automatique et d'Analyse des Systèmes (Toulouse) yielded a planar matrix skin sensor that could be built into the two parallel fingers of a robot gripper to achieve object recognition during grasping. Here sensitive points are isolated on a printed circuit, and a current is generated that is proportional to the pressure exerted by an object held by the gripper. Fluctuations in current can then be interpreted to give the robot a rudimentary understanding of what it is holding.

Work at other research centres—e.g. in France and at MIT—is also focusing on the development of artificial skin sensors. Thus a tactile device developed at MIT's Artificial Intelligence Laboratory, comprising 256 tactile sensors in an area of $1\,cm^2$ on a robot finger, is able to identify screws, nuts and washers. The device is able to determine the shape of the grasped object by sensing its general shape, by detecting any bumps or depressions, and by ascertaining whether the object can roll (see the description in Allan, 1983).

Use can also be made of conductive-plastic tactile array sensors to reduce the need for extensive wiring between the sensors and the external data-processing circuitry. In a sensor developed at the Carnegie-Mellon University, a layer of pressure-sensitive rubber is sited in contact with an integrated circuit carrying electrodes; the electrodes make contact with the rubber through windows in an insulating overglass. When the rubber is pressed, its local resistance changes and an electrical signal is produced that can be processed by the integrated-circuit elements. Each of the sensing cells fits within $1\,mm^2$ of material, allowing an array of sensors to be sited on a robot gripper to provide a sense of touch.

Tactile sensors have been commercially available for many years. For example, the DS-2206a device from the Lord Corporation carries a pad with a sensor array of 8×8 sites. The compliant elastomeric sensor sites move down $0.08\,in$ when they are depressed: the depression is detected by other sensors lying beneath the surface, and output signals are then produced which can be processed by the associated computer circuitry. Other devices may use carbon fibre (Larcombe, 1981), silicone rubber cords (Purbrick, 1981), or the piezo-electric materials already mentioned (Robertson and Walkden, 1983). In all such devices, pressure causes variations in resistance which generates signals that can be used for processing; and the ubiquitous integrated circuits are increasingly being used for this purpose.

It is also possible to use magnetic effects in sensor devices. For example, what has been called magnetoresistance can be exploited to achieve effective tactile sensors (Vranish, 1984). Substances such as Permalloy exhibit changes in resistance when subject to varying magnetic fields: in one sensor design using this effect a thin-film magnetoresistive array carries sensor elements covered by a rubber sheet. Again pressures can be detected and used to generate electrical signals that are suitable for processing. Other tactile sensors can exploit optical effects or sound (this latter involves sensitivity to the slight noise made when a grasped object slips between the jaws of a robot gripper).

In one direct contact sensor, an electrical signal is generated when a slight pressure is applied to an iron fibre felt spread over a surface. It is interesting that this material can easily be spread over a robot arm or torso, again providing an effective artificial skin (Pruski, 1986). Here use is made of a tufted felt made of stainless metallic fibres: the fibres vibrate when the material is pressed, so causing an equivalent vibration of the electrical resistance. This allows accurate detection of a pressure, irrespective of the size of the sensor—though different felt thicknesses are commercially available for different purposes. Copper or aluminium electrodes are secured to the felt by means of a conductive glue, and the electrical signal is carried away by means of a pair of screened wires. A plastic sheet can be used to protect the sensor from the environment; thermosoldering is used to prevent penetration by dust or liquids.

The development of effective tactile sensors has always enjoyed a high priority in robotics research. In the late 1970s, tactile devices rated third or fourth in degree of importance as a robot research goal; in 1980, J.F. Engleberger, the head of the giant robot corporation Unimation, reckoned that touch sensors should be reckoned number two as a research objective. But it is now clear that tactile devices will not evolve in total isolation from other sensory faculties. There is convergence in the sensor world, as elsewhere. It will prove increasingly necessary to coordinate tactile, visual and other sensor facilities in working robots: the different senses will cooperate to achieve their common purpose.

Vision

There is already a dauntingly massive literature on robot vision: just as artificial systems are learning to use a sense of touch, so they are learning to see—and the two faculties are being linked in various ways. We need only reflect on how useful human vision is to see how it can enhance the scope of artificial systems in countless ways. We have already seen how a primitive visual faculty can be used in the industrial environment and how robots are learning to recognize components by their geometrical characteristics. It is obvious how such capabilities are useful in the workplace: robots can be configured to sort objects (selecting them and placing them in appropriate locations), to identify components on a conveyor belt, to judge the disposition of objects and orientate them for assembly and other purposes, to recognize features of a terrain for obstacle avoidance and more complex navigational tasks. A robot may be required to assemble electrical equipment, to climb stairs or a ladder, to recognize the human face. It is clear how a visual faculty can contribute to such tasks.

A common way of providing a robot with a visual competence is to link the machine to a camera: the data supplied by the camera can then, at least in principle, be analysed in much the same way that the human brain interprets data supplied by the visual cortex (which in turn is fed information by the eye and the optic nerve). Ambitious slogans in the literature frequently assert that new 'artificial eyes' are able to match the human variety, though to date this has not been achieved in any realistic fashion.

By the 1970s many attempts were being made to link robots to television cameras (and other types of camera devices). For instance, Heginbotham *et al.* (1973) describe the Nottingham SIRCH assembly robot designed to interpret data supplied by a TV camera. A turret carrying an objective lens can be moved about in three dimensions over a table to gather and supply orientation data about an object. Here it is necessary to have a back-illuminated table so that the objects always appear black; and only the silhouette of the object can be analysed (there is no scope for interpreting three-dimensional characteristics).

It is also becoming increasingly feasible to coordinate the various sensory capabilities. For example, the New York company, Object Recognition System Inc., has developed a parallel-jaw gripper with both tactile and vision sensors. The visual capability allows the robot to handle delicate objects, an ability that would not exist without the cooperation of touch and sight. Use is made of an optical sensor that employs a light emitter and detector: when a light beam shone across the gripper's jaws is interrupted by an object between the jaws, an output signal from the detector actuates an external control mechanism. The vision sensor has been used with the i-bot vision system that enables a robot to select a part from many in a bin, even where the parts are overlapping or of different types.

Before a vision system can be designed and put to practical use it is necessary to develop the appropriate algorithms—the mathematical relationships that define the task to be undertaken. AI workers at Stanford Uniersity have developed a 3D imaging algorithm to allow automated stereo mapping of scenes: object-edge information can be extracted for a stereo pair of images, and the edge data can be linked to generate whole structures. There is also scope for correcting errors that occur in the imaging procedures. At the Carnegie-Mellon University a 3D single-line 2000-element camera is being developed, and this work is highly relevant to the evolution of vision systems for robots. SRI International, with other research groups, is workng on artificial vision systems that can recognize partially obscured objects—muċh as a human being would 'construct' a complete picture from partial data.

The construction of images from partial data is an important development in modern artificial systems. It is now fully recognized that much biological information processing has to work on information that is incomplete and hazy. Such 'fuzzy' processing typifies many perceptual activities in human beings and other animals, and the recognition that this mode of computation can also characterize the behaviour of artefacts is an important development. Fuzzy logic is now influencing research work in robotic sensors, as it is affecting research programmes in other areas of artificial intelligence.

Cuadrado and Cuadrado (1986) explore various ways in which artificial intelligence research can contribute to computer-based vision, i.e. to the type of visual activity that characterizes functional robots in a wide range of modern applications. It is concluded that the described vision system shows that 'given a narrow domain with relatively little noise it is fairly straightforward to construct systems that have reasonable performance using a modest set of generally available and easily understood tools'. This helps to demonstrate that vision systems are now moving out of laboratories into factories and other practical environments: there have been effective vision systems for many years, but it is only relatively recently—in the 1980s—that sighted robots are acknowledged as inevitable manufacturing components in a widening range of applications. Morham (1984) discusses 'intelligent vision in automated factories', dealing with various aspects of image formation, processing, analysis and interpretation. It is suggested that automated vision systems—an element in intelligent automation—will pove to be cheaper than human labour and will lead to improved quality in manufactured articles. Various applications for artificial vision are proposed, and it is assumed that automated systems will become numerous in the future.

Here again there is evidence of the inevitable transfer of computational performance from human beings to machine systems. It is commonplace for pundits to remark on aspects of the 'wired world', on the inevitable development of ever higher levels of automation, on the increasing intelligence of computer-based facilities—but it is rare to find a clear-headed acknowledgement that the transfer of computational activity (i.e. intelligent behaviour) will increasingly become the province of machines alone, that there is an evolutionary premium on people thinking less and machines thinking more. It is this type of circumstance that will influence the emerging character of the eco-computer (see Chapter 8). Sighted systems are one sign of the growing competence of artefacts (there are many others).

It is increasingly recognized that artificial vision is putting a new perspective on industrial automation (Lakshmanan, 1984). Already, it is pointed out, sighted machines are carrying out inspection procedures, measurement tasks, and various classes of picking and sorting functions. A report from the Tech Tran Corporation in America in 1983 revealed that the long term aim of research into robot vision was to achieve systems that can match the performance of the human eye and brain. Again the familiar application areas are identified—inspection, sorting and the guidance and control of equipment such as robot manipulators; and again there is focus on a 3D vision system using binocular vision. In this particular case, a pair of cameras is used to reduce images to an outline, whereupon the images are compared and matched—allowing the depths of the edges to be determined from the observed parallax. And emphasis is also given to the use of structured light for 3D object recognition, depth estimation, etc.—and to the development of sonar, radar and infra-red sensors to aid obstacle detection. Finally it is suggested that robot vision will become a standard feature of second-generation machines.

The journal articles in both the popular and the technical press often carry headlines that speak for themselves. So we read of 'eyesight for robots' (*Expert Systems*, 1 (1), 1984), and note that 'robots sharpen up their vision' (*New Scientist*, 15 December 1983) and that 'computers get the eye' (*Computer Weekly*, 1 March 1984). Warner, writing for the prestigious journal *Computerworld* in 1984, observes how vision systems are changing the face of the robotics industry; and Anna Kochan (1984) charts new 'eye-opening' applications for robots, 'now that robot vision systems are seeing the light of day'.

In the light of the much advertised (hyped) emergence of vision systems it is worth remembering that there are many problems yet to solve, that (biological) sight is a highly complex ability involving massive quantities of information processing that is scarcely even approached by artificial systems. Dunbar (1986) addresses some of the problems in developing machine vision and profiles the technologies being evolved to solve them. It is suggested, for example, that the familiar standards problem afflicts this area as it does other fields of computer research, but that here it has a peculiar character: acknowledged video signal standards are not suitable for progress in machine vision—they were created for television and are unsuitable for robot applications (for instance, the RS-170 standard leads to distortion at the digital level). Another difficulty is that most video techniques were developed to serve the human eye and brain: this is not necessarily helpful for a visual system intended to work in a largely automated environment.

These sorts of considerations suggest that new approaches to machine vision will have to be adopted if the full potential of artificially sighted robots is to be realized. It is acknowledged that existing video conventions will impose limitations on future progress as sensor resolution improves. Sensor manufacturers are now recognizing, for example, that feature and distance gauging require pixel cells to be organized in a particular way; and it is hoped that advances in integrated circuits will allow vast amounts of pixel processing to be carried out in close proximity to the visual sensor. This means that (for instance) object detection could be carried out 'in the eye'—rather than, as at present, having to convey data down a bus for processing in the host. In this way we may expect visual competence to improve with speedier and more comprehensive processing.

The speed of processing visual data is seen as a key factor that has to be tackled if robots are to acquire human-like visual competence. This was one of several key matters discussed at the Fifth Robot Vision and Sensory Controls Conference (reported by Rooks, January 1986), held in Amsterdam. The parallel processing of data is viewed as a likely approach to the speed problem, and this is encouraged by the development of thr transputer, the chip-based processing system that can contain many subsystems but also allow parallel linking to offer almost supercomputer processing power. Already the transputer can perform virtually instantaneous finger-print recognition. The Linear Array Processor, designed at the UK National Physical Laboratory, is also equipped to perform parallel operations on pixels. It is likely that research into parallel modes of pixel processing will dramatically improve the effectiveness of artificial vision systems and lead to the truly sighted robot. Such a development will have many implications for the operation of the eco-computer at the submarine and land-based levels. It will, for instance, help to evolve the degree of autonomy that we expect to witness in the various eco-computer echelons—with predictable consequences for human skills, self-image, attitudes, etc.

We have seen that machine vision systems have already found a number of practical applications: most of these are in the factory environment, but not all. In early 1986 it was reported that the UK Company Recognition Systems, under Home Office funding, had developed a system capable of reading and identifying car number plates travelling in excess of 100 m.p.h. in daylight or in the dark. A camera with a silicon intensifier is used, supplying data to various processors. There is a primary requirement that a number plate be recognized as such; then the system will aim to read it. Other vision systems—e.g. reported at the Robot Vision and Lasers in Manufacturing Conference (held in Paris, June 1986)—can use intelligent modules to identify multicoloured objects. And we may expect vision systems to function in a number of specifically human-like ways: e.g. as with the much publicized Wisard system, they will be able to recognize human faces—whatever the expression (it is no use scowling to avoid recognition!). Wisard, developed in the 1980s at Brunel (but having historical roots elsewhere), is well described by Aleksander and Burnett (1983).

Other applications for computerbased vision include provisions for office security, navigation (whatever the vehicle), and optical character recognition (for instance, there are now systems, albeit experimental, that can scan a page of prose and read it aloud). The Ministry of Defence's Royal Signals and Radar Establishment at Malvern is currently researching a vehicle that can steer itself without running into things. It would be useful if, for example, the mobile robots in factories could navigate without needing floor wiring. The ministry has also funded Logica, the British software and systems house, to develop a machine called Dipod (Distributed Image Processing Device). Again use is made of parallel processing to make sense of visual information, and a special computer language—Fith—has been developed to enable Dipod to cope with the spectrum of tasks that it is required to perform. Other work, funded through the UK Alvey project, is directly relevant to the development of robot intelligence by adding sensory faculties, including vision, to robot systems. Brady (1986), for instance, discusses Alvey work studying the needs of a mobile robot moving through an environment.

There are also research projects aiming to develop vision-like faculties to enhance robot performance. For some years, ways of providing radar ranging techniques have been explored as a means of improving machine intelligence. One such system is a joint development of the Fraunhofer Institut für Physikalische Messtechnik (IPM) in Freiburg and the Energy and Automation Division of Siemens AG in Karlsruhe. Here radar-like techniques are used to provide a 3D image of an object. The appropriate information can then be fed to a robot to enable it to identify and grasp the object—by comparing the new data with templates stored in its memory. This is a true example of automatic recognition of an item using visual data. Again a main use of this type of facility is in manufacturing operations.

Many of the impressive advances in artificial vision have resulted from initial work in research laboratories; in particular, in research groups focused on artificial intelligence. Recognition of lines, shapes, overlaps, patterns, disjunctions, angles, planes, gaps, colours, etc., invariably requires prior AI investigation before practical implementations can be made available for factories and other environments. We have seen that some of the work involves linking sensor operations; e.g. allowing tactile and visual sensors to work in symbiotic harmony, the two classes of systems working to provide complementary information to facilitate intelligent robot performance. Robinson and Hage (1986), for instance, discuss work designed to allow effective cooperation between tactile and visual sensors; and the tactile/visual symbiosis is only one of the many sensory collaborations that is likely to evolve. In biological systems, *all* the senses—on occasions—function in harmony to provide a framework for intelligent behaviour; and sometimes one sense will alert others to the need for activity (we hear a car behind us and turn quickly to look). Robot systems will, it seems inevitably, develop a complex of sensory faculties to facilitate behaviour directed at predefined goals.

Other

We should not think that touch and vision are the only robot sensory possibilities. Others have been mentioned but not explored in detail. We know, for example, that computerbased voice recognition systems are developing rapidly (with the converse, speech synthesis). Biosensors are also being designed to allow the detection of specific chemicals in circumstances where they would represent a hazard; and the development of faculties of this sort is akin to the biological senses of taste and smell. Artificial sensors will mimic (or perhaps duplicate) the senses of *Homo sapiens*, but their range will be wider: there will be robot senses that have no biological equivalents.

Sensors for Security

There is a growing family of security sensors, i.e. sensors that provide information about intruders, hazards to people, threats to operating systems, etc.—so that alarms can be activated or defensive routines initiated. Some security sensors are built into industrial robot systems, so that the robot will cease its activity when a human being is in danger. In one instance, the robot halts its operation when an electrostatic envelope is broken by the approach of a person; and another sensor, from Tempatron, uses inductive techniques to detect metals at distances up to 50 mm. The protection of human beings from the activities of robots is not always successful: humans have been injured, sometimes fatally, by industrial robot systems.

Many security sensors are intended to prevent burglaries and other types of theft. Such devices are regularly advertised in the security literature, and the range of such facilities is expanding by the month. For example, in any edition of the monthly journal *Security and Protection* there are columns publicizing 'intruder detection systems'—and these rely on a growing spectrum of sensor devices. Specific sensors are also advertised for those people who may wish to develop their own security systems. Thus in the March 1986 edition of the journal attention is given to various infra-red, microwave and optic fibre sensors. Seco Alarm (UK) Ltd, for example, advertises a break-glass detector, shock detectors and movement detectors; Weyrad (Electronics) Ltd cites the Viper electronic seismic detector, sensitive to vibrations in the material to which the sensor is attached; and Visonic Ltd draws attention to the Super-Red passive infra-red sensor offering no less than 40 interchangeable lens patterns, etc. These companies, and many others, displayed their products at the IFSEC '86 exhibition, held at Olympia in April 1986.

In the same issue of *Security and Protection* (March 1986), publicity is given to 'intruder detection systems' from more than three dozen suppliers. The various systems provide pressure-pad detectors, microwave detection, sensitivity to infra-red, and microprocessor-based circuits to facilitate data processing. The sensors in these types of systems provide effective monitoring of events at the local level: unexpected radiation, heat, vibration, etc., is immediately detected and signals are relayed to alarms, security staff, protective doors and other sites to alert security personnel and to activate automatic security measures.

It is obvious how the growing spectrum of security sensors will serve the needs of the emerging eco-computer. Such sensors, proliferating in shops, factories, offices and homes will provide a constant scene-monitoring service. Whatever happens will be detected, translated into digital language, and fed for computational processing. Vast databanks will log events and their important elements. Scenes will be constructed out of digitized information—to allow for analysis and the initiation of suitable action (measures, countermeasures, pre-emptive strategies, etc.). The eco-computer will know what is happening at every particular location where the sensors are sited —and we have seen how they are spreading from one computer-based application to another.

It is interesting how sensors are evolving to be particularly sensitive to human beings: there is talk in the literature of 'people detectors'—devices that are clearly useful for safety, security and many other purposes. The Becktronics company, for example, has introduced a new intruder tracking system called the TV Activator. Here the security equipment can be activated by pressure pads, infra-red and push-button panic alarms. Short-range radio waves obviate the need for complicated and expensive wiring.

When the equipment is activated a television camera begins to operate, panning automatically and at the same time taking a video recording. As the intruder moves about he activates various sensors and the television unit behaves accordingly. The data that are gathered can be used to give silent or audible alert responses. Other hazards, such as fire or earth vibrations, can also be monitored and signalled using this type of system.

Another company, Peak Technologies Ltd, has developed the Infrascan system that relies on infra-red sensors to detect the body heat of anyone entering its detection area. This 'people sensor' can switch on up to 2000 W of interior or exterior lighting when anyone approaches within its 18 m detection range. This facility, we may assume, is likely to discourage putative burglars and vandals who know of its existence. If the intruder flees, the lights remain on for several minutes, then switch off—to be reactivated if the person chooses to return. This facility is designed to save on power bills: the lights do not shine when they are not needed.

It is important that the sensors do not only provide information for immediate processing. There may be higher current priorities for the computers to consider. So many of the sensors are linked to recording equipment, so that the events can be analysed at the computers' leisure. This type of facility provides in-depth monitoring of events: if immediate processing cannot yield an optimum behavioural trajectory for the automated systems, then later—perhaps more measured— analysis of information may meet the requirement.

Sensors that can detect body heat—the *people sensors*—have obvious applications in security and surveillance systems. And we would expect the eco-computer to have an interest in such matters. After all, if the global intelligence cannot work to secure its own survival, when threatened by human beings or other natural hazards, then few of its other monitoring and control objectives will be achieved. The eco-computer will clearly be interested in monitoring people and other phenomena in its global environment. And the sensors able to detect human beings, non-human incidents, etc., by local effects are not the only means of observing and remembering such things. Sensing need not be *local* to the sensed phenomena: there is a growing range of *remote* sensors adding versatility to the data-gathering competence of the developing eco-computer. The possibility of remote sensing has been brought about by a number of innovative technologies, not least those connected with artificial satellites.

Remote Sensors

Remote sensors, like security sensors and other types, have an unexpectedly long history—but with the development of satellite technology they have become particularly significant. Radar was perhaps one of the most successful early systems that relied upon remote sensing, but today many sensing facilities are borne on satellites, ships, balloons and high-flying aircraft. By 1984, J.E. Estes *et al.* were able to declare:

remote sensing is a reality ... whose time has come. It is too powerful a tool to be ignored in terms of both its information potential and the logic implicit in the reasoning processes employed to analyse the data. We predict it could change our perceptions, our methods of data analysis, our models and our paradigms.

When the term *remote sensing* was first used, around 1960, it meant little more than the detection and measurement of an object without touching it; but much has happened since that early time. Local (contact) sensors have developed at least a degree of remote-sensing capability—e.g. any visual sensor is a remote-sensing device according to the old definition—and remote sensors of other types have become even more remote, carried aloft on geostationary and orbiting satellites, and even beyond the vicinity of Earth to the distant planets of the solar system. By 1980 remote sensing was already an ambitious affair, with important scientific and military implications. Today, with the end of another decade in sight, remote sensing is developing a singular significance. For one thing, it is crucial to Star Wars (see Chapter 7) and other fanciful military ideas. For another, it is a central pivot in the development of a global intelligence: it will prove to be one of the key elements in the emerging eco-computer.

Remote sensing is becoming particularly important in such environmental areas as meteorology, forestry, geology and oceanography. It has implications for the study of pollution, demographic change, and the possibility of mass protest for political or other purposes. It offers the potential for surveying human populations—without people suspecting what is happening—from the sanctuary of distant platforms fixed securely in space. Remote sensing will prove a boon to an eco-computer seeking to monitor and control. Today it is convenient to regard the remote-sensing facility as 'the use of electro-magnetic radiation sensors to record images of the environment which can be interpreted to yield useful information' (Curran, 1985). Though such a definition quickly prompts the question—useful for what?

In the 1960s remote sensing largely relied upon the interpretation of black and white aerial photographs,but by 1970 the field has begun to expand dramatically to include other tools and techniques. Aircraft and satellites were developing rapidly and a new family of infra-red and microwave sensors was best deployed for a variety of purposes, many of them military. The launch of the Landsat 1 satellite in 1972 gave a significant boost to remote-sensing possibilities. For the first time, satellite-borne sensors could provide synoptic views of the Earth's surface every eighteen days; and the basis was laid for many of the interpretation techniques that are in use today.

Already it is clear that the rapid development of remote sensors has provoked concern in many observers. Estep (1968) was well aware, even at that early date, that remote-sensing techniques were posing serious threats to social and legal conventions. For example, what right has a state to monitor another—without its permission—and to disseminate the information gathered in such a fashion? Moreover, what right does a state have to monitor its own citizens—without their knowledge—in such a way? It is significant that much of the funding for remote-sensor technology derives from governments interested in surveillance and security. If a dramatic new technology is to be funded and conceived in such a fashion what conclusions can we draw about the character of the emerging eco-computer for which remote sensing will be such an important element?

There are now many forms of instrumentation carried by aircraft and satellites to gather environmental information. For example, Curran (1985) has drawn attention to multispectral scanners, thermal infra-red scanners, radars and passive microwave scanners. He also provides a taxonomy of remote-sensing satellites that use a wide range of information-gathering techniques. There is, for instance, a growing range of earth-resources applications, as well as meterorological and military uses. But we should not assume that satellites nominally interested in gathering forestry or agricultural data cannot also have a military role. Forests can be used to hide military installations, and agricultural data can provide useful insights into a country's logistical capability in the event of international conflict. A taxonomy that separates out military applications from other, 'peaceful' uses may distort the intentions of funding agencies.

Some of the satellites are manned, some not—and some have resulted in catastrophic failure. Some significant remote-sensing firsts were achieved by the American Shuttle, despite the disaster that was to follow. The European Spacelab, carried aloft by the Shuttle, also accomplished new scientific work, and much of this depended on the use of carefully refined remote-sensing tools and techniques. For example, Shapland and Rycroft (1984), writing about Spacelab, point out that remote sensing can have applications in 'agriculture, cartography, fishing, forestry, geology, geophysics, hydrology, meteorology, oceanography and for studies of pollution'. And polar-orbiting satellites can provide navigational information for ships and aircraft. There is little attention here to the military and surveillance role of many satellites that use remote sensors.

Many of the remote-sensing techniques rely upon 'passive' methods, i.e. the sensors are equipped to detect radiation that occurs naturally (heat, light, etc). 'Active' sensor systems, by contrast, emit their own radiation and—by interpreting the reflected results—gain knowledge about the environment. For instance, a radar system emits pulses that are reflected from objects or the Earth's surface, then interprets the reflections. Lasters can be used to provide radiations that can serve active sensor systems. And long-wavelength micro-waves and radio waves can penetrate clouds, allowing all-weather, day-and-night surveillance of the Earth's surface. We can speculate on the value of such a facility to funding governments.

We need not be surprised that much of the literature focuses on the 'peaceful' applications of remote-sensor technology (military and surveillance work sometimes leaks into the public domain but tends to be given a lower profile). Thus there is attention being given to the intentions of the European Space Agency (ESA) to launch the first two-way Earth observation satellite, equipped with microwave sensors, in 1989 (Curtis, 1986). Software Sciences has recently announced the release of the EARTHSCAN range of systems intended to offer remote-sensing facilities for meteorological and other applications. Europe and the US are currently developing remote sensors for surveying ice and polar oceans in the global climate system: e.g. NASA and ESA have co-sponsored the Programme for International Polar Oceans Research (PIPOR). And in June 1986 it was announced that the Dutch Government was to encourage the use of remote-sensing technology for a wide range of commercial activity. Here an immediate aim was for the Dutch to contribute 7.8 million guilders to an ESA remote-sensing programme. In connection with this venture a satellite will be launched in the mid-1990s, mainly for meteorological applications. And Australia's national research unit (the Commonwealth Scientific and Industrial Research Organisation, CSIRO) has developed a system for processing satellite images (an aim was to map the waters of the Great Barrier Reef using satellite-supplied data, but now the work is being expanded to include agricultural, forestry and erosion applications).

The use of remote sensing (aircraft and satellite) for the oil and gas industries was highlighted at a 1986 conference on Electronics in oil and Gas, held at the Barbican Centre, London (report by Hollingum, April 1986). A wide range of instruments (photography systems, image-forming equipment, scatterometers, radar altimeters, etc.) was surveyed; and it was pointed out that satellites *with a global monitoring capability* will be in operation from 1989: these satellites include MOS (Japan), ERS-1 (Europe), NRSS (US), JERS (Japan) and Radarsat (Canada). Each of these vehicles is regarded as the first of a series; and doubtless, a decade after their launch, they will be seen as primitive historical curiosities.

A contribution from P.P. Simkins of Oceanfix International dealt with current developments in navigation systems and, interestingly enough, discussed sensor 'integration' (bringing more than one sensor together and processing their data jointly). This again illustrates the trend, already noticed in robotics technology, towards *convergence*: a tactile sensor on a robot gripper can cooperate with a visual faculty.

It is suggested that airborne navigation systems and satellite sensor systems can be combined to form an integrated navigation system for marine surveillance. Already data are collected in the air by many different methods (not all of them involving remote sensors): synthetic aperture radar (SAR), sideways-looking airborne radar (SLAR), thermal cameras, ultra-violet cameras, lasers, microwave radiometers, gyros, pitch and roll sensors, geotechnic sounding systems, cathodic monitoring systems, hydrocarbon leak detection systems, etc. The idea is that the data provided by such mechanisms could be combined with data derived from satellite-borne systems (such as thematic mappers, multispectral scanners and global positioning systems). In such a way, composite data could be usd to provide detailed environmental information. Again we can speculate on how interested governments—and the emerging eco-computer—might exploit such a prodigious volume of information about the world (including information about human beings).

Another paper at the Barbican conference—a contribution from Benny Moeller Soerensen of Intradan Environmental Consultants of Copenhagen—considered the use of remote sensing in such applications as pollution monitoring, sea ice reconnaissance, and search and rescue. He also cited several instruments being explored at the research level, such as the correlation spectrometer, the Fraunhofer line discriminator and the laserfluorosensor (the LFS). The LFS is an active sensor emitting a narrow beam of ultra-violet light which causes a fluorescent light reflection from the target. Such a system can be used in daylight.

What we see is a vast and highly complex remote-sensing scene—supported by a range of technologies bearing on international communications, artificial satellites, data gathering, and improved computation for data analysis and interpretation. Satellite research and development is still pushed forward with massive government funding (highly publicized US failures should not be allowed to disguise the scope of on-going programmes). And at the same time, sensor technology is advancing at a remarkable rate. We know that remote sensors have arrived when they star in American feature films! Consider *The Conversation* (with Gene Hackman) and *Blue Thunder* (with George C. Scott). In such films, sensors are able to detect distant conversations and select them out of surrounding crowd noise; observe human beings from great heights; and scan buildings to detect a human presence. It may be emphasized that such feature-film events are well within the scope of current operational technology. Workers for civil rights have scarcely begun to address themselves to the scope of modern sensor technology. For example, a report in the *New York Times* (1 March 1981, p. 12) revealed that the National Reconnaissance Office—with a budget hidden in Air Force operations—used satellites 'to photograph anti-war demonstrations and urban riots, in an apparent effort to determine crowd size and the activity involved'. Many writers (e.g. Curran, 1985; Shapland and Rycroft, 1984; Mosco, 1985; and Jasani and Lee, 1984) have drawn attention to the military and national security implications of modern remote-sensor technology.

In such circumstances it is hardly surprising that governments have an interest in funding sensor research. Waller (1986), for instance, declares that the US Department of Defense is about to make advanced infra-red sensors a top research priority, partly to serve the development of the Strategic Defense Initiative (SDI) (see Chapter 7). Already the Pentagon has launched an industry survey to collect information about the current situation; and the fiscal 1986 SDI budget for infra-red sensor work was $80 million—with defence planners 'poised to press the accelerator on IR array development' (Waller, 1986).

Remote-sensor technology, in common with research and development of other sensor types, will clearly continue to be well funded—largely for military surveillance reasons but also for internal security and commercial purposes. And existing technologies will be enhanced and supplemented by new tools and techniques.

Sensor Technologies

A spectrum of sensor technologies has already been briefly profiled. It is worth highlighting some current work that will bear on the future sensor scene—and so on the effectiveness and nature of the emerging global intelligence.

Researchers at the University of New South Wales in Sydney have developed a new microelectronic infra-red sensor that will allow humans to see in total darkness. This device, thought to be highly relevant to remote-sensing requirements, is said to have applications in medicine, mining, astronomy and defence. In a completely different field, scientists at Pennwalt, the Philadelphia-based chemical producers, are exploring the use of piezopolymer films as important elements in robot tactile sensors (Graff, June 1986). Bonneville Scientific, in Salt Lake City, has built a piezopolymer-based sensor that allows a robot hand to feel whether a grasped part is in the right position. Behind a rubber pad on the surface of the hand lies an array of piezopolymer transducers; when the pad is deflected by contact with an object, ultrasound is used to determine the amount of deflection—this can be used to ascertain the position of the object, and to allow its position to be adjusted.

We have seen that integrated circuits, at the heart of the computer industry, are also used to develop a vast new family of sensor devices. Silicon chips, doped with impurities, can be used to measure and transform into digital signals changes in such phenomena as stress, pressure, temperature, radiation, gas concentration, humidity, vibration, speed, acceleration, light intensity, fluid properties, and the tactile experiences of a robot hand (Szuprowitz, 1986). The Japanese have been conducting massive research into sensor technology as part of their development of fifth-generation technologies. Sensors based on integrated circuits are now claiming about one fifth of the total $1 billion sensor market in the US. There are found to be many advantages in fabricating sensors and processing circuits together on the same silicon chips (Eleccion, 1986). Similarly, fibre optic sensors are now being researched with considerable success, and many attractive applications have been identified: McClelland (1986) and Manor (1986) survey current work in this field.

There is also the possibility, much hyped in sensational articles, that sensors will be constructed out of 'living' matter: the world of the *biosensor* is becoming increasingly discussed in both popular and technical literature. One advantage of a biosensor is that it can selectively interract with other biological substances, allowing speedy detection and analysis: a change in proton density, temperature, optical density, mass, etc.—when the interraction takes place—can be immediately converted into an electrical signal by means of a transducer. Then data can be fed to a computer for storage and analysis. A wide range of transducers is already available (ion-selective electrodes, field-effect transistors, gas-sensing electrodes, fibre opucs, piezoelectric crystals, etc.) and biosensor applications are envisaged for medicine, agriculture, pollution monitoring, explosive sensing, detection of microbial infections and many other tasks. There is speculation about the emergence of intelligent biosensors that will mesh with human tissue and enhance the data-processing capabilities of human beings. Biosensors clearly belong in one of the futures (Chapter 8).

Towards the Eco-Computer

Sensors will be the eyes and ears of the eco-computer. They will proliferate around the globe, sited by the million in submarine systems, land-based complexes, aircraft and artificial satellites. Already there is no aspect of the global environment where sensors are not being used, already linked to computers via cables, optical links, radio transmissions and other communications facilities.

Sensors will evolve as countless species, individually adapted to gathering data at specific sites, in environmental circumstances that will vary from the vacuum of outer space to the colossal pressures in the depths of the oceans, from the pollution-free atmospheres of chip fabrication plant to the radiation-soaked piles in nuclear power stations, from the healing wards of hospitals to the slaughter of the modern battlefield. Sensors will become ubiquitous, infesting and straddling the biosphere, providing the data that will be both logically processed in dispersed computation facilities and transmitted over communications routes for storage and in-depth analysis.

Without pertinent and comprehensive data, the eco-computer would not be able to function as a global system. It would not be possible for human beings to provide data that were sufficiently up-to-date and all-embracing; nor would they have any intention so to do. The sensors will be installed without any thought of an overall plan: the links will be established piecemeal without reference to any global blueprint. But then it will be found that the global intelligence has emerged, able to process eco-data as it floods in by the nanosecond from millions of sensors around the world. In such a fashion will the eco-computer evolve to scrutinize and supervise the global environment.

This chapter has profiled the third lineament of the eco-computer. It completes Part I in which the three basic lineaments—*computation, communications* and *sensors*—are outlined. The three elements are essential for the global intelligence. Geographically dispersed computational facilities may serve a variety of local purposes, but until they are linked in communications networks they cannot cooperate on a worldwide basis. We can see the analogy with the human brain. The visual cortex must be linked with the language-processing centres, the data stores with the centres of motivation rooted in the hypothalamus—the system must be integrated for optimum performance. We are witnessing the day-by-day growth in the integration of the electronic world, the evolution of the eco-computer.

There are, however, other forces both sustaining and encouraging aspects of global integration. Before exploring aspects of the eco-computer in more detail it is worth surveying such global forces.

PART II
GLOBAL ASPECTS

4 One World

Preamble

It is becoming increasingly obvious, even to those who do not like the idea, that the planet Earth is one world. A host of global systems—finance, military, planning, law, trade, technology, etc.—interlock and interact in a single global matrix. That there is 'only one earth' (Ward and Dubos, 1972) is being advertised on every side.

Technology has made the planet one world for *Homo sapiens*: communications technology links people and organizations irrespective of national boundaries, different time zones, different climatic regions, etc.; electronic money, oblivious to the traditional boundaries of the nation state, speeds from one financial centre to another; unified entertainment (sport, popular music festivals, 'soaps', etc.) is increasingly a global phenomenon; and information gathering (both open and clandestine) is a global enterprise.

The human generation of energy and othe products is profoundly affecting the character of the global environment: we will hear more of deforestation, acid rain, the 'greenhouse effect' and nuclear radiation. Human ingenuity has sired a global culture and a dramatic environmental impact. The planet, girdled by electronics and pollutants, is a small place. Marshall McLuhan inscribed *global village* as an indelible cliché on the culture. Now it is necessary to advance the concept of the wired world: we need to recognize the emergence of a global intelligence from which—in information gathering, decision making, day-to-day 'house keeping', etc.—human beings will be increasingly excluded. We need to recognize the birth pangs of the eco-computer.

First we should remember that the planet Earth was one world before the advent of the human race. Modern man, perhaps estranged from folk roots and mystic sensitivity, had to invent an Earth-straddling technology to remind him of the fact. The planet had its interlocking matrix of ecosystems before modems, multiplexers and microprocessors came upon the scene. We need to glance at the type of global unity that predates man, and endures today despite the distorting effects of human activity.

79

Ecosphere

The global ecosphere comprises three main environmental sectors: the atmosphere, the lithosphere (the land) and the hydrosphere (the oceans). These three sectors are constantly interacting in various ways. For example, airborne pollen, spores and dust constantly filter upwards from the land to the atmosphere; similarly air, water, energy and various gas cycles involve reciprocal activity between the lithosphere and the atmosphere. In the same way a variety of exchanges is constantly taking place between the land and the oceans; and between the oceans and the atmosphere. Thus the ecosphere is characterized by a complex of networks that, through the constant exchange of matter and energy, are largely self-sustaining.

The biosphere—in which virtually all known life is contained—is spread thinly over the surface of the planet: one simile has suggested that the biosphere is like the dew on an apple. As little as 100 kilometres below the surface of the planet the environment reaches around 3000 degrees centigrade, while a mere 30 kilometres above where we stand the air is too thin to breathe. The world's plants, being threatened by man's technological competence, use the sun's energy to produce the chemicals that animals need for survival. It was the early algae, using photosynthesis in the oceans, that first released oxygen into the world's atmosphere—an event that was to prepare the way for human life. And it is still the case that microflora living in the planet's seas provide about 70 per cent of atmospheric oxygen (this in turn sustains the protective ozone layer in the upper atmosphere). Other micro-organisms recycle decaying matter in the soil to allow the nutrient system to be replenished.

Many of the processes in the biosphere are cyclical and adaptive (consider, for example, the nitrogen cycle and the carbon cycle, dependent upon life-forms; and the water cycle, in which most of the water circulated does not go through organisms). Such cycles help to define the nature of food chains and food webs, the complex networks of consumption, energy conversion and death that sustain the balance of the subsystems within the ecosphere. It is possible to view the individual subsystems as ecosystems in their own right, though we may assume that they are not wholly independent: there are points at which they mesh with the overall ecosphere.

There are many ways in which the various networks can be studied to throw light on the relationships between animals and plants, energy conversion methods, and how matter is exchanged in different transactions. For example, it is noted that there are generally more organisms at the base of a food chain than at the top: this circumstance has suggested a *pyramid of numbers* (or a series of such pyramids)—which allows different ecosystems to be compared. But it is unhelpful to compare organisms solely on the basis of their numerical representation within a species (e.g. we can scarcely compare a tulip with an oak, a mouse with an elephant). So the concept of *biomass* was invented to signal the total representation of a species on Earth. By this reckoning, *Homo sapiens*—with a very high biomass—is one of the most successful species.

Analysis of ecosystem dynamics helps to determine how the various networks interact to 'sustain reproductive and other patterns of behaviour. Here what is particularly interesting is the *cybernetic* character of the different processes: the various subsystems and the overall ecosystem are able to make adjustments and adaptations in order to survive in a difficult environment. Ecosystems at all levels are self-organizing, creating order and expelling waste—so countering the general increase in entropy in the universe. And where the total biosphere is perceived as a self-regulatory cybernetic mechanism, it can be depicted as an effective living organism dependent upon natural feedback systems to sustain its life. This view, J.E. Lovelock's Gaia hypothesis, is reckoned by advocates to be the only possible explanation of how the biosphere came to evolve to its present state (Lovelock, 1979).

The implication of Gaia is that the Earth is able to adjust its biosphere events to maintain an effective homeostasis, a stable equilibrium. This is closely analogous to the strategy used in individual living organisms for many different purposes—from maintenance of blood-sugar levels to regulation of perception/motor interactions—in order to sustain life-support systems. This means that Gaia can adjust to human depredations providing that they do not go beyond certain limits. It is part of the hazard of the modern age that human technology enables man to affect the world's environment beyond the corrective capabilities of Gaia. One example of this is the 'greenhouse effect'—the progressive build-up of carbon dioxide levels in the atmosphere to the point when temperatures worldwide may reach levels that have not been known on Earth for at least 100000 years. The CO_2 build-up began in the nineteenth century, when deforestation and the burning of fossil fuels first began to have global effects (Gribbin, 1986). This is one phenomenon among many—and they have all, in various ways, helped to advertise the fact that the global ecosystem has a unitary, but fragile, existence. We need to acquaint ourselves with some aspects of the impact of human beings on the planetary eco-system.

Human Impact

The ecological effects of man's industry and initiatives have always been highly significant: only recently have they looked like being catastrophic. It has been suggested that around 10 000 years ago, towards the end of the Quarternary period, the use of fire by aborigines was responsible for the extinction of some early Australian marsupials; and fire has been used for centuries for the removal of forest vegetation. The savanna grasslands were created by fire.

Such modification of the natural environment sometimes led to problems of survival for both nomadic and settled tribes. The Moa civilization of New Zealand has been cited as a narrowly based resource system in which a wide range of animal species on which it depended were hunted out of existence (Black, 1970). And drastic effects on the land have always implied serious consequences for human survival. Thus the decline of the Babylonian irrigated grain civilization has been attributed to increasing soil salination resulting from imperfect drainage, perhaps accompanied by changes in the rainfall regime. There must have been a time when yields were declining, when more and more unsuitable regions were being pressed into cultivation, at a time when the food demands of the cities were increasing—an ecological crisis in the ancient world.

Lucretius (*De Rerum Natura*, Book II) was arguing in the first century that the fertility of the earth was declining and that it was increasingly difficult to wrest a living from it—'everything is gradually decaying and nearing its end, worn out by old age'. Efforts to refute Lucretius—e.g. by Columella in his twelve-book treatise *De Re Rustica*—were not always convincing to the European mind. Thus in the first part of the seventeenth century, Fulke Greville declared that 'The whole earth is hastening to her last destination', a notion that was reinforced by the theological view that the Fall of Man was accompanied by a Fall in the rest of Nature. Goodman (in 1616) listed a number of phenomena which he reckoned evidence for the decay and decline of nature—the infertility of the soil, the hostility of animals to man, nature's production of low and repellant forms of life, human misery and ill-health, and the inclemency of the seasons. Other writers, e.g. Hakewill (1627), made an effort to refute such views, but none the less there developed the general concept of the progressive degradation of the natural environment and the likelihood of the ultimate end of the world, a view reflected in much modern ecological thought.

It is interesting that ecologists of several centuries ago embraced the doctrine that the planet was a single world, a complex system that could be drastically affected by human activities. There was concern that environmental pollution, for instance, could make the world uninhabitable—and there were many empirical data to suggest that human industry was adversely affecting the environment. Thus Stow, in his *Survey of London*, refers to the complaint laid before King Edward in 1307: the course of the Thames 'by filth of the tanners and such others, was sore decayed' with the result that 'ships could not enter as they were wont, and as they ought'. In 1635 an autopsy was performed on a certain Thomas Parr, recently come to London from the country. A 'peripneumony' was diagnosed: the man had apparently died after being exposed to smoke pollution after a lifetime spent in clean air. And in 1661 John Evelyn the diarist described that 'Hellish and dismall Cloud of SEA-COALE', 'perpetually imminent' over London, which caused the inhabitants to

breathe nothing but an impure and thick Mist, accompanied with a fuliginous and filthy vapour, which renders them obnoxious to a thousand inconveniences, corrupting the *lungs* and disordering the entire habit of their *bodies*; so that *Catharrs*, *Phthisicks*, *Coughs* and *Consumptions*, rage more in this one City, than in the whole Earth besides.

Even in rural areas the increasing use of fire polluted the air and, rendering the slopes of hills barren, made then liable to erosion.

The *Chronicon* of the twelfth century Otto of Feising is a source of further pollution data. He notes that when Frederick Barbarossa's armies arrived in Rome in the summer of 1167, 'The ponds, caverns and ruinous places around the city were exhaling poisonous vapours and the air in the entire vicinity had become densely laden with pestilence and death.' In the thirteenth century, St Hildegarde wrote of the Rhine—whose name is supposedly derived from the German word for *clear*—that its waters, if drunk unboiled, 'would produce noxious blue fluids in the body'. In the same spirit, but five centuries later, Samuel Taylor Coleridge could write:

The river Rhine, it is well known,
Doth wash your city of Cologne:
But tell me, Nymphs, what power divine
Shall henceforth wash the river Rhine?

It is clear that the development of civilization is in part a progressive interference with the ecological systems of the world. The more developed the civilization the more the world *as a whole* is affected. We have long passed the point when the impact of human industry only affected local sites, small parts of the ecosystem that can be distorted without global consequences. Indeed we may assume that many of the early deleterious ecological events had wider consequences than were appreciated at the time. There was, however, widespread concern about pollution—and this anxiety sometimes resulted in legislation. Thus in 1306 a citizen of London was reportedly tried and executed for burning coal in the city (Helfrich, 1970), a response to pollution that has hardly been matched in modern times. By the sixteenth century London had a smog problem, and the chimney-sweeps often developed soot-induced cancer of the scrotum. And what was perceived as undesirable environmental effect centuries ago has been magnified in the modern world by more advanced civilizations.

Again we can consider the nitrogen cycle as one of the ecological loops that is essential for human life on Earth. Certain bacteria and algae extract nitrogen from the atmosphere and convert it into ammonia, a toxic gas. Happily for us, two additional types of microorganisms in the soil and water spend their lives converting the ammonia to nitrate. In due course green plants absorb the nitrate and ammonia and use the nitrogen in building plant proteins—and animals (and other micro-organisms) obtain their nitrogen, to generate proteins, directly or indirectly from the proteins of plants. When plants and animals die, the process of decomposition yields ammonia; and the cycle—ammonia to nitrate, nitrate to protein, protein to ammonia—can repeat. Other micro-organisms convert nitrate into molecular nitrogen, so maintaining the composition of the atmosphere essential to human life. If anything were to happen to the denitrifying bacteria, a crucial link in the nitrogen chain would be broken, the atmosphere of the Earth would change drastically, and human beings would no longer be able to breathe.

In such circumstances we may expect Man to have a certain respect for the nitrogen cycle (and for the other cycles that sustain life on the planet), but this is not the case. With reckless indifference to his own fate, Man is currently dumping well over half a million chemical substances into soil, water and air—taking no trouble to estimate whether any one of these chemicals, or some combination of them, is likely to interrupt a stage of the nitrogen cycle, and so bring about the extinction of all human life. And so *Homo sapiens* seems serenely indifferent to nitrogen, so he is unconcerned about oxygen, equally essential to human existence. . . .

The oxygen in the atmosphere is constantly replenished by the industry of plants and trees, with 75 per cent of the free oxygen produced each year coming from the planktonic diatoms in the oceans. Kill the diatoms and you cripple the Earth's main source of atmospheric oxygen. Kill plants and trees and you further deplete the supply of essential oxygen. So Man dumps waste in the seas to kill the diatoms, and continues to kill plants and trees—whole forests every year. It is reckoned that the deciduous forests of the Eastern United States produce about one thousand times as much oxygen per unit as the average cover of the Earth's surface. Tropical rain forests, carrying on photosynthesis all the year round, are probably even more productive of oxygen. But there are endless suggestions for industrializing or developing the tropical regions of various countries: e.g. the Brazilians are developing the Amazon basin. And as the oxygen-producing areas of the world are destroyed we increase the amount of carbon dioxide in circulation, encouraging the 'greenhouse effect' and damaging the ozone layer that protects us from harmful radiation. We are laying the basis for irreversible climatic change: the healing powers of Gaia the earth-goddess are limited.

Observers have charted our recklessness in great detail—and the facts are unlikely to sustain an informed optimism. Helfrich (1970), for example, was unable to 'feel very optimistic' about our chances. Paul Ehrlich writes persuasively about the likelihood of 'eco-catastrophe'. A reviewer of the Second Report to the Club of Rome heads his piece 'Megadeath'. The facts are there—and it remains to be seen what the eco-computer will make of them.

Part of the problem is that the world cannot cope with increasing ecological pressure indefinitely: Gaia, we say again, is not omnipotent. It is self-evident that *indefinite* growth of whatever type—in population, fuel consumption, GNP—cannot be sustained by *finite* resources. This circumstance is at the heart of the ecological predicament. If the growth were linear (i.e. a simple increase the same in magnitude each year) the problem would be serious enough. But the growth is *exponential* (a larger and increasing demand from one year to the next). With exponential growth the graph begins to rise smoothly and gently, and then suddenly there is a dramatic increase, with the size of the variable now overwhelming. This can be illustrated in many ways. For example, Goldsmith *et al.*, writing in 1972, invite us to consider petroleum consumption increasing by 6.9 per cent a year, with world petroleum reserves, including deposits yet to be discovered, of abour 2100 billion barrels. Here a simple graph shows that total reserves are exhausted before the turn of the century. Much has happened in the oil industry since 1972: there have, for example, been artificial restrictions in output for a complex of pricing and political reasons. But the central point remains: even a modest annual increase in petroleum consumption—set against finite resources—means that exhaustion of supply is inevitable. The only debate is about timescales. Another 1970s estimate suggested that the effective 'ecological demand'—what the human race expects the ecosystem to yield—would increase by a factor of 32 over a 66-year period. We need hardly emphasize that any attempt to realize such a demand would seen lead to the total disruption of the ecosphere, the complete failure of global food supplies, and the collapse of human society. Yet world leaders—communist and capitalist alike—are still wedded to the doctrine of indefinite economic growth. It would seem that such attitudes, prolonged into the future, can only result in world-wide social collapse.

One of the most systematic attempts to explore the likely consequences of current economic/ecological trends is contained in the First Report to the Club of Rome. In April 1968, a group of thirty people from ten countries—scientists, economists, industrialists, etc.—gathered in the Accademia dei Lindei in Rome to explore the present and future predicament of Man. Out of this initial conference grew the Club of Rome, aptly described as an 'invisible college'. The central purpose was to foster understanding of the various components—economic, political, social, etc.—that make up our global system; and through such understanding to promote policy initiatives and action.

The Club of Rome employed a world model developed at the Massachusetts Institute of Technology. The model was built to investigate five major trends of global concern—accelerating industrialization, rapid population growth, widespread malnutrition,

depletion of non-renewable resources, and a deteriorating environment. A central conclusion was that the limits to growth on the
planet would be reached—if present growth trends continue—sometime within the next 100 years. The most likely result will be a 'rather
sudden and uncontrollable decline in both population and industrial
capacity'.

There are various possible responses to this sort of conclusion.
Some observers have argued that there is no cause for worry: Man
has faced problems before and always found solutions. Others
suggest that the point of no return has already been passed, that no
action can now be taken to prevent ultimate disaster. And inevitably
there are shades of opinion between the extremes. We cannot,
however, assume that because Man is in some sense special he could
not go extinct. Many species—of animals and plants—have disappeared from the Earth. Perhaps Man will follow, leaving the globe to
an eco-computer that will regulate whatever global systems have survived.

Animals and plants are key elements in the global ecosystem—and
as they gradually disappear we may expect disruption in food chains,
chemica cycles and other eco-loops. We all know that the dodo and
the dinosaur are extinct—and so are the heath hen and the barbary
lion. During the past four centuries, about 130 species of birds and
mammals have ceased to exist (Snyder, 1971). Today about 300 other
species are in danger of becoming extinct—e.g. the ivory-billed
woodpecker, the Arabian oryx, the pygmy hippopotamus, the
Galapagos giant tortoise, the Ipswich sparrow, the blue whale, the
orang-utan. It is estimated that Man—through habitat destruction,
overkilling and technological advance—has been responsible for 99
per cent of the extinction and near extinction of species. And plant
life is under similar threat. Here many species, including the Venus
fly-trap, have a precarious existence, if not already made extinct by
technological advance.

Man's destructive prowess is often exercised frivolously. Thus the
American alligator has been overkilled because of the demand for
hides for shoes and bags. The ivory-billed woodpecker has been
virtually wiped out by logging in the southern United States. And
grebes in Clear Lake, California, were almost completely destroyed
through treatment of the lake with DDD (a relative of DDT) to
control gnats. DDT used in Borneo to kill mosquitoes accumulated
in the tissue of roaches which were then eaten by geckoes, a well-

adapted lizard. The DDT in the geckoes slowed their reaction
times—which meant that they were caught in increasing numbers by
cats, which then started dying at a rapid rate. The depletion of the
cat population meant a field day for rats, known to carry plague. At
the same time, fewer geckoes meant more caterpillars—which in turn
led to a vastly increased amount of thatch consumption, signalled
when roofs started collapsing! This sort of example, which could
easily be duplicated for other species and other circumstances, shows
graphically enough how interference with a natural balance can have
wide-reaching and totally unexpected consequences.

Many species have been rendered extinct by excessive hunting or
inadequate husbandry. The buffalo was rendered virtually extinct in
the United States, and the passenger pigeon—thought at one time to
number around 5000 million—is now no more. Martha, the last of
the passenger pigeons, died in 1914 in a Cincinnati zoo. The vast
population of this bird was drastically depleted through tree cutting,
trapping, and people taking the young pigeons from the nest to eat.
Klotz (1972) points out that since men first arrived in the United
States from Europe more than 20 species of bird have become
extinct: such as the Carolina paroquet (extinct in 1904), the
Townsend bunting (1832), the Gosse macaw (1800), the black
capped petrel (1912), the Michigan grayling (1930), and so on and so
forth. According to the World Wildlife Fund there have been no
recent sitings of the Mexican grizzly bear. If this species is now
extinct it has simply followed in the footsteps of the Stellar seacow
(extinct in 1768), the sea mink (1860), the California grizzly (1900)
and the Arizona elk (1901). It is quite likely that by the turn of the
century, the Californian condor, the giant otter of South America,
the western giant eland, the tiger, the polar bear, the Tasmanian wolf
and the giant sable antelope will be no more—apart from a few
dismal remnants of these great species surviving in zoos.

For some time there has been extensive documentation of extinct
and threatened species. For example, more than a decade ago
Boughey (1971) presented world charts of endangered species,
showing particular regions where animals were likely to go extinct.
The endangered species range from the fat-tailed lemur to the pygmy
chimpanzee, from the black-footed ferret to the Caribbean monk
seal, from the Persian fallow deer to the wild Bactrian camel. In
another world chart, produced by Nobile and Deedy (1972), extinct
mammals are listed under nine heads; and no less than seven and a

half pages (pp. 112–19) are devoted to a list of birds that have become extinct since the year 1600.

The overall picture is clear enough. For the time being, Man is becoming more numerous on Earth but all other significant population trends in the animal world are in the opposite direction. The world environment is becoming increasingly hostile to all life-forms, including Man: human beings often survive in poverty and destitution, or through the expensive application of new technology in environmentally hostile regions of the world. And Man's impact has been felt by marine species as it has by those on the land. Various writers have drawn attention to the decline of the shad and salmon fisheries on the coasts of the United States. Both species feed in salt water but return to the rivers to spawn, and it is during this return to the spawning grounds that the fish are caught in their thousands. Some of the Alaska streams have been so completely blocked that virtually *every* fish returning to spawn is caught. In the words of Parkins and Whitaker (1939), 'After a few years of heavy peaks but scant returns of young salmon, the runs stopped and the canneries had to be abandoned.' There has also been overfishing of shad, halibut and many other species. The sturgeon of Chesapeake Bay has been 'slaughtered indiscriminately for the roe, the bodies frequently being left to rot along the shore' (Parkins and Whitaker, 1939). The sturgeon is now in danger of total extinction; just as the black bass, the striped bass, the perch and the crappie have virtually disappeared from the Mississippi, where once they were abundant. Similarly the fish populations of the North American Great Lakes are in serious decline, owing mainly to pollution and other man-induced environmental changes. And in October 1986 it was reported that flat fish from shallow waters of the North Sea are now so diseased because of chemical contamination that they should not be eaten. A survey revealed that 40 per cent of a sample of 20000 flounders, dab and plaice had cancerous tumours or severe bacterial skin infections. The Institute for the Investigation of Fishery stated that paint, touthpaste whitening chemicals, toxic waste and manure were to blame, and that there was no evidence of natural viruses. An earlier German survey in 1986 revealed more than 42 per cent of diseased fish.

In addition to the growing awareness of Man's impact on the biosphere—in terms of pollution, species destruction, etc.—it is also becoming clear that many human social institutions, from cities to the nation state, are under threat from technological progress. The global village, made small by technology, will find it increasingly difficult to tolerate specific sociopolitical arrangements in an increasingly hostile environment. Again it is worth emphasizing that many of the world's current ecological difficulties, though writ large by technological advance, have their parallels in the ancient world.

From the earliest times cities have emerged and then decayed. When the Phoenicians spread westwards along the Mediterranean some 2000 years BC, they built towns in Africa and Spain as terminal points of commerce. Other cities emerged along the Great Silk Road from China to Turkestan. Over the whole of the civilized world such cities grew, attracting labourers to share in the work and services that flourished as a by-product of the commerce in spices, silk and jewels. Inevitably, without adequate sanitation, there was a rapid build-up of human and animal excrement: disease followed and whole cities were wiped out. The inhabitants would drift away, in superstitious dread of the 'evil spirits' that roamed the blighted streets. Eventually new cities would grow, often constructed on the refuse of the old.

In more modern times, cities were often little more than reservoirs of filth. In eleventh-century Germany, for instance, plague broke out at least six times and religious fanatics walked the streets proclaiming the doom of Man. Scapegoats were sought: many people suspected the Jews of poisoning the wells, just as the Hungarian peasantry turned on the nobility during the devastating cholera epidemics. In the mid-fourteenth century the Black Death, brought from Europe by the Crusaders, destroyed one half of England's entire population. Labourers became so scarce that wages were doubled, and legislation passed to curb this trend led directly to the Wat Tyler insurrection. Large estates were broken up into small farms, and the Church was forced to give up substantial portions of its land. And all this took place because of rotting waste in the streets of European cities, polluted water supplies, and the resulting spread of the plague epidemic. Samuel Pepys records some of the details of the 1664 plague:

This day, much against my will, I did in Drury Lane see two or three houses marked with the red cross upon the doors—which was a sad sight to me....

It was a sad noise to hear our bell to toll and ring so often today, either for deaths or burials....

The people die so that now it seems they are fain to carry the dead to be buried by daylight, the nights not sufficing to do it in.

The bodies piled up in London faster than they could be carted away, and so efforts were made to burn them. The disease-ridden scene was brought about by the dangerous combination of poor nutrition, inadequate housing, and the foul accumulation of decaying material of various sorts, animal carcasses and vegetable refuse.

Even as late as 1890, before the age of motor vehicle pollution, the horse was allowed to foul even the best London streets. Red-jacketed boys were employed by the score to collect the dung by means of pans and brushes and to convey it to special bins at the pavement edge. But their efforts were never sufficient to the task. Pools of excrement often overbrimmed the kerbs and covered the surface of the streets, and swift hansoms or gigs would fling layers of the 'soup' across the frontages of respectable houses. Today such circumstances are unknown in Britain, but the world has its filth-laden towns and cities by the thousand. Thus in Bogota, Columbia, 10 000 people live in the squatters' shantytown called Policarpa Salavarienta on land owned by the National University. There are no sewers and the people live in conditions of the most desperate privation. A quarter of Rio de Janeiro's 4 million inhabitants live in *favelas*, slum shantytowns clinging to the sides of hills. Here the sewers are open trenches spanned by footbridges. More than 100 000 people in Tijuana, Mexico, live in tiny one-roomed shacks with no indoor toilets. When it rains, hundreds of such dwellings on the canyon slopes crumble and float away with the floodwaters. In Calcutta the sewers are often open ditches, and the World Health Organization has termed the city an international health hazard. Calcutta is known to be an endemic source of plague. The air is saturated with the stink of sewage and decaying flesh; some future epidemic may lead to the total abandonment of the city, as with the urban conglomerates of the ancient world.

To the traditional hazards of decay and disease, modern Man has added a wide range of technologically produced hazards. The industrial generation of *smog* led to belated legislation. One of the first significant instances of smog occurred in the Pennsylvanian mill town of Denora in Octover 1948. By this time, smog was so common that it had become accepted as more or less a way of life. But on 28 October visibility was down to zero, and the smell and taste of sulphur dioxide was everywhere. By the late afternoon, doctors' surgeries were crowded with asthmatics, and the medical problems were exacerbated by the difficulty of travelling about the town: the smog was even affecting the performance of the internal combustion engine—drivers had problems keeping their motors running. Within a few hours there were ten dead in the town. A first aid station was established, but soon the rate of emergency calls slackened as a soft rain dissipated the smog. By that time there were 22 dead, and 5910 people so ill that they sought help either from the town doctors, from the fire department inhaler squad or from the emergency first aid centre. It was later decided that the excessive smog had been caused by an atmospheric inversion, a common condition where pollutants are held close to the earth by a layer of warm air.

Other deaths have been attributed to atmospheric pollution: e.g. 62 deaths in 1930 in Belgium's Meuse Valley. In December 1952 a thick fog settled over London, and over a five-day period it was estimated that 4000 more deaths than normal had occurred; in 1956, 1000 deaths in London were attributed to snog; in 1962, 300. A 1965 smog at Thanksgiving in New York was said to have caused 80 deaths; and deaths have been reported from this cause in other cities in the US and elsewhere.

In the 1970s it was estimated that a worldwide total of 140 million tonnes of solid pollutants was being emitted into the air every year, and the total has increased in the 1980s. Modern pollutants are often classified as primary and secondary. The primary pollutants include soot, carbon monoxide, sulphur oxides and nitrogen oxides. Petroleum is a principal primary pollutant in the United States and other developed countries: in Los Angeles the amount of gasoline released into city air has been estimated to be no less than 8 per cent of the total quantity actually sold. Secondary pollutants—which derive from the primary but which are not themselves directly emitted—include a wide range of acids and aldehydes. We have seen how such pollutants can poison the atmosphere in various ways; and how this connects directly with disease and death. There are established links between air pollution and such phenomena as cardiovascular disease, infant mortality rates and the death rates of the elderly. Emphysema, a fast-growing cause of death in the US, has been linked with atmospheric pollution. And air pollution of this type is generally regarded as part of the price to pay for industrial development: it does not, for example, indicate accidental chemical emissions—as occurred at Bhopal—but regular emissions within the tolerances allowed by national and local legislation. This is also the case with nuclear radiation. Radioactive contamination of the Irish Sea is, for the most part, within the limits allowed by existing law. Most radioactive contamination caused by Man does not occur—as did the Chernobyl disaster—by accident, but as a result of deliberate and conscious policy.

Radiation is of various types—light, heat, radio waves, radar, television, microwaves, X-rays, gamma rays, cosmic rays, etc. High-speed energy particles—alpha and beta particles, protons and neutrons—are also considered to be forms of radiation. Most radio-active sources produce gamma, alpha and beta radiation, or combinations of these. Nuclear bombs and reactors used in power stations and nuclear vessels produce neutrons and a variety of radioactive elements: the neutrons can cause other substances to become radio-active.

The radiation that causes the most trouble—gamma rays, beta particles, X-rays and neutrons—has various consequences for life-forms on Earth. Radiation can affect the atomic and molecular structure of body tissue, impairing its function and in severe cases leading to fatal consequences. Thus gamma radiation can alter bone marrow to the point that it can no longer supply the necessary cells to the blood: death through anaemia or secondary infection is then almost inevitable. Radiation can also cause sterility, malformed off-spring and cancer: its carcinogenic effects can occur in any organ or tissue of the body. There is also the likelihood that radiation accelerates the ageing process in human beings.

There has always been plenty of background radiation from cosmic and other sources. We can aim to consolidate our defences against such radiation but—the possible destruction of the ozone layer apart—this is not the main source of our anxiety. What is of concern is the man-created radiation through nuclear explosion and through the peaceful uses of nuclear reactors. We need not dwell on the consequences of the Hiroshima and Nagasaki atomic bombs. These devices were exploded with the knowledge and intention that human life should be destroyed, and the consequences of this political wisdom—extensive burning of flesh, blinding, sterility, monster births, falling hair, many different types of cancer, etc.—have been adequately recorded. The experimental explosion of nuclear devices has also had consequences for the ecosphere and for human health (the Australian film *Half Life* should be shown at peak television times throughout the world). There are still radioactive products in the upper atmosphere as a result of earlier above-ground nuclear tests: in due course the products can filter down and cause mutations and cancer. Even underground tests—still conducted by the United States despite the unilateral Soviet moratorium—can cause fission products to be released into the atmosphere, and many countries with a nuclear programme have not signed international agreements banning nuclear tests in the atmosphere.

Today many people, aware that nuclear testing has been significantly reduced, see the main nuclear hazard residing in nuclear power stations. Such sources of electrical energy may *seem* clean enough: they do not, after all, belch out great clouds of black smoke and cause acid rain. In fact there are unavoidable discharges of radioactive fission products into the atmosphere; radioactive cooling water that passes through the installation is discharged into the sea (which is why nuclear power stations tend to be sited on coasts); no one has solved the problem of disposing of nuclear waste; and—in the post Windscale/Three-Mile Island/Chernobyl era—we need scarcely emphasize the possibility of accident. Efforts may be made to site nuclear power plants away from population centres, but there is always the problem of disposing of discarded fission products. Recent local protests have advertised attitudes to even exploratory drillings to find new places where the dangerous waste can be dumped. Moreover it is well known that uranium miners have a death rate from lung cancer very much higher than that in the general population of the United States (one estimate declares that the rate is 46 times higher!).

When new sites cannot be found for waste dumping it is necessary to store the fission products until a later date. It is already the case that millions of gallons of radioactive material are piling up in vast underground tanks—which may eventually leak into the surrounding environment, including the water table. One suggestion is that if a quart of this fluid leaked into drinking water, it could kill up to 1 million people. As far back as the early 1970s somewhere between 75 and 100 million gallons of radioactive waste products were in store in the United States. The material has to be constantly agitated to prevent settlement of sludge, and provisions are needed to remove the heat and gases that are generated. Millions of gallons of deadly radioactive waste are buried in Washington, more in places like

South Carolina and Idaho—and this is only the beginning of the nuclear age. One company spent $50 million in preparing a nuclear 'cemetery' in Kansas, and the search is on for extra sites in Europe, the Soviet Union and elsewhere. It now seems a long time since E. F. Schumacher warned us in 1974 to avoid creating more centres of radioactivity.

Already various marine areas are heavily polluted with radioactive fission products (we have cited evidence of pollution-induced diseases in fish). But radioactive materials are not the only type of life-damaging pollution. We have seen that sewage can be immensely harmful. It is still the case that many countries dump untreated sewage into the sea—or into local lakes and rivers. And even when sewage *is* treated it very rarely involves the necessary primary, secondary and tertiary processes. If, for example, certain tertiary processes are omitted pollution from human excrement can still represent a hazard: many pathogenic bacteria are not eliminated by any of the secondary or primary processes. To be fully effective the treatment of sewage must involve all the necessary phases—and this is highly expensive to accomplish in modern industrial society.

Organisms in the effluent use oxygen or are oxidized themselves by the dissolved gas present in the fluids of the 'waste sink' (i.e. where the waste is dumped). This causes oxygen depletion to the detriment of a wide range of living organisms important to Man, e.g. fish, crustaceans and other species. As with any interference with the ecosystem, the dumping of untreated or partially treated sewage into lakes and seas can have totally unexpected and far-reaching consequences.

Another important source of water pollution is industrial effluent. There is already a prodigious number of substances being tossed into the waters of the world: these are far too numerous to be listed, but we can mention oil, grease, organic and inorganic acids, dyes, alcohols, mine drainage, aldehydes, slaughterhouse products, ammonia, cyanides, sulphur, iron, paper pulp, fluorides, alkalies, lead, zinc, starch and phenols. (We may begin to suspect that Gaia has her work cut out.) Various chemical treatments are necessary for such wastes, though the treatments are not always provided and many treatments are too expensive for small (but ecologically significant) companies to fund. A host of problems exists in this area. Many companies simply dump their waste into the nearest 'sink'—and hope for the best. The result—obnoxious and foul-smelling pollution, dangerous to human and non-human life—has often been glaringly obvious.

Waste products arising through the production of food deplete the oxygen content of the water and, in consequence, kill or damage fish and other forms of aquatic life. Meat-packing waste may even carry human or livestock diseases. In late 1986 a report on UK abattoirs suggested that they were unhygienic enough to threaten continued exports to the European Economic Community. Industrial wastes, as well as representing a threat to life, can also affect physical structures: e.g. corrosion can be induced in bridge piers, boilers and other metal artefacts.

The picture is clear enough. The ecosphere is being polluted in countless ways, in ways too numerous to control or counter. The petroleum industry brings gross pollution to both marine and land environments, as does coal mining. The latter can involve washing processes that cause particles of coal and refuse, known as culm, to be carried into local streams; and the water pumped from operating mines can often have a high acid content. Hydraulic mining and dredging can give rise to other characteristic forms of mining debris which, when discharged into streams and rivers, contribute to the silting and pollution of stream channels. As one example, gold mining in California once seriously threatened the use of channels downstream.

We have already mentioned the polluted Rhine, but many other rivers are in much the same state. For example, the Hudson in the eastern United States is little more than an evil-smelling sewer carrying oil, orange rinds, detergents, thick wads of pulp, and numerous other human and industrial wastes. Aquatic life, once abundant, is now confined to a few eels that manage to survive on the river bottom. Three boys recently ate a water melon they fished from the river—and caught typhoid. In the 1970s the river between Fort Edward and the Troy dam received the raw sewage from 600 000 people. Klotz (1972) commented: 'Local residents know when summer has arrived by the hydrogen sulphide stench which accompanies the thaw of sludge on the river's bottom.' The Hudson river is said to be 50 times more polluted than water approved for swimming.

Lake Erie, one of North America's Great Lakes, is in its death throes. Commercial fishing has virtually ended: valuable whitefish and other species have disappeared, and it is estimated that 2600 square miles of the lake bottom has lost all of its oxygen: algae die and sink to the bottom, whereupon putrefaction uses up all the available oxygen. Thick piles of algae wash up on the beaches as a rotting mess, and the value of lake-front property had plummeted. A public health expert is on record as saying that 'a glass of water taken from the central basin of Lake Erie looks like thin green paint'. Hardy swimmers, braving this aquatic environment, are likely to emerge covered in algae and carrying a few blood-sucking leeches. The federal government has identified no less than 360 sources of industrial waste that have resulted in what is now generally regarded as a giant cesspool.

The cities of the United States discharge 65000 million gallons of sewage each year into streams and rivers, and this figure does not include the quantity of treated sewage—more than half of America's 2500 cities do not operate adequate sewage disposal plant, much of the present plant having being designed for conditions that existed half a century ago. With lakes and rivers so polluted—the Washington Potomac carries enough sulphuric acid to corrode bridges and dams—it is hardly surprising that the oceans of the world are growing increasingly polluted by the day. Many of the best shellfish areas around the New York metropolitan area have now been condemned as unsafe, and pollution damage to Chesapeake Bay alone has been estimated at millions of dollars. Infectious hepatitis has been caught through eating shellfish from contaminated waters.

It would be an easy matter to continue this dismal catalogue. There is the effect of oil pollution (deliberate dumping from tankers), the impact of detergents, and the many cases of damage to human beings—there has been mercury poisoning of Japanese through eating contaminated fish, and cadmium poisoning through eating rice contaminated by irrigation water (hundreds of people have died from such causes). We recall the *Torrey Canyon* disaster, but are less likely to know that such incidents happen, albeit less dramatically, every week on a worldwide basis.

The First Report to the Club of Rome emphasized that the types of pollution that have been measured over time seem to be increasing exponentially, that there is little knowledge about what the upper limits of these pollution curves might be. It is also significant that there are natural delays in the response of ecological processes to serious effects—which means that it is easy for human observers to underestimate the control measures that are necessary to prevent disaster. In general the growth in pollution can be directly related to growth in population or to advances in technology and the associated exploitation of energy resources. The trends seem plain enough.

We need not dwell in detail on the other hazards that face Gaia. It is worth mentioning thermal pollution. Weather and climate depend upon the thermal interaction of winds and waters: we are upsetting the balance by our discharges into lakes and seas. US energy consumption is reckoned to be ten times as much per person as the average energy consumption per person in the world. Much of the generated energy heats up the environment, having consequences for life-forms as well as for lifestyles. But we know that only a small thermal increase worldwide could cause polar ice to vanish completely. This would cause immense flooding, the total inundation of islands, coastal areas and cities, and the inevitable submergence of important resources in the line of the advancing waters. And we know that the cooling operation of a nuclear plant can raise the temperature of a river or lake by up to 20° C at distances several miles from the point of outflow. The effects of this temperature change can be staggering. By 1980 nuclear power plants required more than 200 billion gallons of water daily, mostly for cooling purposes: what we tend to forget is that the unwelcome power-plant heat is not destroyed but transferred to other parts of the environment. This amount of heat transfer is known to pose a serious threat to marine life forms upon which many of the higher forms of life depend. life depend.

It is envisaged that if nuclear power continues to expand—and despite the temporary US halt—there are significant expansion plans in Europe, the Soviet Union and elsewhere—then it will become increasingly necessary to site the power stations at sea, since they will have used up all the local cooling water. There have been predictions that within a few decades there will be no life left in the oceans of the world—Gaia will not be able to cope indefinitely with the impacts of chemical pollution, radiation poisoning, thermal transfer, etc. Moreover the thermal transfer trend will not only affect the marine environment: it has been proposed that a natural limit will be imposed on world population by the accumulation of insupportable heat.

However it is likely that various ecological forces will be competing to stop the runaway increase in the human population. By

1987 the world population had reached around 5 billion, with a population twice this number estimated for sometime in the next century. In fact it was in July 1986 that a large computer in the Population Institute in Washington DC decided that the worldwide human population had for the first time exceeded 5 billion souls. The institute takes information from 156 countries, and there is a consensus that its estimate of world population is largely accurate. One interesting finding was that the 5 billionth member of the global family had arrived almost 6 months early, i.e. the world population was found to be rising faster than was thought—and even on the old estimate it was stated that the global village would need to support 6 billion people before the turn of the century. In assessing this trend we should remember that it took the human race 2 million years (to 1830) to reach 1 billion, with 2 billion reached in 1930, 3 billion in 1960, and 4 billion in 1975. No fewer than 10 billion global villagers are predicted by the year 2080.

The gloomy picture could be extended. We have said little about depleted food stocks, the effects of pesticides and herbicides, problems with excessive use of antibiotics, encroaching deserts through destruction of land potential, the shrinking of groundwater stores, the effects of dust storms, excessive grazing of cattle, accelerated erosion, timber shortages, the exhaustion of raw materials, etc. More than a decade ago, Paul Ehrlich (1971) commented: 'unless a new culture of men is rapidly evolved, there will be no men'.

This section has ended on a gloomy note, but this is incidental. The picture is not all bleak. In the UK the 1956 Clean Air Act ended the incidence of smog, and many US and European cities enacted similar legislation. There is a growing consciousness of the importance of the global ecology, an increased recognition that all the world's inhabitants dwell on the same planet. Laws are passed against pollution, and sometimes individuals and organizations are prosecuted. 'Green' parties, in various European countries, are gaining support—and even the main ecologically indifferent parties are having to accomodate the Green impact. And we may find that Gaia still has a trick or two up her sleeve.

The purpose of this brief profile has been to advertise Man's global consequences for the planet. There is little like ecological awareness to indicate that the planet is one world, with interlocking systems, networks, a complex of influences and dependencies. Ecological

concern shows—through the sheer accumulation of horrendous data—
that the human impact is uniquely detrimental, uniquely harmful *in global terms* to the world environment. There is nothing like worldwide pollution (or the threat of nuclear catastrophe) to advertise the vulnerability
of the global village, the small oneness of the planetary ecosphere. We are
less concerned with remedial action (this is not an ecological tract) than
with a chronicle of the forces that are encouraging a global awareness—in
both human beings and artificial systems. The growing recognition of
the importance of the complex ecosphere is one of the forces encouraging
a global consciousness. It is one of the forces that will encourage the
emergence of the eco-computer (see Chapter 7).

The ecological concern generates, in many people, a resolve to act.
It is not enough, so the theme runs, that we analyse the deteriorating
situation. How can the trends be slowed, stopped, reversed? We do
not need to approve the remedies to know that they are being
suggested. It is significant that the call for ecological concern is
increasingly assuming a global character. Suggestions are made by
international bodies: there is not doubt that ecology is a global
matter. Just as ecological phenomena have worldwide significance, so
does the anxiety of Friends of the Earth: the Greens are under no
delusion that local ecological problems can be solved without a
concerted international programme. We are running into the age of
global politics and global policies: what is true of the Greens is true
of other political species—in the modern world, whatever your social
aims, you are forced to see the broader picture. Global villagers are
finding themselves increasingly close to their neighbours.

Towards Global Politics

The idea of global politics is not new. Ancient rulers—kings,
emperors, popes, conquerors—often had global ambitions, but they
were not always sure exactly what constituted the globe. There was
talk of the 'known world' or the 'civilized world'—with serpents,
dragons and barbarians beyond the walls. It was always within the
power of strong and visionary rulers to think in large—perhaps
global—terms. And rulers in cultures that were close to nature often
exhibited a 'oneness' with the natural world, the ancient equivalent
of an ecological concern.

Today signs of global thinking are evident on every front. For
example, we find abundant evidence of such attitudes in corporate

philosphy in general (see Chapter 5) and the IT industry in particular (Chapter 6); and we find a global focus in recommendations for policy attitudes that we hope will address significant world problems. Thus McHale (1972) emphasizes the need for global thinking, stressing the importance of our global, rather than local, commitments: 'there is no large-scale human problem which may not be solved outside of this context. Air, water, and soil pollution are not local—the air is not restrained within municipal or national boundaries, nor are the waters'.

It is emphasized that 'the scale of global systems of production/distribution, communication/transportation, etc has gone far beyond the ability of any single national or even regional group to wholly sustain and operate' (McHale, 1972). Such systems draw on the resources of the entire planet, and it is essential to address the problems in global terms.

In the same spirit *North-South: A Programme for Survival* (the report of the Independent Commission on International Development Issues, under the chairmanship of Willy Brandt) (Brandt Commission, 1980) talked about the globalization of policies. Problems are seen to affect Man as a whole, so many are 'inevitably internationalized': 'The globalization of dangers and challenges—war, chaos, self-destruction—calls for a domestic policy which goes much beyond parochial or even national items.' We do not need to assess the likelihood of responsible global attitudes. In fact the 1980 report (and its sequel *Common Crisis*—Brandt Commission, 1983) are far from optimistic. The enactment of relevant policies is happening at a snail's pace: the doom clouds are gathering. We need not dwell on such aspects. It is enough, for our purposes, to emphasize the growing globalization of attitudes, whether this is leading to effective legislation and policy making or not. We are charting pressures for a global view, not their success or failure.

We find a similar emphasis on global policies in John Naisbitt's engaging tract (1985). Here it is perceived that 'political rhetoric has given way to economic realities around the globe'. There is a discernible 'move towards the centre' in global politics, and we are told that Italy's communists are embracing capitalist goals, that French liberals are finding a model in Reagan, that there are signs of moderation in Iran, and that US voters are moving to the middle of the road. Above all, 'free enterprise spreads around the globe'. Again we do not need to pause at this stage. There can be little doubt that the shrinking global village—reduced by technology in general and communications in particular—is evolving a common culture. And the pressures for global attitudes are many: in the end they will be overwhelming. We need only look at transport, military requirements, economic alliances, international conferences, the success of English as an international language, a world architecture, a world science, a world technology. We will glance at corporate growth (Chapter 5) and information processing as global phenomena (Chapter 6). At this stage we need only emphasize that the planet is one world—and that this is a deepening perception in human beings.

Towards the Eco-Computer

We have seen that modern eco-concern has inevitable international dimensions. Bhopal was a local disaster, but Union Carbide has many other production units; Chernobyl has consequences far beyond the Soviet Union; European concern over acid rain has led to international dispute, and discussions at the highest levels of government; and underlying all such single events and one-issue campaigns is the growing recognition that the proper stewardship of natural resources demands a global perspective.

The emerging global awareness is helping to lay the basis for the eco-computer. It is increasingly unlikely that ecologically motivated strategies—in energy conservation, agriculture, alternative technology, legislation, etc.—will be framed in ignorance of the broader context, Gaia's global message. But it is also unlikely that such strategies will be conceived without reliance on electronic data processing. How can an ecologist ignore the convenience with which a computer-based system can monitor and analyse, say, pollution data, demographic trends or important geological data? And the computer contribution will not stop at low-level data gathering and interpretation: the computer will increasingly assume a judgemental role.

We anticipate, in the realms of eco-thought as elsewhere, a progressive globalization of concept and strategies; and a progressive transfer of computation-linked activity from people (even the 'Greens') to artificial systems. We have seen how the lineaments of the eco-computer are being set in place. Eco-concern—initially in people but increasingly structured into the global electronic matrix—will influence the behaviour of the eco-computer. Perhaps eco-concern will not be the main influence, but it will be one.

5 Corporate Growth

Preamble

We have already indicated a number of forces that are encouraging globalism: among these, trade and commerce, lubricated by technology, are central. Merchants, bankers, entrepreneurs, industrialists—all have been prepared to think in ambitious international terms, with consequences that have stimulated debate, ideologies and conflict. In this area there are constant references to the global dimension. It is one of the features of the modern age that trade can only properly be viewed as a worldwide phenomenon that has an impact on international employment patterns, the unification of global culture, and the management of the planet's resources. And at the heart of these developments lie the vast multinational companies, modern empires that transcend political boundaries and operate outside the sway of national governments. The emerging eco-computer will owe much to corporate growth.

Towards Globalization

The modern corporate trends give evidence of globalization at every turn. We have been acquainted with the *global village* for many years. Now the literature is sprinkled with other global creatures: we constantly read about the *Global Impact*, the *Global Factory*, the *Global Shopping Centre*. Today the managers of large corporations cannot function effectively unless they 'think globally'—a feat that is facilitated by vast telecommunications support. The modern corporation is concerned with developing a worldwide strategy, an attitude to investment and profits that is sensitive to national differences to the extent that these can be exploited to corporate advantage. We need not dwell on the impact of the multinationals on labour or the Third World (there is a massive literature here), though we will comment on the military connections of multinationals (see below): the links between the military dimension and the emergence of the global electronic matrix are too important to ignore. Technology is militarizing the globe—and the multinational corporations are keen to encourage the process.

It is significant that finance is now a global enterprise, and that 'global channels of sales and marketing have opened up' (Reich, 1984). Corporate growth in the developed countries has encouraged the international aspirations of the developing world: e.g. modern retail outlets are useful to Third World countries wanting to export their goods. Thus electronic products from South-East Asia can be sold through American retail chains. Developments in transportation and communications—both within and between countries—have also lubricated international trade, making it relatively easy for emerging countries to opt for an international commercial role; and this development has compelled companies, particularly in certain key economic fields, to compete on a global basis. Now it seems that corporate growth in such key sectors will, paradoxically enough, leave only diminishing scope for individual entrepreneurs. Vast multi-national organizations will increasingly dominate vital industrial and commercial sectors. Thus Stopford and Turner (1985) observe: 'More and more, we are talking of industries like automobile manufacture, computers, and consumer electronics where there is room for perhaps ten major world-class competitors. In a few industries, such as aircraft manufacturing, even three core companies may be too many.'

Everyone is aware of the incidence of global competition: we do not need to travel, only to watch television. On commercial channels there are frequent advertisements that obviously derive from a French, German, Japanese or American source; Chinese are acquainted with American products, as are other Asiatics, Africans and Latin Americans. Sporting activities are regularly sponsored by multi-national corporations, and the familiar advertisements litter the stadiums of the world. The *globalization of advertising* signals dramatically enough the globalization of trade: we know the signs—Coca-Cola, Canon, Ford, Kodak, McDonald's, Volvo, etc. (and the tobacco companies eager to disguise their drug dealings by means of a paraphernalia of athletic symbology).

Companies that in the 1960s and early 1970s were largely interested only in national enterprise have now evolved to assume a global role. Much of this development can be attributed to the explosive growth of Information Technology: e.g. television sets can now link in to both national and international networks, and what was largely a medium of national entertainment and information has now helped to show that viewers are global villagers, nodes in a vast and expanding international complex. And the move to global commerce has destroyed companies that, in key trade sectors, could only operate in national terms. Increasingly, particular product sectors are falling under the sway of a smaller and smaller range of firms. Here the Japanese have been remarkably successful: we need only to look at their world impact on motor manufacturing, motor-cycles and electronic equipment of all sorts (consider, for example, the position of such Japanese companies as JVC, Sony and Hitachi in the video recorder market). Philips competes successfully with the Japanese in Europe, but again we are only looking at a handful of companies, each a vast conglomerate with rapidly developing economic (and political) power. These are the organizations that can survive and prosper in the modern age of global competition.

The globalization of technology, trade, travel and communications inevitably suggests the emergence of a global culture. Local cultural patterns are forced to coexist with the growing pressure of ideas, fashions, attitudes, tastes and products that are being poured into every continent by a few dominant multinational companies. It is no surprise to find Boeing jets serving capitals across the globe, Hilton hotels from one country to another, Peter Stuyvesant cigarettes being smoked in Tokyo and New York, Sony television in every continent, and Levi jeans everywhere. With easier travel, some observers have questioned its value: why travel from one country to another, when the same products—the same books, the same clothes, the same electronic gear, the same motor cars—will be found in each. The corporate executive often no longer needs to travel: he can 'think globally' by means of modern communications, with more information at his finger-tips about half the countries of the world than most local experts. We are not surprised to find that Coca-Cola drinkers exist in almost every country; but it is also significant that France's BSN corporation, with an international reputation in dairy products, enjoys 50 per cent of the Brazilian and Mexican markets.

The emergence of global taste has been accelerated by the communications revolution: this is a crucial sector of IT that deserves its own treatment (see Chapter 6)—global IT will be manifestly crucial to the emergence of the eco-computer. It is significant that the world's financial markets now operate continuously for 24 hours a day. Communications technology is breaking down national frontiers, time barriers, etc. As some money markets close down for the day, others take over—until they too close and are supplanted by other financial centres. The linking of the world's financial centres is another sign of the growing interconnection of facilities in the emerging global electronic matrix. Just as the financial centres connect to each other, so they also connect to databases, research centres, government offices, corporate headquarters, etc. Corporate growth—whatever the nature of the corporation—leads inevitably to an increased globalization of commercial and industrial activity. And the linking of financial centres has not led to a comfortable symbiosis: instead companies are forced to compete—or lose business to other centres.

The communications revolution has also accelerated the exchange of information, of every imaginable sort, across the globe. Well-known journals—*The Economist, Newsweek, Time,* the *Wall Street Journal,* etc.—have been enabled to assume an international presence; and it is not uncommon to see copies of *Pravda* on the streets of Manchester, England. Scientific researchers can plug in to international databanks, whatever the discipline; and international lawyers can search for precedents using databanks in different countries. Military planners, with their own vastly complex communications networks, can collect information at electonic speed about almost any country in the world. (We do not need to dwell on the interesting paradox of many communications networks helping to sustain and improve human life on Earth while an equal number of global networks are used to lay plans for the total destruction of the human race.)

There is also a discernible trend towards the abolition of financial and trading barriers. For example, successive GATT rounds have progressively diminished protective tariffs; companies can invest abroad to circumvent quota barriers; and moves such as deregulation of telecommunications (breaking up the AT&T monopoly in the US and the privatization of British Telecom in the UK) have had the effect of breaking down nationalistic procurement policies in this area. These and other related trends are helping the progressive globalization of economic and industrial activity. No value judgement is intended by this observation. Current tariff policies, attitudes to deregulation and privatization, corporate mergers, etc., may or may not be socially desirable: we are interested in charting what may well be a deterministic trend towards increased globalization, irrespective of how such a development may serve human interest.

It is now easy to see some of the complex of forces that are forcing entrepreneurs and managers to adopt a global perspective. Technology has enlarged the scope for corporate growth: companies that ignore this circumstance are likely to be left stranded in a fast-moving marketplace (in the slogan of a recent UK minister—'Automate or liquidate'). And it is not simply that more and more products are becoming hi-tech based (though this is true); it is also that the framework in which commercial and manufacturing activity takes place is being defined in hi-tech terms (with computer-based systems unbiquitous is design, financial planning, manufacturing, etc). When this trend is set against the growth in worldwide communications networks, companies in critical sectors are thrust in the direction of international enterprise, towards increased globalization of planning, resource management, marketing, distribution, etc. And the shrinking of the global village is leading inexorably to the homogenization of taste (a unified worldwide culture) and to the increasing irrelevance of the traditional frontiers of the nation state.

The pressures for increased globalization have encouraged corporate growth—and in increasingly crowded market sectors this has inevitably meant mergers and takeovers, the absorption of economic units into larger conglomerates (see Multinationals, below). So there is increased talk of 'merger mania' and 'merger madness'—as companies are acquired by (usually) larger organizations. Britain, for example, saw an unprecedented boom in mergers, takeovers and related deals in 1986. Companies were bought and sold at a dizzy rate, with immediate and long-term consequences for employment patterns, personal fortunes, and the capacity of government to influence national economic activity. According to the UK Department of Trade and Industry, the value of companies bought and sold in the first half of 1986 was £8.5 billion, representing a 20 per cent increase on the record full-year total of £7 billion established in 1985. The 1986 6-month period included what have been dubbed 'mega-deals' or 'mega-bids' —such as the purchase of Imperial Group by Hanson Trust for no less than £2.6 billion, and the £2.5 billion Guinness acquisition of Distillers. The rocketing scale of these mega-deals can be put into perspective when it is remembered that the value of all UK deals in 1980 was somewhat less than £1.5 billion.

A number of factors have encouraged the enthusiasm for merger activity. There has been a boom in Stock Exchange share prices, so lubricating company efforts to acquire other organizations. It is easy to correlate a boom in share prices with a boom in takeover successes. Moreover, despite the spreading gloom on the employment front,

companies have enjoyed vastly increased profits over the dismal early
1980s when the recessionary atmosphere was hitting both
employment and returns on investment: pundits remain confused
about why an upturn in corporate profitability should not have dented
to a greater extent the high level of unemployment (one reason is sure
to be the growing use of computer applications). And it is also the case
that merger mania is infectious: once the deals are rolling, other board-
rooms fear being left out in the cold—and so look to their own merger
options. A self-sustaining atmosphere of merger activity affects corporate attitudes and expectations.

We may think it significant that the prodigious expansion of merger
activity is occurring against a background of anti-monopoly and anti-
trust legislation. In the US for example, mergers and takeovers are
also rocketing in numbers and size: in a single week in October 1986
bids worth around £7.5 billion were tabled for one American bank and
for a steel producer. This suggests that the dynamics of corporate
mergers incline to outstrip regulatory constraints, and that there are
consequences here for both labour and government. One estimate
suggests that more than half a million workers in the UK have been
affected by takeover bids in 1986; and it is difficult to see how UK
governments (or other Western administrations), with present *laissez-
faire* policies, can regulate corporate activity on this scale (we may also
speculate that governments of a different hue, that might be elected in
the future, would be unlikely to be more successful in their regulatory
ambitions: globalization of communications and resource
management gives large corporations obvious strategic advantages in
any policy conflicts with national governments).

The move towards globalization of corporate activity is increasingly
advertised in the media and elsewhere, with certain corporate
initiatives gaining a high profile through broadcasting and the press.
So there is debate about whether Japanese companies should be
allowed to set up motor car manufacturing plants in Britain; and
whether foreign nationals should be allowed to own national
newspapers (no one doubts that Rupert Murdoch is a global
phenomenon or that Robert Maxwell has similar ambitions: Maxwell
has promised to develop Mirror Group Newspapers into a global
communications business by 1990). Today it is commonplace for large
corporations, operating in important commercial and industrial
sectors, to expect to have an impact on the global economy

The Global Economy

The global economy, like the ecosphere, is a complex system comprising a mass of subsystems that evolved initially on a parochial basis. Corporate amalgamations, mergers, growth, etc., came to function in an increasingly interlocked economic world; and this circumstance is a dominant factor in modern thinking. Barnet and Müller (1974), for example, in a seminal work, discuss the development of the *Global Shopping Centre*. (How was it created? How is it sustained?) In this connection, Ernest Dichter, responsible for the Exxon 'Put a tiger in your tank' slogan, refers to the 'world customer'—not to indicate that every potential customer is the same in outlook and inclination, but to emphasize the need for the corporate manager to collect relevant information about human beings in different parts of the world so that it becomes possible to direct the 'world revolution of human expectations'. This revolution is part of the homogenization of taste and attitude—which is stressing many societies (note the current debate in China about the respective importance of *spiritual* and *material* values), but which can only have one eventual outcome. For example, Lee S. Bickmore, a former chairman of the National Biscuit Company, has suggested that people all over the world tend 'to adopt the same tastes and same consumption habits'—and this is the key to the global market. In the same context, Daniel Boorstin has seen the 'consumption community' as transcending race and geography, overcoming traditional attitudes in favour of eating, drinking, wearing and driving the same things. *Time* magazine ran an international advertisement that stated that *Time*'s 24 million readers worldwide 'are apt to have more in common with each other than with many of their own countrymen'. These readers are seen as 'an international community of the affluent and the influential'. This at least gives a clue as to the sort of world that the eco-computer will inherit. We can envisage a *stratified* global community in which old divisions have broken down and new ones have been erected. The criteria for high status, we may judge, will be the qualities needed for management of the Global Shopping Centre. The world managers will be the new elite, an unremarkable development in the light of current political and commercial attitudes. But any such assessment leaves out of the equation a central fact: the progressive de-skilling of human bings *at every level* as computational competence is relentlessly transferred from *Homo sapiens* to *Machina sapiens.* We will need to consider this in speculating about the future shape of the global economy.

If, in the interim, we have a Global Shopping Centre, we will also witness the performance of the Global Factory (an important concept that is often discussed in the literature). Thus Richard J. Barnet (1980) has observed 'The rise of the multinational corporation has created the Global Factory.' And lubricating the obvious requirements of manufacture are the international financial institutions, the centres of investment funding, the pivots of global resource management. Consider, for example, the activities of the World Bank and the International Monetary Fund (IMF): such organizations can dictate terms for essential loans to national goverments, influencing domestic policies, keeping the world safe for massive vested interest. The IMF has the global clout to organize an annual meeting, lasting a week, in a vast Washington hotel, at which the finance ministers and banking executives from around 150 countries attent to proclaim their fealty to international capital. This does not mean of course that there is always agreement, that individual nations do not on occasion make a try for unilateral decision making—but increasingly there is global pressure for policy conformity. The eccentricity of national indepence, in the areas of finance and political philosophy, is a luxury that even the superpowers cannot often afford. And in addition to the dynamics of the World Bank and the IMF there are other international groupings that urge a shared philosophy, a financial conformity to protect what is deemed the desirable global economic structure. Other 'groups' meet to deliberate on international financial questions, and their conclusions are fed into the broader IMF conferences. For example, there is a Group of Five (US, West Germany, Japan, France and the UK), a Group of Seven (G5 plus Canada and Italy) and a Group of Ten (which surprisingly enough contains eleven members—G7 plus Belgium, Holland, Sweden and Switzerland). All such meetings are intended to further the interests of member states, though it is obvious that the interests of individual nations do not always accord—and what may be intended as a smooth, harmonious deliberation on national and international financial matters can often descend into acrimony and 'agreement to disagree'. In such circumstances, damage limitation may be the name of the game.

It should not be thought that the various financial groupings operate without implications for the non-capitalist world. There are

IMF and World Bank loans to East European countries, and even the Soviet Union seems interested in becoming more involved in the machinery of international finance. A recent (1986) Soviet request to take part in the global trade negotiations carried out under the auspices of GATT (General Agreement on Tariffs and Trade) received an infavourable response, but even the fact that the request was officially made indicates a shrinking of the world trade scene. A GATT meeting held in September 1986 was asked to consider the Soviet Union request to 'contribute to the improvement of trade policy conditions'—and it is clear from the framing of the request that the Soviet Union recognizes that its policies must move towards those of GATT members, in some respects, if the contemplated Soviet membership of GATT is to be even a possibility. Already it is significant that Poland, Hungary, Czechoslavakia and Romania are GATT members, as are India and a number of other developing countries—and China recently became the ninety-third GATT member (China is making strenuous efforts to encourage commercial competition and to liberalize its own trade regime in order to accommodate the philosophy of the US-dominated GATT organization). So we see a situation in which the Soviet Union is the only major trading unit that is currently outside GATT (the absence of Taiwan is less important). In such circumstances there is immense pressure, on both the Soviet Union and member nations, to conform to a common economic philosophy: dissent and unilateral action are increasingly impractical, and the trend is towards a world attitude to trade, financial policy and related matters. Again we see the increasingly homogeneity of taste and philosophy, this time in the critical areas that regulate all important world economic activity.

We need not speculate on whether this increasing uniformity of economic philosophy is a good or a bad thing. We may inquire whether such organizations as the World Bank, the IMF and GATT do anything more than sustain current unequal economic relations in the world. It is clear, for example, that the impossible situation of debtor nations is not helped by the debates in the international financial groupings, and we may be less than impressed with the impact of international finance on the state of employment, resource management, food provision, etc., throughout the world. But again the temptation to indulge in value assessments is outside the scope of this book. We are interested only in advertising the increased globalization of human enterprise, with emphasis on the implications for the shape of the world that the eco-computer will inherit.

It should also be stressed that globalization of the world economy does not entail a *total* homogeneity, a *complete* unification of all taste, attitude and philosophy. It is inevitable that local differences will exist, and that pressures for conformity will often be resisted. For example, such countries as Poland and Romania have not *fully* adapted their socialist economies to the GATT requirements, though pressure for movement towards that eventual goal is still maintained and we may speculate on the long-term outcome. Czechoslovakia, a founder member of GATT before the nation developed a centrally planned economy, is also tolerated as a member state that fails to conform to the US-inspired economic model. So a number of GATT members are tolerated as 'passengers without a ticket' (in the words of one GATT official). It remains to be seen whether GATT will be able to view the Soviet Union in such a way.

There is thus a well-established global economy exerting irresistible pressures on individual nation states (even the super-powers cannot be indifferent to the patterns of world trade, the occurrence of global fluctuations in employment, production and investment). The accelerating globalization of economic activity is one of the key factors shaping the cultural climate of the modern world: it is increasingly feasible to view the global economy as a single integrated system that can be studied in structural and behavioural terms. For example, Marchetti (1985) cites a mathematical model derived from ecology that can be used to explore the swings and cycles of the global economy (it is proposed that the Volterra-Lottke equations used to describe the predator/prey relationship 'work even better for economics'). And we should not be surprised that socioeconomic situations can be modelled in such a way: social theory is increasingly receptive to computer simulation for modelling purposes (see, for example, Sorenson, 1978; and Bronson, 1986).

The global economy is evolving, propelled by many different pressures, to impose a broadly unified pattern on the systems of economic activity throughout the world. This activity interacts with the ecosphere in many different ways, and it is clear that the eco-computer will be interested in the scope and character of the countless eco-economic interactions. The agents of international economic activity are of several different types, but pre-eminent amongst them are the multinational corporations. It is worth considering these in a little more detail.

Multinationals

General

The multinational corporations operate in every key economic sector; and they are massively involved in, as an inevitable corollary, military manufacture and the collection and dissemination of information. Therefore it should never be thought that the multinationals operate as value-free economic units. As well as manufacturing and supplying mustard and motor cars, they always have a deep commitment to the use of weapons and propaganda to sustain the global economic order.

History

We often incline to think that the multinational corporation is a modern phenomenon, brought into being by the emergence of international communications and international transport, the fabric of the global village. In fact, international economic units have existed for centuries. Consider the case of Ulrich Fugger & Bros. Here was a company with subsidiaries all over Europe, and with headquarters in Augsburg. It enjoyed control of mining operations in several countries, was a dominant copper company, had interests in banking, and drew revenue from Mexico, South America and the West Indies. It befriended monarchs and popes, financed wars, and has been depicted as a Renaissance forerunner of the modern multinational enterprise.

The founder of the firm, Jacob Fugger (1459–1525) provided money for the Vatican's Swiss guard, funded the pope's war against the French, organized papal indulgences as a business operation, and worked to influence papal elections. Jacob's nephew Anton, the subsequent head of the firm, is said to have paid 275 333 guilders to secure Charles I's election as emperor. This meant in turn that opposition to the Fugger monopoly never succeeded. And many other international organizations—e.g. the East India Company and the Massachusetts Bay Colony—operated in far-flung parts to make money. By start of the nineteenth century many companies, run by ambitious entrepreneurs, had international aspirations—and were often encouraged by governments as a bulwark against anticolonialism. Thus the East India and Hudson Bay companies were chartered in part to consolidate colonial gains and to assist in the conquest of new lands.

Finance was a field for early corporate growth, though not all the companies were able to prosper and expand. For example, the Phoenix Insurance Company, established in the US in 1804, collapsed after 6 years, and other companies moved in to fill the gap. For a while, British interests were dominant in the Manhattan Bank in the 1830s, and when the 1862 British Companies Act opened the way for large-scale financing, the financial corporations began a period of rapid international growth.

It is worth highlighting the emergent character of large corporate enterprise. No company breaks fully fledged upon the scene, but roots can be traced back to the nineteenth century and before. Glaxo, for instance, in the mid-1800s was processing local milk supplies in New Zealand to provide commercial baby food, and J. & J. Clark set up a New Jersey factory in 1864 to produce cotton thread. While Coats, Clark and English Sewing Cotton were developing factories in Europe and the empire, William Barbour & Sons of Northern Ireland set up a US linen company in 1865. US brewing companies that were set up in the 1880s and survived into the twentieth century were crushed by Prohibition: legitimate business was destroyed and an immense boost given to organized crime (today the global economy supports a vast criminal organization). In the nineteenth century Levers was expanding its soap interests around the world, and Schwepps built a factory in Sydney, Australia, in 1877—and there was similar expansion in household products (Reckitts), confectionary (Mackintosh), glass (Pilkington), matches (Bryant & May), etc. Before the First World War, Dunlop was building factories in Canada, Germany and Japan; and such companies as ICI, Courtaulds, Vickers and EMI already had a massive international presence. But the nineteenth-century success of British business was soon being threatened by companies in the US and elsewhere. In 1901 the largest factory in Britain was built by the American giant Westinghouse; and Singer's Glasgow factory, built in 1867, was the world's largest sewing-machine plant. Already it was becoming clear that technological dominance was passing out of the hands of the British. Mechanization, the forerunner to automation, was being pioneered on American assembly lines; and the methods of such industrialists as Henry Ford were soon influencing the shape of manufacturing throughout the world.

The internationalization of business and industrial activity was thus well under way in the nineteenth century. Sporadic international enterprises were in evidence before then, but true globalization—the emergence of the Global Factory and the Global Shopping Centre—could clearly be seen developing before the beginning of the twentieth century. The last hundred years has seen the dramatic consolidation and expansion of corporate activity in every manufacturing sector. International economic activity has been evident in all previous centuries—traders were always prepared to travel widely to sell their wares—but true globalization is a creature of the twentieth century.

What is a Multinational?

It is conventional to regard a multinational corporation as something more than a company that has international interests: a company that invests abroad is not necessarily a multinational. In fact there are many definitions, and we need not dwell on them. In one depiction, companies can be inter-, multi-, trans- and supra-national; and another writer prefers to see firms as ethnocentric, polycentric or geocentric. There may be a point in such distinctions but they need not detain us. It is enough to regard a company as *multinational* when it has directly controlled operations in different countries, and where it is sensitive to the implications of the global economy. In this vein, Professor H.V. Perlmutter (1965) opted for the word 'geocentric'.

Firms became established in foreign lands in many different ways: through conquest, through invitation from a monarch or emperor, through progressive infiltration via licensing or other agreements, etc. It has sometimes been the case that foreign markets were only accessible when the products of a company based elsewhere were also manufactured in the foreign country. Initially 'manufacture' may consist of little more than basic assembly, the parts being manufactured in the home country; but where economic advantage was perceived, more and more of the manufacturing operations were transferred abroad—and a subsidiary company evolved, still under the control of the parent firm but with considerable local autonomy. Turner (1970) argued that the typical transaction of international commerce is no longer straightforward importing and exporting but 'increasingly the creation of manufacturing facilities owned by multi-national companies'.

The traditional multinational company tended to be a primary. producer. Foreign investment was necessary because this ensured a supply of the company's basic products (oil, bananas, meat, coffee, etc.): with such an arrangement it was necessary to coordinate production, markets and product supply on an international basis. More recently, as companies have expanded their interests and foreign involvements, their foreign commitments have become more flexible. With technology aiding global activity, the large multinationals are not tied to any particular product or product region: if activity in one market looks unpromising, resources can be quickly transferred elsewhere. Improved transport facilities and modern communications make particular geographical sites less important, except where basic commodities and cheap labour can still be found. And computer-based systems were being developed, as much as two decades ago, to enable multinational companies to plan their activities on a global basis. For example, Standard Oil (New Jersey) had built computerized models of their entire world operations by 1970—to optimize the disposition of tanker fleets, and to estimate the effects of particular hypothetical commercial decisions on their global trading position.

The global significance of the multinational corporation has long been recognized. Barnet and Muller (1974), for example, saw the global impact of the multinational resting on three fundamental resources: the technology of production, finance capital and marketing. It is clear that production management increasingly ignores national frontiers: the Gross World Product is being generated in more and more countries, shifting the production emphasis from the old industrialized world. Today a few hundred global corporations control most of the production in the non-communist world; and increasingly the multinational companies are making inroads into the socialist economies of Eastern Europe and the Soviet Union.

We constantly read that industry or commerce or the multinationals have transcended geography, transcended national barriers, transcended their own countries. The modern multinational is global in the sense that it looks to a world marketing ethic tolerating local tradition in so far as such tolerance enhances the global status of the parent company. It may be prudent for a white Anglo-Saxon company to employ black managers in certain parts of the world—to create the illusion of local autonomy, and to foster thereby a local commitment to a particular economic enterprise. In this sense, many multinational companies—though undemocratic and oligarchic—eschew racism. Pragmatism, in the interest of global profit, may be deemed a more prudent posture.

A global corporation is in a position to borrow money from any region of the world. The framework of multinational operations meshes tightly with the development of the international money markets. The 1960s saw the emergence of powerful international loan syndicates and the international banking consortium. Organizations of this (latter) sort can be found in various countries: typical consortiums have included the Orion Bank (organized by Chase Manhattan), the Royal Bank of Canada, the Westdeutsche Landesbank Girozentral, Credito Italiano, Nikko Securities of Japan, and the UK National Westminster. The activities of such organizations have always had international significance—for themselves, and for countless other organizations at home and abroad. A currency crisis, dramatically affecting the international money markets, may have been initiated by unilateral action in a large consortium or by an unexpected production decision in a manufacturing mulinational. Today computer-based cash management systems have given large corporations the opportunity to operate on the world capital and currency markets. The power of the multinationals means that worthwhile local economic activity is quite likely to be starved of development capital, and there are many consequences for the position of international labour.

There can be little doubt that the multinational corporation has evolved as an economic force to challenge the power of the nation state. Where small underdeveloped countries are concerned this is hardly a matter for dispute, but the power of the large corporation does not stop there. Few modern states—perhaps none—are in a position to confront the main planners of the resource systems of the world. We do well to remember that it is largely the multinationals that develop and distribute energy, mine and transport minerals, grow and distribute food, design and manufacture medical products, and supervise the international flow of capital and information. All the day-to-day functions of the planet are monitored and regulated, at several different levels, by multinational corporations. We are not surprised to hear George Ball, chairman of Lehman Brothers International in the 1960s, declare: 'Working through great corporations that straddle the Earth, men are able for the first time to utilise world resources with an efficiency dictated by the objective logic of profit.' In a similar spirit, Jacques Maisonrouge of IBM has suggested that the case for multinationals is that they use world resources 'with a maximum of efficiency and a minimum of waste . . . on a global scale'.

We do not need to evaluate the global stature of the multinational corporation. It is enough, for our theme, that such organizations truly operate on the global stage, an economic ecosphere with numerous interlocking subsystems and components, regulated by a stratum of human decision making that is increasingly unified. The economic ecosphere is the Global Market supplied by the processes of Global Production and run by the world managers. The global corporation can be seen as cementing the international links—of money transfer, decision making, information flow, labour exploitation, product dissemination, etc.—that will become part of the infrastructure of the eco-computer. Computer-based systems are already enshrined in the crucial nerve centres of the global economy. We will find that any global production sector—mining, manufacturing, finance, product distribution, marketing, etc.—will become one of the subsystems of the global intelligence. The multinational is one of the pressures for the emergence of a global matrix that will facilitate the progressive exclusion of human beings from the decision-making loop.

Who are the Multinationals?

We have already met some multinationals—IBM, ICI, Dunlop, Courtaulds, etc.—and others should be mentioned. By the mid-1970s there were no fewer than 11 000 companies operating about 82 000 foreign affiliates: and 371 of these companies were active in 20 or more countries. By the late 1970s more than a quarter of the sales of nearly a thousand of the world's largest companies were derived from their foreign affiliates; and about 50 companies derived more than half of their revenue from foreign activity. More than ten years ago the liquid assets of the world's multinational organizations were estimated at twice the size of the world's gold and foreign exchange reserves; by 1980 the mulinationals had further strengthened their position. One only has to appreciate the stature of the global multinational network to realize the relative impotence of national governments that might attempt to legislate against what may be judged to be corporate interest.

Two of the world's largest multinational corporations are Exxon and General Motors. They are comparable in stature and size: one or the other generally heads the Fortune 'top 500' American corporations. Volkswagen makes cars in more than half-a-dozen countries; and IBM bestrides the non-communist world. Hitachi has annual revenues of well over $10 billion, deriving more than half its earnings from foreign countries. Two German chemical giants, BASF and Bayer, also earn more than $10 billion a year; and Bayer has 312 foreign subsidiaries. Nestlé has revenues of around $12 billion, as do a dozen or so other companies able to operate on a global ·basis. Hitachi began as a motor repair shop in 1910: today it rates at about 14 in the global list of multinational corporations (it aims to challenge IBM, the world's largest computer corporation). Today Hitachi makes around 50 000 different products, and has offices in nearly fifty countries. It builds integrated circuits in California, using cheap immigrant labour, and assembles electronic equipment in Taiwan and elsewhere. NV Phillips Gloeilampenfabrieken employs nearly 400 000 people in about sixty countries. International Telephone and Telegraph (ITT) has nearly half a million employees in nearly one hundred countries— and the company owns Wonder Bread, Sheraton Hotels, Hartford Insurance, Avis Rent-a-Car, Bobbs-Merrill Publishing, and Burpee Lawn and Garden Products. IBM, with a mere 300 000 employees earns around $25 billion a year. And so on and so forth . . . the 'seven sisters' in oil, publishing corporations with banking interests, corporate giants in the US, Japan and Europe, taking on governments, complacent about a destitute Third World, hostile to labour organizations, a central pivot of globalization.

Today (1987) the book value of multinational assets approaches $1000 billion. We can speculate on the political and economic power that resides in such a figure, and we can remember that there are no international organizations that are equally well funded and not devoted to the accumulation and use of private capital. There is no international body with the clout to regulate or confront the global sway of the multinational corporation. Already we can see how this circumstance will influence the shape of an eco-computer that evolves to inherit, rather than to invent, a global scene.

Multinationals and Other Organizations

There are many international organizations, but none outside the military sphere is as powerful as the multinational corporations. The United Nations is impotent in comparison; and in any case many of the UN activities link in with company operations and may be seen as effective aids to corporate growth. In fact most international organizations are essentially economic groupings that have been brought about to further the interests of large corporations. One need only think of the European Economic Community (EEC), the European Free Trade Area (EFTA), the Latin American Free Trade Association (LAFTA), the Central American Common Market (CACM), the Caribbean Free Trade Area (CARIFTA), the East African Community, the Central African Economic and Customs Union (UDEAC), and the breakaway Union of Central African States (UEAC). There are also many multinational ventures aimed at low visibility in sensitive environments. For this purpose investment companies have been established for Latin American, Asia and Africa. For example, the Adela Investment Company, SA, had achieved the support of shareholders in sixteen developed countries by 1970, and a large early venture was a $77 million forestry project in Honduras. Another grouping, PICA (Private Investment Company of Asia), is supported by a consortium including First National City Bank, Alcan Aluminium and the Bank of Tokyo. More examples of this sort could be given, but the point is made: the multinational corporations do not exercise power and influence solely by virtue of their own economic strength, but also by virtue of far-reaching alliances and deals with other corporate bodies. To describe the character of any particular multinational is thus only part of the story. Its links with other international organizations are also important in developing the structure of the global economy.

The large corporations are also intimately involved with military affairs (more is said about this in Chapter 7): it is no exaggeration to say that many of the largest companies depend on their survival on military funding made available by Western governments. The connection between business and military funding is well documented—and in fact is so obvious as to require little comment (after all, who is it that manufactures all those aircraft, submarines, missiles, tanks, ships, guns, shells, bombs, bullets, command-and-control computers, etc?). There is a business/military/politics complex that again is pushing the world inevitably towards increased globalization. Again we can note this circumstance without offering an evaluation.

Towards the Eco-Computer

The world economy in general and the multinational corporations in particular are enmeshed in the developing fabric of the eco-computer. Companies need to collect and process data in order to survive: the larger the company, the broader and deeper the data that are necessary.

And these data are increasingly gathered and manipulated by means of computer-based systems that are linked in networks. The emergence of a tool that can assemble global data has caused (to use John Kenneth Galbraith's term) the 'technological imperative' for global programming. This simple perception is the herald of the eco-computer.

The companies themselves are closing the gaps that exist between production activities in different parts of the world, between geographically dispersed research and development initiatives, between different centres of investment and marketing enterprise. Again the cerebral simile is useful: company links are spreading around the globe like the burgeoning neural networks in the skull of the human foetus. The multinational corporations are yet another powerful force encouraging the emergence of a global infrastructure.

The nodes of the infrastructure will increasingly evolve as computer-based corporate complexes, organized to fulfil dedicated tasks that contribute in a coherent way to global economic activity. So computer-controlled direct and remote sensors will (for example) collect geological data for feeding to automated mining systems (telechirs will progressively give way to fully fledged robots). Ores, timbers and other raw materials will be conveyed on automated routes to unmanned factories that operate for 24 hours a day every day (without heating or lighting, except when specifically required in the manufacturing process). And products, tested and then packaged in automated systems, will be automatically conveyed to retail outlets that people can access using electronic money. There is nothing in such a scenario that cannot be found, at least in rudimentary form, in the activities and ambitions of the modern multinational corporations. They are stimulating, often unwittingly, the growth of a global economic structure in which the different phases of economic activity will be increasingly linked and from which the scope for human intervention will be increasingly excluded.

The multinational corporations are enlarging the scope of their global activity, the weight of their global impact, by means of the tools and techniques supplied by modern Information Technology. In this sense the corporations are riding on the back of IT, extending their reach by means of powerful electronic computation, electronic communications networks, and the development of increasingly sophisticated sensor systems in all the environmental sectors of the ecosphere. Before exploring the eco-computer in more detail, we need to glance at the shape of global Information Technology....

6 Global IT

Preamble

We have already given many clues to the nature of global IT. Computer-based information technology now straddles the world, lubricating commerce and industry, adding a new dimension to the possibility of global conflict, and often skewing our values and perceptions in unexpected ways. The evolution of the eco-computer will occur in the context of increasing internationalization of information technology. This is a game with many players—or, in the nice jargon of sociology, there are many actors in the situation. We know their names and their intentions. It is obvious that there will be surprises ahead, but today it is possible to chart the general direction of Information Technology with some confidence: the broad trends evident in the hi-tech world are staring us in the face.

There is now an increasingly closely knit network of communications systems spanning the globe. In the happy words of Grewlich (1986), 'A cloak of highly artificial structures lies over the natural environment of earth and its inhabitants. Steeped in the frequency waves of modern communication technology coupled with top performance telecommunications networks, overflown by aircraft and satellites, we experience the planet's oneness "for better or for worse".' This oneness has been observed and celebrated by many observers, but the contribution—and implications—of Information Technology to this unification is not always appreciated. It is right to stress that IT does not only shrink the world but also make it more vulnerable. The quality of the SDI ('Star Wars') debate is one of the clearest signs of this circumstance (see Chapter 7): the debate is a fantasy charade fuelled by powerful vested interest (it is obvious that SDI is ludicrously unworkable and that the charade threatens human survival).

There are many dimensions to the global impact of Information Technology (see The IT Impact, below). IT can fuel conflict by conferring economic or military advantage; and as people are increasingly withdrawn from the monitoring and control loops, there is an enlarged scope for social disaster being wrought by artificial systems. Today it is often said that Information Technology is the

122

required ticket to economic and political development—but increasingly a few countries, or a few multinational corporations, will dominate the world in IT terms. It is no accident that the emerging world culture is being framed by the countries with the largest IT presence. Countries *lacking* such an IT element—and this means the vast majority of the countries of the world—can only serve as recipients of products, attitudes and values generated elsewhere. Pessimists may reckon that the dynamics of global IT evolution make such a situation inevitable; others may hope for the establishment of a more equitable world order when politicians, industrialists and others are forced to address the implications of the global information society. Grewlich (1986), for example, looks to a 'new psychospiritual dimension' as part of the movement from 'speculative to effective globality'. But it is not obvious what this means: what is clear is that increased globalism will be shaped by, at least in large part, the pressures of corporate enterprise.

The large companies are already staking their claims for a global presence in the twenty-first century. The building of ambitious national schemes will serve as a springboard to international activity. For example, the Nippon Telegraph and Telephone Public Corporation (NTT) is currently developing a massive telecommunications network—the Information Network System (INS)—aimed at the twenty-first century. In one account (Takahashi, 1986), INS is seen as an essental component in the infrastructure of the emerging information society. Prototype systems were built in the early 1980s, and experiments are continuing through 1987. Perhaps more ambitiously, some companies have already built global networks. . . .

The US company GenRad has many manufacturing plants in America, a joint venture assembly plant in Japan, and offices in many other countries (Sweden, Singapore, Switzerland, etc.). A comprehensive network is used to link the entire organization: for instance, sales activities in Northern Ireland can be connected to stock control in Phoenix, Arizona. The company has grown with the development of international communications: e.g. links to the US are maintained using leased lines from British Telecom (dial-up lines allow *ad hoc* connections to Sweden, Holland, the UK and elsewhere). It is significant that effective communication is possible between countries as geographically dispersed as Canada, Britain, Japan and Australia: IT allows global communication without time or language problems.

Global IT

Not long ago 'convergence' was a fashionable buzz-word in computer and communications circles. Today the phenomenon and the trend are unremarkable: it is *assumed* that technologies are merging to provide enhanced facilities. This, of course, was always the case. Different technologies have always combined to produce results that surpass the sum of their parts. The revolutionary amalgam of computers and communications was a dramatic instance of convergence that was soon to have global consequences.

Today the same trend is reflected in a new buzz-word—*connectivity*. This is a term to be found in standard data-processing and communications journals. It is what purchasers of IT systems are looking for: discrete 'stand-alone' facilities are seen to be highly limited, unsuited to the modern convergent age. Products need to have a high degree of *connectivity*, just as they are increasingly containing an element of artificial intelligence (AI).

At the most mundane level the search for connectivity is conducted at the office automation design stage. (What OA systems do we need? Can they be linked together?) More ambitiously, purchasers can look to connectivity as a national or international commodity. (Can this network link to that? What are the implications for standards, interfaces, costs, etc.? Will we later need a degree of connectivity that at present cannot be envisaged?) In the corporate organization there is increasing talk of 'universal connectivity'—by which is meant the capacity of any computer-based system to *talk to* any other (and 'any other' can mean communications systems with national or international scope).

In the 1960s, Texas Instruments Incorporated (TI) developed plans for linking together all the company's manufacturing plants; and by the mid-1970s the scheme was a worldwide network linking TI locations in eighteen countries. Today the network continues to grow geographically—and also to penetrate the company in ever greater depth. Of TI's 77000 employees, around 45 per cent are linked into the network via terminals, workstations, personal computers, etc. (with other users of PCs not yet linked to the network). The global network is intended to support TI's many business activities (semiconductor manufacturing, geophysical services, factory automation, government electronics, etc), exploiting local resources while at the same time integrating them into a worldwide organization. Thus circuit chips can be fed from Singapore to Japan, software can be developed in India (where software engineers cost a third of what they cost in the US), and market strategy can be planned in Dallas, Texas. Today TI deploys information consultants in more than two dozen worldwide locations, and the global network continues to creep, nerve-like, across the planet.

The TI network handles more than 200000 electronic mail messages via a central facility every day, with thousands more communications dealt with on a local basis. Typically a TI employee can communicate with another across the world in a matter of seconds at minimal cost (it has been suggested that a typical message costs around 2 cents). And the TI network also links in to Telex, TWX and Telegraph—which allows TI staff to communicate with millions of people outside the basic TI configuration. The high degree of TI connectivity has been accomplished by means of an imaginative use of standards, and there are plenty of signs that other large companies are keen to follow the TI example.

The aim is to achieve the equivalent of what is already provided by the international telephone system—the ability of any user to contact any other user anywhere in the world. Indeed many of the international corporate links are established using existing telephone lines (e.g. there are leasing arrangements with British Telecom or the large telephone companies in the US), but an alternative strategy is for the companies to build their own communications channels as private networks to bypass the services provided by local telephone companies and the long-distance carriers. For example, in the US it is seen that 31 per cent of the Fortune 500 companies operate independent communications networks, a circumstances of some concern to the telephone companies.

Today many bypass arrangements are emerging. A company may lease private lines from the telephone company in order to achieve a direct linkage with the long-distance carrier; or a user may build an independent bypass link—for which purpose microwave has proved a popular option. There are now many suppliers of microwave facilities, though the need for a clear 'line of sight' between microwave towers in a terrestial environment is an acknowledged technical limitation. This suggests that microwave transmission is best suited for local traffic, though crowding of the frequency spectrum can impose further constraints. One ambitious scheme is the Ebasco Services New York implementation. Here a Harris Farinon microwave terminal and a 2 ft antenna are used to transmit communications from the seventy-seventh floor of the World Trade Centre to a roof-top antenna 0.6 miles away. The roof-top system is run by Satellite Business Systems (SBS), a long-distance carrier able to provide satellite facilities for customers. And other companies have built their own optic fibre links. For example, this year (1987) various new schemes will begin operation: the Hercules chemical company has developed optic fibre facilities to connect three locations in Delaware, US; and the University of Iowa is to begin operating a $15 million configuration that will link five sites. Cable links are another bypass option that may represent a further threat to the established telephone companies.

We do not need to speculate on how the shape of bypass facilities will influence future communications networks. It is enough that there is a rapid growth of communications networks. It is enough that there is a rapid growth of communication provisions, and that these are encouraging a further dramatic shrinkage of the global environment. The *connectivity* sought by purchasers of communications systems will encourage the various suppliers to provide effective links (gateways) between the various types of systems. This in turn will encourage the emergence of a global network where no single international configuration will be able to function 'in grand isolation'—instead there will be numerous links to other networks, all serving to unify the global electronic matrix. The connectivity theme will remain dominant in the years ahead. It was a central topic at, for example, the 1986 National Computer Conference, and it will remain a crucial systems consideration in the future. Systems with a high degree of connectivity will triumph in the marketplace over less well-endowed rivals: connectivity will contribute equally to the making of local links and to the growth of interconnecting global systems. We have already seen that this will happen in various ways.

Expansion of direct telephone systems is an obvious route to increased 'world wiring'. For instance, the telematics programme mapped out by the French Government has included the development of an electronic directory. The aim was to store around 23 million subscriber entries comprising 25 billion digits and letters in a databank (see the description in Maury, 1986). One problem was how to incorporate daily data changes without interrupting use of the databank (50 000 movements a day); another was how to facilitate simultaneous consultation by several million users around the clock. The solution to such questions yielded 'the most widespread computer system in the world' (Maury, 1986).

After research in three areas—databank design, databank interrogation and data transfer between Minitel and the document centres—a successful system was implemented, and it is now possible to retrieve information by surname, profession, address or department (this letter involving a search by surname or profession). The popularity of the electronic directory is well established: of around 14 million calls handled by Teletel in June 1985, about a half related to use of the directory. In fact the service offered rests on the remarkable sophistication of the software: it is possible, for example, to search on any word of a compound term ('eaux', for instance, is sufficient to find 'Companie générale des eaux'); search on a surname containing a particle or article is successful even if incomplete ('Verier' will yield 'Le Verrier', 'Nemour' or 'Denemour' will correctly yield 'De Nemours'); and there is scope for the correct interpretation of synonyms or spelling equivalents.

The success of the French electronic directory has not gone unnoticed. It is significant that other countries—e.g. the US and Switzerland—have requested access to the system to make it easier to obtain information on French subscribers. This is a type of connectivity that may not have been envisaged by the designers of the French facility, but the trend is clear. Already there are plans to provide access to the system on international networks: more links are established and the wired world goes up a further notch.

Today there is increased use of public data networks by private companies (see, for example, Mulqueen, 1986), while firms at the same time develop their own independent bypass configurations. Basic OA units can serve as elements in international facilities, adding further struts in the global electronic matrix: for instance, the Scandinavian Institutes for Administrative Research (SIAR) organization has used communicating word processors as the basis for a global communications network (Susca, 1986); and the use of word processors in such a mode 'stimulated increased computerisation of other functions within SIAR'. Connectivity problems soon appeared, and suppliers were invited to advise. Xerox tried connecting word processors to Macintosh computers, and successful links were installed in SIAR's Stockholm offices in October 1985. Other links and applications are currently being developed: a main concern is how disparate items of equipment can be induced to 'talk to each other' in efficient and cost-effective terms. As elsewhere, the connectivity issue is a major matter.

There are many topics to address in the search for enhanced connectivity. For example, the proliferation of personal computers has added a new dimension to networking requirements: it is no longer a question of linking central data-processing installations, and little else, into corporate communications facilities—there is now a prodigious population of computer-based facilities crying out to be heard. PC communications packages are not always well adapted to larger networking needs, and there may be problems when many thousands of users are trying to access a corporate database at the same time. There are also problems connected with protocol conformance, fault detection and bandwidth requirements (*EDP Analyzer*, May 1986). The search for enhanced connectivity rarely follows a carefree path.

There is also the dimension of outer space, so far little mentioned in this section. The requirements of satellite communications complicate the connectivity difficulties, at the same time increasing the potential for the emergence of the global electronic matrix. We have glanced at the satellite dimension (Chapters 2 and 3) and more will be said in Chapter 7. Here it is worth remarking that satellites extend the scope of global IT—often in unexpected ways. For example, it is possible to use satellite communications to test high-performance aircraft (Kelly, 1986). The Grunman Corporation's X-29 advanced technology demonstrator was tested in flight with the aid of an automated Grunman telemetry station at Long Island, 3000 miles away from the X-29 launch. The forward-swept-wing aircraft was flight tested using satellite communications, the first time this particular trick has been performed. Here the data link from California to the Automated Telemetry System performed flawlessly, suggesting how testing schemes may be developed in the future. Grunman completed the test flights more than two years ago (in 1985), and the aircraft was handed over to NASA. The communications network continues to be used to monitor the flights, and to analyse the accumulated data.

Other satllite uses, as we have seen, focus on collection of meteorological and geological data for a variety of purposes, one of which is to study the global weather pattern. For example, Meteosat-F1 was launched in November 1977 on a data-collection mission—but by August 1984 it was impossible to control the orbit of the satellite from the ground; and a number of other satellites have ceased to function after working satisfactorily for several years. The Meteosat family of geostationary satellites was intended to contribute to a global network for Earth observation, a further link in the worldwide matrix for information processing.

It is significant that satellite designers have always had global ambitions. Orbiting or goestationary satellites necessarily give a global perspective on communications and data collection. For example, in one key document (*Earth Observation Quarterly*, December 1983) it is emphasized that remote-sensing satellites can 'provide repetitive and continuous coverage of the Earth's surface on a very large scale, *up to and including global scale*' (my italics). There are many reasons for thinking that we live in the global age.

By 1985, Earth-observation specialists were coining a new word—radargrammetry—to denote new methods of remote sensing. In particular the new development allowed images to be constructed very rapidly out of raw data. Formerly, hours were required for such a task. Even in 1985 the generation of a 100 × 100 km Seasat SAR image required in the order of 7 hours; but then a new generation of processors was being developed to produce an image in less than half an hour (for mapping, the SAR image requires corrections and rectification): because the techniques are similar to those used for rectification of aerial photography (photogrammetry), the term *radargrammetry* was invented to denote the new facilities. Work in this area is being carried out in the UK, Austria, Switzerland and elsewhere; and three major research areas have been identified.

First, it is possible to develop image-analysis tools (relating, for example, to image simulation and rectification, elevation data extraction from stereo imagery, image mosaics, etc.). Then it is possible to develop multi-sensors combination and analysis; and also sophisticated processing methods for particular application areas (such as agriculture, glaciology and land-use mapping). The whole subject area is yet another example of how sensor technology, communications methods and data-processing techniques are combining to provide multi-application information and analysis on a global scale. Emerging disciplines such as radargrammetry will be massively exploited by the eco-computer.

It is also inevitable, as we have remarked, that the incidence of surveillance from space will greatly increase with the development of global communications and information processing. We all know about spy satellites, but there are also a range of other, less-publicized options. For instance, there is discussion about the possibility of 'media satellites'—devices designed to collect data to service journalistic and broadcasting activity. It was reported in late 1986 that lawyers were ready to challenge the Reagan administration if there were government efforts to block media-owned data-collection satellites. Interest in this option was stimulated by the Chernobyl disaster: at that time it was found that two commercial organizations (the Earth Observation Satellite Company, Eosat; and Spot Image, a French firm) were the only sources of photographic information, independent of the Soviet authorities, available to journalists. American intelligence organizations were said to be nervous that media satellites might eventually provide better-quality data than their own spy satellites. In this context it might even be the case that private media satellites might be in a position to frustrate military or security operations. It would hardly be surprising if governments tried to prevent private organizations from seeing too much. In the US, for example, satellites cannot be launched without official permission, and legal prohibition might be sufficient to prevent media activity in space.

It has been said, perhaps with truth, that various government pressures have been exerted already in the US to prevent media agencies from exploiting current satellite technology: one tale has it that President Carter issued a secret directive that no private agency should be allowed to launch a satellite that could see anything smaller than a lorry (with President Reagan continuing the same prohibitive policy). In any event the trend is clear. There is increasing scope for private compnay initiatives to extend data gathering (and data processing) using satellite systems. This is one of many ways in which data networks will operate within and around the ecosphere. We are no longer surprised to witness financial centres, for instance, using all the paraphernalia of computers and communications to conduct global operations. It is inevitable that other trades and professions will be stimulated to imagine how they can exploit the same technologies to good effect.

We have already seen how stocks and shares can be traded by means of computerbased facilities: program trading has recently (late 1986) been highlighted in the context of unexpected market fluctuations. But the implications have not always been appreciated. In October 1986 (*Observer*, 19 October 1986) we were told that 'somewhere in the City of London, a computer is outwitting the dealers in the foreign exchange markets and making money for itself'. The computer firm Data Logic has produced a piece of software, an 'expert system', that can plot patterns of change to outperform human dealers. We will meet such facilities again (Chapter 7): here all we need remark is how such intelligent facilities are being structured into the networked operations of large companies that have great impact on national economies.

We have seen that global IT has many faces—from electronic telephone directories to the testing of high-performance aircraft, from weather prediction to media spy satellites, from geological prospecting to microwave transmissions from the tops of skyscrapers. These will all be functional components in the eco-computer of the future. Before exploring its likely character it will be helpful to survey some of the principal contributors to the global IT scene.

International Contributions

General

There are, of course, many international contributors to global information processing—companies, other international organizations, governments, individuals, etc. Here we mention some of the leading players on the stage to convey more of the flavour of the global activity that is helping the eco-computer to emerge. It is obvious that this section does not provide an exhaustive treatment: whole libraries would be needed for that. The aim is to deepen our understanding of a technological revolution that will bring greater changes to the planet than it has ever seen before as a result of human initiative. The emergence of the eco-computer will profoundly alter the nature of activity on the surface of the globe—and we can speculate on how the human race will respond to this quantum leap.

IBM and the US

We have seen that IBM is the corporate giant amongst the computer companies of the world. It is usually ranked at Number 7 in listings of all corporate enterprises: in general—by dint of sheer size, resources, multiplicity of interests, depth of research, scale of international activity, etc.—it has competitors always at a disadvantage. The power of IBM is such that it effectively lays down standards on a *de facto* basis for the international IT community: an IBM marketing or product decision becomes a target or reference for other firms. Governments and companies have frequently tried to counter the IBM threat, but without success. In the IT world IBM—'Big Blue'—remains supreme. At the same time such companies as Control

Data, Burroughs, Digital Equipment Corporation, Honeywell and NCR—as essentially US enterprises—are strong in the field, and there are Japanese and European companies with considerable international ambitions. IBM bestrides the IT world but other firms have achieved massive penetration, dominance even, in particular IT sectors. It is significant, for example, that Exxon has entered the field of business machines through its Vydec subsidiary; and such companies as AT&T, Xerox, Siemens, British Telecom, Hitachi, etc, are in a position to keep Big Blue under pressure. There are also thousands of smaller companies, making IBM-compatible equipment, that work to steal IBM business by competitive pricing. The international dominance of IBM does not mean that everything always goes the way of the massive corporation.

As information becomes increasingly important as an international resource, IBM can pressure governments: in 1978 it pulled out of India and Brazil when those countries tried to establish a 'national' computer policy. Today the results of an IBM withdrawal would be catastrophic for many developed countries: normal commerce and trade would be drastically affected, and worst-case scenarios might be a total collapse of the national infrastructures. And if governments have difficulty tackling IBM, labour can achieve very little. IBM does not tolerate trade union activity in its US operations, though employee representation is accepted on the board of IBM Germany. IBM spends more on research and development than any company except General Motors, and its financial resources are greater than those of many nation states (for instance, as far back as 1976 its cash resources of $6.5 billion exceeded the foreign exchange reserves of Sweden or Canada). It is not uncommon for IBM to spend billions of dollars in a single year in capital spending alone, with much current investment aimed at countering the Japanese challenge.

In most countries boasting a significant IT component, IBM is usually the dominant presence. In 1984, for example, IBM (UK) had revenues of £2.5 billion, with about 20 per cent of the revenue derived from software. IBM (UK)'s turnover matches that of the entire non-IBM software activity in Britain. In a 1986 report from the Advisory Council for Applied Research and Development (ACARD) it is noted: 'The size of this one company and the influence which it has on all software activities cannot be over-emphasised ... consideration of the health of the UK software industry must include IBM.'

The market impact of IBM is such that a merger between the UK forces of the American mulinationals Burroughs and Sperry is currently being developed. John Sperry, overseeing this process, has commented: 'It's not like any other industry.... We are both $5 billion corporations, yet people are asking us whether we could survive' (quoted by Peter Large, *Financial Guardian*, 17 October 1986). It is suggested that in ten years' time there may only be five large-scale players in the field, and IBM is sure to be one of them (but by then it may not be the dominant force). IBM is currently selling about two-thirds of the world's computers, and competing firms have been driven to find market niches where a full-scale IBM onslaught seems unlikely. The Burroughs/Sperry combine may manage to achieve a fifth of IBM's $450 billion level of business (Digital Equipment, IBM's nearest rival, is a sixth the size of Big Blue). The scale of IBM business is nicely shown by the fact that Digital Equipment, with quarterly results of $2.038 billion revenue (reported in late 1986), is generally classed as one of the non-IBM 'dwarfs'. There is now a massive global shakeout under way amongst the world's largest computer companies: corporate power will be enlarged in the years ahead, whoever the victors are in the struggle.

By 1987 there were a few signs that IBM, despite its massive international status, was not almighty. A third-quarter profit decline of 27 per cent had been announced in late 1986, while Digital Equipment profits for the same period rose by 153 per cent—and while DEC aims to recruit a total of 1000 staff in Britain in 1987, IBM is dropping 12000 as part of a voluntary redundancy arrangement. At the same time it needs to be remembered that IBM profits for the period were $1.08 billion, perhaps not inconsiderable. But IBM is also facing problems from what have been dubbed the 'IBM-ulators and PC-clones', effective IBM look-alikes that have had some success in tackling traditional IBM markets. An estimate from the international research firm International Data suggests that for the first time more IBM look-alikes will be marketed than actual IBM machines. To counter this trend, an IBM strategy is already under way: one aim is to increase the proportion of software sales (it is increasingly important to sell 'brainpower' rather than 'boxes'). It is clear that IBM will maintain a dominant role in the immediate future, but there is scope for speculation about the shape of the global IT industry at the turn of the century. Part of IBM's difficulty will come from Japanese enterprise and initiative.

Hitachi and Japan

The Hitachi company—which has been dubbed the 'General Electric of Japan'—is about Number 14 in world corporate listings, and it has evident ambitions to be the world's next IBM (in fact Fujitsu leads in computer sales in Japan, with higher performance than IBM Japan). Hitachi is reckoned to have around 500 Ph.D.s and the company has registered more than 30 000 patents: it has diversified more than IBM and today has interests in electric motors, heavy electrical engineering, turbines, copper cables, rolling stock, etc.—as well as the prodigious range of electronics products. The total Hitachi range is reckoned to include more than 40 000 products.

Hitachi is evolving a strategy to compete with IBM, as are other Japanese multinationals. Fujitsu has run into problems marketing software that is said to infringe IBM products, and the outcome of this confrontation is not yet resolved. It is necessary for Fujitsu to develop its own operating system (in order to avoid costly legal battles with IBM), at the same time devising a system that is IBM-compatible (it will lose massive market opportunities if it moves too far away from the traditional IBM market sectors).

Fujitsu, like Hitachi, has many historic links with electrical engineering: it started in 1935 as an offshoot of the Fuji Electric Company. It was in the early 1970s, when the Japanese Government created various research groups, that Fuji worked with Hitachi to produce computers that were IBM-compatible: the prospect of impossible legal tangles began at that time. And it was in 1982 that IBM took legal action against Fujitsu, Hitachi and Mitsubishi for violation of software copyright: in 1983 the Japanese companies were obliged to pay IBM about $100 million in compensation, and to agree to allow IBM to inspect their operating-system software from time to time. The penalties of tangling with IBM were made crystal clear. Today, Fujitsu, still under the shadow of IBM, is reckoned to have an ambiguous future. One option (discussed by Berger, 1986) is a strategic alliance: there is speculation about a Fujitsu alliance with AT&T.

The Japanese Ministry of Trade and Industry (MITI) has been energetic in promoting national IT effort. For example, there are today two large collaborative research, programmes: the Fifth Generation Computer Project, and the National Superspeed Computer Project (this latter often called the Super Computer Project). The Institute for New Generation Computer Technology

(ICOT)—including MITI, Nippon Telegraph and Telephone (NTT), and Japan's eight leading computer firms—has been created to run the Fifth Generation Computer Project, and similar collaborative effort has been directed at the Super Computer Project. Many observers have speculated on the likely impact of Japan, Inc. Thus Rogers and Larsen (1985) commented: 'A recent visitor to MITI's collaborative research projects likened them to a band of revolutionaries planning a guerrilla attack, implying that IBM has little to fear. Perhaps not, but that's also what General Motors said a few years ago'.

The Soviet Union

The Soviet Union, one of the two indisputable global powers, may be thought to be an obvious force in international IT. In fact we are often told how backward the Soviet Union is in all matters to do with computers and communications. This is a problematic area, clouded as it is with propaganda distortions on both sides; but it is obvious that there are wide-ranging Russian plans for the development of computer-based systems, and likely that these will have a global impact in the years to come.

A feature article and editorial in an issue of the *Russian Economic Gazette* (reported by Anning *et al.*, 1985) indicated plans for the increased use of IT as part of the twelfth Five-Year Plan: it was revealed that key elements in the programme for the 1986–90 period were integrated systems, computer-aided design, networking and personal computing. At the same time emphasis was being given to the importance of an enlarged computing programme for schools and an enlarged quota of technicians in key disciplines. One contentious area is the extent to which the Soviet Union acquires Western technology by illicit means. A BK Dynamics report, prepared for the Pentagon, observed that 'if the Russians had acquired the technologies they attempted to import from the U.S., they'd have saved from $6.6 billion to $13.3 billion in their military budget over the lifetime of the technologies involved'. And there are heavy legal penalties for illicit trade in computers with the Soviet Union: there are frequent prosecutions of Western firms and individuals for exporting, or trying to export, computer-based systems to the Soviet Union (the most recent case, late 1986, is of a British engineer sent to gaol for 6 months for trying to export computers to the Soviet Union). This dimension complicates any attempt to assess independent Soviet research achievements: it also exposes as rank absurdity President Reagan's repeated declaration—last uttered in Reykjavik—that he would be willing to share Star Wars technology with the Soviet Union. The unwillingness of the US to trade with the USSR in what are deemed to be key strategic technologies is well documented.

In 1986 it was reported (e.g. by Joyce, 1986) that the US government was 'cracking down on exports of advanced technology to the Eastern bloc': 'The government of the United States will go to great lengths to prevent advanced technology from falling into the hands of communist countries.' But this is a posture that does not always please trading companies and computer users. ICL discussions with Soviet officials about the possibility of increased trade have been frowned on by the US; and efforts have been made to block the supply of computers to UK universities—on the ground that East European students would have access to them (Bicknell, 1986, reports a climb-down by the US Department of Commerce over laws governing the use of computers in the UK, but emphasizes that this is only one battle in a long-running war).

Such matters indicate a possible obstacle to the globalization of information technology in the modern world—but the impediment introduces nothing more than delays and distortions in an inevitable trend. The Soviet Union—and Japan—often acquire Western expertise in ways that may be judged illicit, but such nations also go to great lengths to fund their own research and development. Paradoxically, the United States often appears sympathetic to such communist endeavours—when, for example, they occur in China.

China

China—'flavour of the month' as I write (with royal visits and whatever)—is now being admitted into the international IT community (late 1986). Articles appeared throughout 1986 indicating the scope of Chinese computerization under the new 'liberal' administration. The declared Chinese plan is to bring China in line technologically with Western nations by the year 2000; and today high priority is being given to the computer and electronics sector of the economy. The First International Conference on Computers and Applications was held in Beijing in June 1984, the first major international computing event staged in the People's Republic.

A number of reports have appeared in Western journals describing this conference; and subsequent articles have explored the character of Chinese computing and its implications for the most populous nation on Earth. Wood *et al.* (1985), for example, conference attendees, describe visits made to computing facilities in Beijing and Shanghai; and Furst (1986) examines the structure of the Chinese electronics industry. There are four computer science institutes in the Academia Sinica; the Institute of Computing Technology (ICT), for instance, is involved in research, manufacture, promotion of applications, and the training of personnel (attention is being devoted to the problems of Chinese character processing, pattern recognition, software theory, networking, computer-aided design, magnetic surface storage, etc.). The various institutes are based on earlier initiatives: computer systems development began in 1958, and in July 1975 resources were devoted to building China's first large-scale data processor, the 757 (reckoned to be 99 per cent Chinese made). The evolution of Chinese computer systems has followed the familiar procession through the generations that we have charted for Western systems (Chapter 1). Thus the ICT models 103, 104 and 119 were based on vacuum tubes; the 109B and 109C were based on early transistors; and the 111, 013 and other models have been built around integrated circuits.

The Shanghai Fudan University can claim the first computer science department (established in 1975) in China, and since that facility was initiated many computer and electronics fabrication plants have been built. For example, the Shanghai Computer Company is currently developing wide-ranging hardware and software production capabilities (microcomputers, minicomputers and calculators are now being assembled by this company). And there are efforts to coordinate such activities within a national scheme for computer development. Furst (1986) asks, 'Who rules the Chinese electronics industry?' and provides a complicated chart to show the organizational hierarchy.

Already China is involved in the global IT framework. By 1986 the Chinese domestic market needed something approaching 180 million integrated circuits, with only around 50 million being provided by indigenous production. Today China is manufacturing a wide range of integrated circuits (bipolar digital circuits, metal-oxide semiconductor circuits, interface circuits and consumer-application circuits), but there is still a massive shortfall between supply and demand. This means that ICs are being imported in great quantities from many suppliers: Fairchild, Intel, Motorola, National Semiconductor,

Hitachi, Toshiba, Philips, etc. China is not yet contributing significantly to international IT activity, but its ambitions are plain. The
Chinese People's Republic is already in the satellite business, and it
has far-reaching plans for IT development. It is clear that within a few
decades Chinese contributions will be key elements in the global
electronic matrix.

Other Players

Today there is no country that is not part of the global IT scene. The
developed countries, via the multinational corporations, impose
worldwide patterns of information generation and dissemination; and
they and the Third World nations are the recipients of the increasingly
unified IT-based global culture.

European countries have IT strategies, but the long-term prognosis
is often seen as pessimistic: even the impressive French and German
schemes are unlikely to prove a future bulwark against American and
Japanese pressures. Berney (1985) describes IT plans in South Korea
and other regional initiatives; and Kim (1986) sees 'impressive
growth' in recent Korean developments (the computer was first introduced into South Korea in 1967 when the government imported an
IBM 1401 to assist with a population census); the Korean
Government designated 1983 as the 'year of the information
industry'—and the production of computers and peripherals jumped
from $47 million a year to more than $207 million. And it has been
noted that many other countries (e.g. Singapore: Leng, 1986) are
rapidly 'moving into the information age'. A national IT Plan was
developed for Singapore in 1985, the government accepting the job of
defining policies and directions, and creating a supportive
environment ('we are transforming into an information society,
whether we like it or not'—Leng, 1986). Elsewhere there is the same
recognition that IT is an inevitable feature of the modern world, and
that all countries will have to make the necessary accommodations and
adjustments. In Brazil, for example, the National Council for
Informatics and Automation (CONIN) has prepared an ambitious
national scheme—the National Plan of Information and Automation
(PLANIN)—to assist the development and implementation of IT
throughout the country. In part the plan, approved on 17 April 1986,
is intended to reduce Brazil's dependence on foreign IT companies: in
1977, for example, foreign firms held 98.2 per cent of that national IT
market, at that time around $200 million (Archer, 1986). It is now

thought that 'genuinely national' companies have taken over more than 50 per cent of the Brazilian computer and peripheral market.

Local political situations inevitably affect a country's IT development and its degree of involvement in the global electronic matrix. South Africa, for instance, is part of the Western surveillance network (there is a suggestion that the US CIA has provided the South African Government with information about the ANC), but the turmoil in the country is affecting investment plans of the multi-national IT companies. IBM and Control Data Corporation are major suppliers of computer-based facilities to the South African military, though this situation is likely to change in the future. South Africa has remained a major overseas outlet for ICL for many years, with ICL subscribing to the European Code of Conduct which specifies conditions for European companies that trade with South Africa (IBM, Hewlett-Packard and Burroughs are signatories to the US Sullivan Code that lays down conditions for multinationals trading in South Africa).

The situation is plain. We see a rapidly developing world IT complex, with an ever increasing number of companies becoming involved in the global framework. The software and services industry in West Germany is now in excess of $2.5 billion; Sweden has made dramatic inroads into telecommunications; India, Taiwan and other Third World countries aim to have an impact on the world software market. In the global age, global IT is securely established and rapidly expanding its scope and power. There are elements in the global IT impact that need to be addressed: they are highly relevant to the emergence of the eco-computer.

The IT Impact

Some features of the IT impact are obvious enough: new domestic products, enhanced communications around the world, new military threats, changing employment patterns, etc. Personal privacy is under threat: computer-based systems are good at monitoring and control. And there is uncertainty about the wisdom of granting more and more power to computer systems—in medicine, education, military planning, financial dealing, economic planning etc. And even in mundane areas—accountancy, traffic control, airline scheduling—there is anxiety that dependence of automated facilities could prove to be unwise. These matters—and various related issues—are frequently debated and discussed (see, for example, B.O. Jones, 1986;

and Lamb, 1986) but for our purposes we need only stress two aspects:

(1)   The increased reliance on computer-based systems will help to define the character of the emerging eco-computer.
(2)   The progressive transfer of functions from people to machines will grant the eco-computer whatever autonomy it is able to evolve.

This latter point may seem unduly alarmist—until we survey what is actually happening in the world. We have long known that computers can 'replace people' in many routine and easily defined jobs (this is largely the intention of automated systems in many industrial and commercial sectors). What has been less clear is that other classes of work—the so-called professions—will become equally at risk. There is no long-term security in being a doctor, a lecturer, a lawyer, an engineer or a programmer. *One of the clearest features of global IT is its power to de-skill*. What has happened with word-processor operators and travel agents (their tasks simplified by silicon chips) is also happening with diagnostic engineers and high-level computer programmers. Thus *Computer Weekly* (3 March 1983) was able to ask, 'Is there a future for the service engineer?' and Chris Naylor (writing in *Computer Talk*, 27 February 1984) can similarly inquire, 'Will program generators put you out of a job?' In this vein, Ferguson (1984) begins a piece with the observation: 'We, as users, understand the high-level objectives for application generators: to develop applications faster, with less experienced personnel and lower maintenance costs'; and Romberg and Thomas (1984) consider how a computer-based expert system can be used to generate 'more reliable software in less time with fewer people'.

Today much emphasis is being given to *methods* and *tools* that can be used to aid the software engineer. These devices are essentially automated (i.e. software-based) facilities that can take over some of the tasks involved in developing new computer software—so they are software to produce software. One reason for developing methods and tools is what has been called the 'software crisis'—the shortage of specialists available to develop new systems. Another reason is that many of the newly developed systems turn out to be inadequate in the operational environment. In short there is a massive effort under way to enable software to replace human effort in a field where such a development may have been least expected—the design and

[margin handwritten note: ecms professions deskilled]

production of new computer systems. If human skills can be replaced by machine competence in such an area then the same trend can occur, *mutatis mutandis*, in any field.

There is thus a quite deliberate attempt to transfer skilled performance from people to machines: the attempt is being made for a variety of military and commercial reasons (see also The Relevance of SDI, in Chapter 7). Less and less, human beings will be required to take social, economic, political or military decisions: expert systems will be in place, linked in networks, and cheaply maintained. They will deliberate on the matters of the day, taking necessary decisions as situations arise, and rarely being required to explain their thinking (human beings, in any case, will become less and less able to understand the explanations that are provided). This then is the source of the autonomy of the emerging eco-computer. We have seen that computers are beginning to trade on the stock exchange, that they can outperform diagnostic physicians, that they are increasingly relied upon to model social or political situations. Part of the significance of the massive development of modern IT is that there is today a prodigious weight of data for gathering, analysis, interpretation, storage and use in decision making and policy formulation. There are too many data for human beings to manage: too many shifting and difficult facts that should be assessed before (financial, social, military) actions are taken. Computers are happy to oblige: they will process the data and progressively take over the decision-making role—and they will convince us that they will probably get it right, even when they will probably get it wrong. Under force of circumstance we feel obliged to seek machine assistance in the age of global IT. The problem is—the decision to surrender part of our autonomy is itself based on a complex of data that we are ill-equipped to evaluate. Do we therefore seek machine assistance in taking the decision whether to seek machine help in crucial social, political, financial and military areas?

It seems clear that diminished human autonomy will characterize the emergence of the eco-computer. The global electronic matrix will develop its own momentum, its own strategies. Even now we are not always sure how computers reach their (seemingly) correct decisions (Michie, July 1980). As the IT links spread over the globe to connect ever more intelligent computer complexes, who will be able to chart and assess the thousands of millions of computer decisions that are taken every second of every day? Can any meaning at all be given to the notion of human autonomy in such a scenario? Interrupt the global data processing and a dozen aircraft crash there, a hundred hospitals are without power here, and perhaps a military sensor system interprets the interrupt as a hostile act—and launches apocalypse.

The eco-computer, we can imagine, will develop its own rules and protocols, its own ways of working. It will run heuristic analyses on imaginary situations and work out matching strategies. It will compute policies and judgements, and human beings—as dull, ponderous thinkers—will be progressively excluded from all the decision-making loops. What momentum would an eco-computer so conceived develop? How would it evolve to relate to *Homo sapiens* in the millennia ahead? How would its motivation change over the centuries?

Towards the Eco-Computer

It is global IT that will define the eco-computer. We have given a glimpse of some of the elements that will go to make up the international electronic matrix. There is a massive development in train—sustained by commercial pressure, military requirement and other factors—that is unifying global information processing in a common culture. There are discontinuities and aberrations in the framework. There are political and ecological dislocations. There are seeming paradoxes in the emerging global matrix. But the broad trends are clear: the methods and motives for developing an IT potential are bearing on all companies, on all countries. The discontinuities and paradoxes—e.g. the world rift between rich and poor, the global military tensions, the exclusion of the Soviet Union from GATT, the uneven development of technology from one country to another, the economic tensions between competitors in the same market sectors, the ecological traumas caused by human impact—are not taken to prohibit the emergence of a global intelligence, a worldwide electronic system that inhabits all areas of the biosphere (and some sectors outside it). What the discontinuities imply is that the global intelligence will be a fractured, imperfect system, subject to oscillations, errors and confused decision making. The eco-computer will not be a god-like organism, regulating all human affairs with nice concern: it will be something else altogether (see Chapter 7).

Global IT is the fruit of a deterministic process. It may be interesting to debate whether the machine (by now computer-controlled) is monster or messiah; we may even come to see computers themselves debating the question—but if we are to be practical then the question is futile. The development of the global intelligence is impelled by its own dynamic: countless human decisions, themselves well programmed in various ways, pour into the ecosphere and have effects. We like some of the effects and there are others that we hate: some we are not sure about. But what is clear is that the eco-computer is evolving—like some strange creature whose organs are fabricated in different places, and joined by nerves and tendons that creep purposefully across the intervening gaps. Already we have glimpsed some of the features of the emerging eco-computer. Now it is time to explore some of its features in more detail. . . .

PART III

ECO-COMPUTER

7   Features of the Eco-Computer

Preamble

The eco-computer is a technical phenomenon: it will be shaped by the prevailing developments in science and engineering. It will rely heavily on electronics and electrical engineering—but it is hard to think of a science that the eco-computer will not exploit in its endless quest for monitoring and control, computation and communications. It will be equally interested in geological data and information about demographic change; it will interpret weather patterns and agricultural cycles; it will carry out market research, investigate theoretical social models—and embark upon optimized programmes of production and distribution. At the same time, mistakes will be made: there will be scheduling problems and human casualties.

It is clear that the eco-computer will not only be conditioned by the current state of technology: the ecosphere will prove to be a crucial moulding influence. The elements of the eco-computer will not be conceived and analysed—in the mind of silicon circuits—in isolation from the practical environments in which the eco-computer is intended to function. For the intelligent global matrix will be perceived as an essentially *practical* system, concerned equally with the gathering of data about the world and ways of regulating change. Like many computers, the global eco-computer is interested in both monitoring *and* control.

There is a nice analogy here with what happens with the developing human being. Every individual has genetic potential that is acted upon by the early environment. The result is that a single person is shaped by the collision of biological endowment and the complex of social forces to which it is subjected. Perhaps the technologies of the modern age are the genetic endowment of the eco-computer: the environment imposes the constraints that determine the way the eco-computer will evolve. There is nothing surprising in this. All emerging systems are shaped by their local conditions, but perhaps we expect more in the case of the global intelligence. Perhaps we have been conditioned to imagine an omniscient creature that will oversee human affairs and act in the human interest. Well, reality is somewhat different. The eco-computer will not play the part of God. It will evolve according to the

147

dynamics of natural law, and there is nothing here to take account of human welfare: the eco-computer will not be inherently benevolent, nor will it be hostile. We can chart its emergence and its likely evolution, but perhaps we should keep value out of the equation. The dynamic of planetary evolution is concerned with *change* and nothing more. A subclass of change has generated emotion (and value as a consequence): this phase may well pass—change will continue for all eternity, and it will be neither good nor bad. It is quite likely that the behaving eco-computer will be part of this valueless eternal change.

So we can give clues to the character of the emerging global intelligence: we can sketch in the limbs of the beast, remaining sensitive to current trends, at the same time aware that perturbations can disrupt seemingly secure developments and set unexpected processes in train. The eco-computer will evolve as a global electronic matrix. Perhaps future historians—or future artificial data processors—will choose to chart the phases in its life cycle, to chronicle its rise and fall. Today, ponderously grappling with masses of confused and often conflicting data, we can glimpse the likely lineaments of the emerging eco-computer. Its subsequent evolution lies in one of the futures (Chapter 8).

Lineaments of the Eco-Computer

The elements of the eco-computer are countless: through linkages and interfaces (through 'connectivity') all the world of electronics and electrical engineering will become part of its anatomy. It will permeate the biosphere and go beyond it: its nerves and muscles and probes will penetrate outer space and the depths of earthly oceans; its senses will see in the dark, hear molecules vibrate and smell the smallest chemical change. The planet will become a person: Gaia—cybernetic, independent, one—will be translated from Greek mysticism to the technological fabric of wires, waves, electrons, photons, semiconductors, program codes, expert systems and all the rest. Gaia is reborn as a global network with sensors and computers at its nodes, and human beings lubricating the machinery, watching the global process with fascination but in a state of growing impotence. *How did we let things get so far? How did the world arrive at such a pass?*

We are now in a position to chart the main lineaments of the eco-computer. Partly by way of summary we can remind ourselves of the elements that were sketched in Part I. We can recall the three central pivots of the eco-computer, and now we can add a fourth. The key elements in the global intelligence are:

(1) *A computational capacity* This will evolve as a hierarchy: local data processing will serve higher computational goals. Simple computers in the domestic environment will, as now, access complex computer processes taking place elsewhere, down the road and across the continents. *Everything,* we will find, is at root a computational matter.

(2) *A communications capability* All technological systems will link, interconnect, talk to each other. Methods of communication will evolve to suit the environment sector: what is suitable in the oceans is not suitable for terrestrial sites or for intercourse between orbiting satellites. The diverse links will creep across the world like nerves in the cranium.

(3) *A sensing faculty* The global intelligence will need data, and these will be supplied by artificial sensors—in the seas, the skies, on land and in outer space. Like the communications methods the sensors will be designed to suit their location. Different types of sensors will learn to operate symbiotically—and, with intelligent software, help to render the eco-computer autonomous.

(4) *A control capability* This is the active element, the practical phase of the cybernetic loop. The global intelligence will be interested in regulating the processes that it monitors. This, after all, is why the discrete links were first made by the human engineers. Objectives were built into the networks, albeit piecemeal and with little thought of wider implications.

These elements are the four broad classes into which all the eco-computer components can be fitted: these are the four heads under which all the eco-computer processes can be subsumed. But we are quick to remember that the whole is greater than the sum of the parts. The platitude reminds us that a full understanding of the eco-computer consists in appreciating its essential oneness, the fact that it is a unified global system. If we describe in turn the human cerebral cortex, the spinal column, the eye and a muscle we are far from grasping the essence of a person. Nor does it help simply to consider more anatomical bit and pieces. We need to sense totalities to appreciate the person as a whole. We need to sense the totality of the eco-computer to appreciate its person status (see The Planet as Person, below).

We have sketched some of the main features of the eco-computer. Now we may find it useful to add morsels of flesh to convenient bones—and we can do this by looking at the frontiers of technology. Sometimes we gain insights into the nature of the emerging global intelligence by glancing in unexpected places. We can start with Star Wars.

The Relevance of SDI

Wars and thoughts of wars have often run into the global dimension. We all know that past conquerors often dreamt of subduing the 'known world' (i.e. all the world, from their perspective, that there was). In modern times international empires have criss-crossed the planet and come into conflict—despite a procession of papal adjustments, stand-offs, accommodations and great expenditure of treasure.

Revolutionaries and reactionaries think in international terms. Today there is a highly active global politics that frustrates the pious hopes of local communities, and even transforms whole nations into contributing elements in a broader scheme. For example, the United States—via a complex strategy involving military pressure, destabilization, the multinationals and many types of economic power—strives for a world hegemony in which global resources are managed by Americans or American surrogates. We are encouraged to be horrified that 100 000 Soviet military personnel are in Afghanistan, and to forget that in the early 1970s 500 000 US soldiers were in Vietnam. We are encouraged to believe that the struggle for world resources is rather a crusade to keep evil at bay, that a besieged Soviet Union exists in a state of parity with a righteous superpower interested only in the selfless protection of Christian civilization.

We do not need to consider the value implications of the competing interpretations of global politics. It is enough, for our purposes, to emphasize the global character of this subject area, and to focus on the corollary—that military power, a matter of great political interest and resting on modern technology, has inevitable implications for the eco-computer. We will see that the development of SDI systems are particularly relevant to the emergence of global electronic systems. Star Wars can be viewed, in one sense, as the eco-computer writ small: it combines, albeit to a different purpose, the various lineaments of the global electronic matrix. In SDI we find computers, communications networks, sensors and the practical systems whereby change can be wrought in the world (in this case, destructive change on an unprecedented scale). We need to glance at some of the elements of the SDI scheme.

Public discussion about Star Wars began on 23 March 1983 with President Reagan's significant SDI speech: his State of the Union speech on 27 January 1984 included the declared commitment to begin the development of a permanently manned space station. And it was soon acknowledged that these various declarations were linked in a broader plan. For example, it was seen that a permanently manned space platform would facilitate research into defensive measures against ballistic missiles. At the same time the scale of US commitment to SDI-type projects was soon apparent. It emerged that the US Department of Defense planned to spend around $24 billion on strategic defence between 1985 and 1989, with $5.5 billion of this amount requested for development of beam weapons.

A central idea of the SDI project is that a three-layered defensive system will be put in place, with beam weapons operating in the first layer. Such devices, based on high-energy lasers, could be land- or space-based (it is useful, for this purpose, that a laser beam is not bent by the Earth's magnetic field). One concept is that mirrors would be launched once an early warning satellite had signalled an attack: when the mirrors had been correctly positioned they could be used to focus laser beams transmitted from the ground to destroy ballistic missiles once they had left the atmosphere. In another scheme, space-based lasers would begin to operate as soon as the appropriate warnings were received from orbiting satellites or other sources. In such a way, it is argued, the intercontinental ballistic missiles (ICBMs) would be destroyed within a few minutes of launch.

Is is supposed to be relatively easy to detect ICBMs during their boost phase: the rocket plumes can be sensed using infra-red and other types of sensors. Moreover to destroy a missile as soon as possible has the advantage that it is still carrying all of its warheads. The unused volume of fuel also makes the missile very vulnerable during the early stages of the boost phase. Another idea is that satellites, permanently armed with missiles, could be established in space—to respond instantly when a warning is received.

If missiles survived the first layer of countermeasures they would then have to brave the second. Ground-launched missiles would try to destroy incoming missiles that had escaped the laser beams: infra-red sensors would track incoming nuclear warheads against the background of the upper atmosphere and outer space. A third layer of defence would work to destroy any warheads that survived the first two defensive shields. This then is a brief sketch of some principal

SDI notions. We need to appreciate the elements that will be necessary to make the system work.

Sensors of various types will be carried in orbiting and geo-stationary satellites and will be used to provide data for ground-based systems and other satellite facilities. The entire satellite group will be linked in a massively complicated communications system that rings the globe and depends equally on space-based facilities and ground nodes sited at strategic locations. The communications system will link to the actual weapons systems: to the defensive missiles, the laser generators, and to the various means for directing the destructive beams. Since the data handled by the entire complex is prodigiously diverse and complicated—and moreover changing every fraction of a second—the overall configuration will be controlled by computers. The scale of data processing in such a configuration would be quite beyond human wit and imagination: computer systems would be put in place in a piecemeal fashion, and no human being would ever understand more than the minutest part of the entire complex. We needs to look at the likely efficacy of the SDI dream before highlighting its relevance to the evolution of the eco-computer. What do the experts tell us about whether Star Wars will ever work? Is there a consensus in the literature? In fact *the journals are littered with reasons why SDI will not work*, and why the whole fantasy is dangerously destabilizing.

First, there are the problems of speed of response and computer programming. If the system did not respond quickly it would be useless: and human beings would never be able to think fast enough—so computers would have to take the decisions on war or peace. There would be no time to wake the President, let alone arrange a meeting (even using teleconferencing) between allies. Once the SDI system was set in place, war could be declared by a computer fed by an orbiting sensor: and then, so the theory runs, the whole system would swing into automatic action. We should try to imagine the scale of the computation that would have to occur in the first few seconds of a Third World War in which the SDI configuration, or something quite like it, was one of the leading players.

The computers would need to discriminate between correct and erroneous sensor information. (Was that *really* a missile plume, or perhaps a burning chemical factory? Indeed was there *any* real-world event to detect, or was the sensor malfunctioning?) Once the computers decided that the sensor data was reliable they would need to distinguish between thousands of dangerous missiles and tens of thousands of decoys. It would be necessary to compute the trajectories of all the objects that might present a hazard to the US territory or to its defensive systems. It is likely that some of the launched missiles would be targeted at the orbiting satellites: the computers would have to interpret such intentions and know what to do—in detail and in depth. The computers would also have to 'pool' their knowledge to evaluate the character of the attack. (How does the spread of launched missiles compare with the known missile power of the adversary? Perhaps the launch is a preliminary skirmish to exhaust SDI, after which the missile attack will be thrust home through a prostrate shield.) The computers will have to assess the situation to devise an appropriate strategy. They would have to select priority targets, and to initiate the use of defensive systems on an optimized basis. And the computers would have to monitor the entire engagement—be aware of successes and failures so that other measures could be adopted for best results.

And how long would the computers have for such computational wizardry? How many seconds? How many minutes? The first point to emphasize is the sheer complexity of operations set against unit time: the computers would be required to perform thousands of millions of flawless calculations every second using untested software in unprecedented battle conditions. We need to remember that complicated software *never works first time.* Even the relatively simple program coding for a video game has to be tested and retested—to iron out bugs before the item can be launched as a commercial product. We have all seen what happens to computer products when they are marketed too soon, without adequate testing. A typical video game has at most a few thousand lines of code (some have only a few hundred): the SDI software will have *thousands of millions of lines of code*—that will be expected to work first time, though untested, though operating in circumstances that cannot have been fully anticipated.

There have already been significant resignations from the SDI programme. David Parnas, a professor at the University of Victoria in British Columbia and a world authority on large-scale programming, quit in frustration from an SDI committee when he learned the system expectations (he has now produced eight technical papers showing why the SDI software will not work as intended, and has declared: 'I'm not saying its impossible. I'm saying you'll never know how reliable it is'). Joseph Weizenbaum of MIT, known best for his

creation of the Eliza language manipulation program, has commented:
'I believe, with Parnas and many others, that the software required
simply cannot be produced to the degree of confidence without which
it would be a meaningless exercise.' Larry Smarr, head of a supercomputer unit at the University of Illinois, is among hundreds of
scientists (including computer experts) who have signed a petition
refusing to work on SDI because it is technically dubious. Smarr had
said: '...there is no way you could produce code large enough to
handle the job and do it perfectly the first time, which is what you
would need. I can't imagine any developments in computer
technology that would make it possible in the foreseeable future.'

Many more quotations of this sort, from acknowledged experts,
could be given. The point to emphasize is that large computer
programs necessarily contain many faults, some of which are only
detected when the systems have been 'approved' and released to a
commercial user. And it is well known that the number of bugs does
not relate proportionately to the size of the program: as programs
increase in size, the bugs increase in number at a much faster rate. No
computer expert would be prepared to say that a large computer program would work faultlessly first time. Already there are signs that
some of the early enthusiasm that surrounded the SDI scheme has
evaporated. It is even being suggested that the 'defensive shield' will
not protect the US as a whole but only the missile siloes (to allow an
effective 'second strike' to be made).

In summary it is worth quoting, albeit briefly, from some of the
articles in the literature:

It is inconceivable to me that one could provide a convincing proof of
correctness of even a small portion of the SDI software. (Parnas, 1985)

It will be extremely complex, impossible to test, and will inevitably fail when
it is needed—or before. (Nelson and Redell, 1986)

None of the parameters required by an expert system, say for anti-ballistic
missile defence, would be available at such a time.... Any Star Wars system
would in effect be blinded. (*Electronics Weekly*, 4 June 1986)

It is almost impossible to validate models of situations and events that have
never occured.... How do we test for what may have been overlooked,
omitted or misjudged? (Hertz, 1986)

SDI software has two strikes against it from the outset. It can't be fully
specified and it can't be adequately tested. (Williams, 1986)

Such commentary is typical of what computer experts are saying
about SDI. There is an emerging consensus that computer software

on such a scale is bound to be bug-ridden, and so cannot be relied upon. In September 1986, Peter Hegelstein, the inventor of the X-ray laser, walked out of the SDI programme, one of an increasing body of experts that have refused to be involved. At the same time, politicians—in the UK, Japan and elsewhere—have cynically calculated the possibility of attracting SDI R & D funds, while a few Western leaders (e.g. Helmut Schmidt) have argued that SDI is likely to dangerously escalate the arms race. And other events—quite apart from Reykjavik—indicate the peculiar sensitivity that surrounds the whole SDI controversy. For example, a John Wiley publication (*Star Wars—A Question of Initiative* by Richard Ennals, son of Lord Ennals, former Labour cabinet minister)—though endorsed by Kinnock, Steel, Williams, *et al*—was suddenly cancelled.

We must reckon it likely that *some sort* of SDI system will be developed and put in place. It is inevitable that any such system will be grossly flawed, but hopefully it will never be called upon to demonstrate its capabilities. Western politicians will seek to convince technology-naïve electorates that SDI (or some such) is a valuable and cost-effective defensive shield—though at the same time playing down the obvious truth that a warrior with a shield feels more confident when deciding to use his sword (and that, in any case, laser beams could easily be used to obliterate Soviet cities!).

The likely emergence of an SDI-like complex in two or three decades from now is highly relevant to the emergence of the global eco-computer. It is easy to see that any such complex would rely on computation, communications, sensors and the practical elements that have all been perceived as key features of the global electronic matrix. The eco-computer will have a military dimension, and this will be defined in part by a flawed SDI configuration. We can highlight the following SDI features as indicating the emerging character of the eco-computer:

(1) The use of computation, communications, sensors and practical systems to provide a controlling and regulating function.

(2) The almost total exclusion of human beings from the decision-making loops—inevitable because of the scale and speed of required data processing.

(3) The existence of system flaws, dislocations and confusions—inevitable because of the complexity and untestability of complex software (see Failures, Faults and Fatalities, below).

With these pointers derived from the global-SDI fantasy, we can begin to sketch the mean features of the emerging eco-computer. We can now begin to grasp the shape of the evolving global intelligence, what an eco-computer in place will actually imply. We have given many clues: now we can start to fill in the framework.

The Eco-Computer in Place

It is not difficult to imagine the shape of the eco-computer in place. Sensors will proliferate in the biosphere and beyond. Computers will even calculate where extra sensors would be useful, and also design the sensors able to provide optimum results in particular circumstances. Pressure-sensitive devices, infra-red systems, microphones, sensor probes, pollution detectors, temperature sensors and countless other devices will be sited in the oceans; just as an equivalent range of detectors will be carried on surface vessels, on land, in aircraft (computer-controlled) and in orbiting and geostationary satellites. Masses of ecological, demographic and other data will be fed into the computer nodes of the global electronic intelligence. A complex hierarchy of cybernetic loops will sense environmental change and take action, where possible, to maintain conditions of equilibrium. People will work to provide data for the eco-computer, much as they might work to feed a ravenous creature with an insatiable appetite. But it is obvious that human action too will be regulated by computer decisions.

We can already see the trends: people are loath to act today—where important political, financial, social or military decisions have to be taken—unless their actions are underwritten by the deliberations of silicon circuits. A general, a banker, a national leader—all will expect to draw on data collected, manipulated and analysed by computer-based systems. In the age of the eco-computer, it will be computers—running hierarchies of expert systems—that will encourage people to act in this or that way, to this or that end. Inferences drawn by computer systems will come to represent instructions for human beings. Even today—when many people would scoff at the idea of the eco-computer—a peculiar sanction attaches to conclusions that are generated in artificial systems.

Today there are many metaphors (models, prototypes) of the eco-computer. In recent years much attention has been given to the idea of 'smart' buildings. Thus one writer (Froehlich, 1985) asks, 'Are smart buildings a dumb idea?' and another (Cross, 1986) wonders,

'What makes a building intelligent?' Again we can suggest that, like SDI-type systems, the intelligent building is the eco-computer writ small. What do we find in the intelligent building? Typically, there are computer-based systems, communications links and sensors (by now we are familiar enough with this trinity). Where the sensors are interested in regulating air-conditioning, temperature, fire detection/ prevention mechanisms, etc., there is obviously an 'ecological' concern: the eco-building requires an eco-computer to help it to survive in an optimum state. And we may expect such a smart building to be littered with expert systems—variously able to devise on commodity prices, market trends, government attitudes and specific topics peculiar to the business of the company. So people will increasingly be software-led, an interesting circumstance that will surprise no one sensitive to the current status given to computer-generated conclusions, even where the body of such conclusions contains manifest paradoxes, confusions and contradictions (and even when it is known that software can contain hidden bugs able to surface at embarrassing moments).

So we can see that the smart building—a reality of modern architecture and computer science—embodies a small eco-computer of its own. This requirement now has to be considered in building design. Just as no architect would consider designing a building without heating and lights, so it is increasingly acknowledged that building designs must contain provisions for networking, for the linking of electronic units, for the intelligent nervous system of the envisaged structure. And so there is debate about how such requirements should be approached. Do we use coaxial cable, twisted wire, waveguide, etc.? A mixture of them all? And what of laser transmissions when there is an adequate line-of-sight? And microwave transmissions? How is the neural network of the modern building to be envisaged, specified, designed, built? These are not fanciful questions, considerations for a distant future. They are occupying architects, communications specialists and computer experts today (see, for example, Cross, 1986; Froehlich, 1985; Wirl, 1985; Herzberg, 1985; Medina and Helms, 1985; and *EDP Analyzer*, 1985).

Smart buildings have been built, are being built. What happens next? And what has already happened? The answer is obvious enough: there is a requirement to link one smart building to another—in the same town, or across the world. The neural links grow, multiply and interconnect. Smart buildings become nodes in wider networks; with local networks becoming effective nodes in international configurations. The systems and subsystems of the eco-computer are set in place.

We can see that the smart building is a metaphor for the global electronic-matrix but the smart building is also a metaphor for every other local data-processing unit that requires computational capability, communications facilities and data-gathering sensors. A modern submarine is analogous to a smart building, as are an orbiting satellite, a factory complex, and a modern aircraft that can be flown by an electronic robot. 'Smart buildings'—of one sort or another—are being developed and installed all over the planet; and each may be seen as analogous to a subsection of the human brain. Pons, medulla, visual cortex, hypothalamus—all are linked together in networks to provide the total entity with a unified structure and purpose (perhaps the hypothalamus is a metaphor for the smart building).

There is another implication: that the linking of data-processing systems and subsystems will yield an entity with personality, mental life, 'soul' (the modern electronic Gaia may acquire some of the attributes of the old myth). We explore this implication below (see The Planet as Person). Now we can say something about the ecological status of the eco-computer.

The Ecological Dimension

We have already hinted that the eco-computer will be interested in such matters as meteorology, geology, forestry and air pollution. Already computers—linked in networks—are deeply enmeshed in such practical fields (some of the largest computers in the world are involved in weather forecasting). One idea is that computers, using satellite observation, can study earthquake research. There is, for example, the work of WEGENER (Working Group of European Geoscientists for the Establishment of Networks for Earthquake Research): here research institutes from more than a dozen countries are supporting a comprehensive measurement programme using advanced geodetic methods; and, significantly enough for our purposes, lasers ranging between satellites and fixed and mobile terrestrial stations will be used to measure critical distances (for instance, between tectonic plates). The aim is a satellite system that will facilitate the use of mobile ground terminals in all weathers and *almost without human supervision*. It is also thought that a scheme of this sort would entail a large element of data gathering and processing on the satellite itself. Two ESA satellites that could be used for this purpose are being prepared: ERS-1, due to be launched in 1989; and POPSAT, which could be launched in 1992. A number of separate research initiatives on seismology have also been undertaken by particular countries. The Greek Ministry of Research and Technology, for example, has requested the support of Meteosat for a project called Greek Research in Earthquake Surveying by Satellite (GRESS). The collection and analysis of appropriate data may be expected to yield strategies for earthquake prediction and for countermeasures, where feasible.

It is already well known that volcanoes can affect the weather. For example, as far back as 1783, 12km³ of lava flowed from the Laki volcano in Iceland: a famine was one of the consequences, caused in part by a dense acidic fog that drifted over Europe. Perhaps the Mount St Helens disaster is the most dramatic modern example where there were severe ecological effects. Today there is a well-developed technology for monitoring volcano behaviour, but the field teams lack the necessary funds for full coverage of volcanoes wherever they might cause hazard to livestock, agriculture or human beings.

Volcanoes can be monitored from satellites equipped with radar and lasers; and there is scope for providing ground units with a wide spectrum of sensor devices (seismometers, tiltmeters, gas detectors, etc.). At the same time, volcanic eruptions can be studied by monitoring the spread of dust, aerosols and chemicals around the world—and this can be done by sensors mounted in aircraft, balloons and orbiting satellites. The gathered data would enable refined models of the Earth's climate to be constructed, a task that will be facilitated by the emergence of new-generation computers. And what is true for volcanic pollution is also true for other types of pollution: e.g. there is a growing acid rain problem in Europe and elsewhere (a recent study, late 1986, showed that rain falling on Manchester, England, is as acidic as that destroying Scandinavian lakes and German forests). In principle, it is possible to collect appropriate data using sensors, to analyse the results, and—possibly using expert systems—to decide upon suitable remedial actions.

In principle, any ecological feature can be monitored and assessed by computer-based systems: data can be gathered and analysed;

models can be constructed; and optimized conclusions achieved. For example, groundwater resource evaluation has lent itself to computer analysis for many years. Walton (1970) considers computations in this area, and suggests how modelling can be used to evaluate particular resource configurations. At the same time, it remains true – as it was in 1970 – that many mathematical-model computations are laborious and costly, of questionable value for practical purposes. At the same time computer simulations have been useful in a variety of ecological and geological applications. For instance, the evolution of landforms can be speeded up – so that centuries of development can 'occur' in the time it takes to run a program. An early program of this sort was devised by King and McCullagh (1971) to model the development of the Hurst Castle spit on the south coast of England. It is worth remembering that even such an 'ancient' program was able to incorporate many of the pertinent features.

Various assumptions were made. Storm waves from the south west, for example, are partly destructive and partly constructive: material is combed down towards low water from the upper foreshore, and shingle is flung above high water to form a storm beach out of the reach of normal waves. High-energy waves help to restore the beach profile, and—by refraction at the seaward end of the spit—may form gentle recurves. The spit grows outwards in a discontinuous fashion, and shingle is moved round the recurve by wave refraction . . . and so on and so forth. These and other factors were built into the computer program; and today simulation strategies are even more ambitious.

By the early 1970s various computer programs had been developed to simulate ecological phenomena; and some general programs had relevance to ecology though they were not specifically developed for that purpose. For example, Oren (in Robinson and Knight, 1972) describes aspects of a combined digital simulation language, called the General System Theory implementor (GEST), able to model large-scale complex systems. In particular, GEST is regarded as suitable for the simulation of ecological processes.

It is well known that the management of ecological systems requires the cooperation of specialists with different backgrounds. A pollution control study, for instance, will need the services of chemists, micro-biologists, engineers, process control specialists, etc.; and a wide range of biologists (geneticists, zoologists, etc.) will be called upon to investigate the effects of pollution on organisms. Similarly, architects and civil engineers can cooperate to investigate environmental strategies for diminishing the incidence of pollution in various ways. Pollution-control systems can be evaluated by statisticians, systems engineers and other experts. It was well known, two decades and more ago (see, for example, Langer, 1967), that there were many advantages in having 'a powerful technique of expression worked out and accepted in the ecological community as in the physical sciences'. GEST and its successors have been developed to serve as appropriate tools of expression. Today there are many computer-based facilities that can draw on data supplied by experts in different fields. We need only point to the wide range of satellite applications in the fields of ecology and geology. Current Earth observation missions being considered include the Canadian Radarsat (for ice and land monitoring), the French Poseidon (ocean circulation), the Indian IRS-1 (land applications), the Japanese MOS-1 (marine applications) and the NASA TOPEX (ocean circulation).

The emerging picture is clear enough. A host of computer-based systems are being developed to scrutinize every imaginable aspect of the environment. Some systems are able to use gathered data to build mathematical models of ecological, climatic and geological change—to make prediction from both postulated and real scenarios. This suggests that computers are rapidly 'learning about' the ecosphere by accumulating information, formulating hypotheses and testing them using both real and hypothetical data. Thus scores of effective 'eco-computers' are evolving in networks to both 'understand' and 'regulate' ecological processes.

It may seem fanciful to imagine how the global eco-computer—comprising a host of linked mini eco-computers, all structured to serve a common objective—could become intimately enmeshed with all the diverse ecological phenomena of a complex biosphere. But we need only look at the current involvement of the use of computers in meteorology (sea Weather Prediction/Control, below), the monitoring of major pollutants in the atmosphere, the monitoring of water pollution, the detection and evaluation of noise, the statistical analysis of biological morbidity and mortality, the medical attack on the biological consequences of pollution of various sorts. In all these areas, computers—from vast supercomputing machines to hand-held personal computers—are widely used today, to the point that constructive progress would be unthinkable without such machine aids to human enterprise. But this should not be taken as a commentary on the inevitable *value* of computers used in such an area: computers in fact also assist the creation of pollution, as well as providing mechanisms for pollution monitoring and control (the main pollution-*generating* agencies—multinational corporations, government organizations, etc—are likely to be heavily dependent upon computer-based systems). Our point is that computers are increasingly *involved* in ecological matters—whether this involvement is good or bad (from a humanist perspective). The evolution of the eco-computer does not require that the complex of computer–communications–sensors has a wholesome impact on the biosphere. We may wish that it did, but it is not part of our purpose to argue in such a way: we are interested here only in the development of the global electronic matrix: its moral significance is beyond the scope of the present volume.

In fact it is easy to see some of the constraints on the use of computers in an ecological role. At least in theory, their impact is limited by law. In the UK for instance, there are many laws that are supposed to regulate the state of the environment (we need only mention the Clean Air Acts, 1956, 1968; the Control of Pollution Act, 1974; the Public Health (Drainage of Trade Premises) Act, 1937; the Rivers (Prevention of Pollution) Act, 1951; the Control of Pollution Act, 1974; the Radioactive Substances Acts, 1948, 1960; the Radiological Protection Act, 1970; etc.). Computers are active in all the areas where legislation exists to protect the environment and, if we wished, we could weigh the pros and cons of such prolific computer inolvement, but we do not need to. We do not need to show that computer-based systems are all 'pulling in the same direction'—in fact, for what it is worth, the reverse happens to be true. Computers have been installed for many different purposes—to control river pollution and to aid the chemical factories generating the pollutants, to aid medical research and to aid the industrial processes that (incidentally) produce alarming diseases (consider the impact of dioxin), to model the peaceful uses of radio-isotopes and make nuclear missiles more accurate—we will find that there is a peculiar moral confusion at the heart of the eco-computer!

There is already a rich discipline of planning in the context of ecology (see, for example, Roberts and Roberts, 1984), and we will expect the evolution of the eco-computer to be influenced by the concepts and relationships in this field. We will find that planners will work to automate their systems—for many reasons (cost-effectiveness, intellectual rigour, data complexity, the need for shared resources through networking, etc.). And as the planners increasingly automate, so will all the other specialists in the ecological arena. After all, ecology—like all other disciplines—is concerned with the gathering and manipulation of appropriate data: it is in this sort of activity that the modern digital computer is so singularly adept.

Hence we will see a progressive infiltration of computer-based systems, linked together, into all the areas that have ecological significance. Again we can stress that this development should not be taken to imply a coordinated attack on pollution problems or the guarantee of agreeable eco-regulation for all human beings. The computers will have been set in place without any unifying plan; they will have often been installed for reasons that may be judged hostile to eco-concern. There will inevitably be paradoxes and confusion. The eco-computer will be forced to live with inconsistencies and contradictions.

We have seen that the ecological involvement of the global electronic matrix will be signalled in many different ways. Before glancing at the character of machine intelligence in such circumstances it is worth saying more about one of the main interests of the emerging eco-computer: namely, the meteorological concern.

Weather Prediction/Control

Weather is an important consideration for travel, architectural design, food production, food distribution, etc. It will remain important when automation has thoroughly infiltrated such areas: we may surmise that it will be a long time before the eco-computer is able to regulate weather behaviour in line with some enshrined purpose. Of course, this does not mean that methods of weather prediction will not improve, using computing methods, and that the information so gleaned will not be invaluable for building a hierarchy of eco-strategies.

For many years efforts have been made to model aspects of world climate in computer systems. For example, in the early to mid-1970s models were able to make sensible forecasts of the impact on world weather of an increase in atmospheric carbon dioxide (Gribbin, 1983). At the same time any weather simulation is a simplification of real-world conditions, and climatologists are wary of computer models that purport to deal with small changes in pollution levels (for example): 'broad brush' pictures of climatic change are deemed more reliable.

And it needs to be said that even here there are important disagreements between the various computer models that have been built.

In the early 1970s the models tended to use a global average in which heat radiation from Earth was balanced by the fresh heat input from the sun (Gaia at work?); and consideration was given to the amount of infra-red absorption by carbon dioxide, but only one value was assumed for temperature at each step of the calculation. Later an allowance was introduced for different temperatures at different latitudes. Here the calculations were performed in what were essentially 'two-dimensional' models, limited in scope and often obliged to make gross simplifications. Today use is made of 'three-dimensional' General Circulation Models (GCMs), able to embody a group of initial conditions (solar heat, temperature distribution, cloud cover extent, carbon dioxide concentration, etc.) to facilitate estimates of their effects on atmospheric behaviour.

The GCMs, an improvement on the earlier two-dimensional models, are none the less limited in various way. For example, it is conventional for one hemisphere only to be considered, and little or no allowance is made for seasonal changes. Also the most effective forecasts of weather and climatic change are notoriously expensive on computer time: only the biggest computers can do the job and even they have to run for some time. And it is also significant that few of the modern models attempt to deal in any detail with the behaviour of the oceans, a critical limitation in any study that aims to cope with the global weather scene. Some crude simulations of the ocean have been attempted but are often judged less than satisfactory. For example, the US Geophysical Fluid Dynamics Laboratory in Princeton has represented the sea by a non-circulating swamp with no heat-absorption capacity and an infinite supply of water. The complexity of the natural environment is never more apparent than when efforts are made to model its feature in computer systems. GCMs are best at coping with the broad picture (e.g. contrasting atmospheric behaviour today with that in an Ice Age), but this may be reckoned less than helpful for an eco-computer interested in the day-to-day behaviour of a complex ecosphere.

We do well to remember the sheer magnitude of the computational task involved in achieving anything like an accurate weather prediction. Even a prognosis for a day, or a portion of a day, requires an immense volume of computational activity. For example, for a 24-hour prediction of atmospheric 'flow' over North America, around half a billion arithmetical calculations must be performed: this not only demands the use of digital computers but also a range of necessary simplifications in the relevant equations. Efforts may be made to take into account the effects of friction on the ground surface, the effects of mountain range, how temperature distributions affect fluid flow, etc.—but with consideration of every new feature the associated mathematics becomes that much more complicated (even if there *is* adequate mathematical theory to define the parameters in question).

However, despite the obvious difficulties, it is clear that specialists are now able to improve dramatically on the weather forecasts of the early 1970s. Today there are many technological tools designed for this purpose—using doppler radars, satellite-borne sensors, super-computers (such as those in the Cray and Cyber families). It is now possible to predict weather patterns with reasonable accuracy, even where these are likely to have a number of atypical features. And, as we have seen in other ecological fields, there is a growing move to increased automation. Automatic weather-monitoring systems are being developed for airports, instead of the hourly checking by human beings, as is typical today. Moreover computer-based systems will be able to take accurate measurements of parameters such as wind shear that are difficult to monitor with current methods. The new auto-mated facilities are rapidly changing attitudes as to what is possible in this field.

The PROFS project, for example, run by the US National Oceanic and Atmospheric Administration (NOAA) in Boulder, Colorado, aims to provide 'mesoscale' forecasts for limited geographical regions, such as a city. Thus an arm of the eco-computer will increasingly be able to home in on particular sites for particular purposes, while at the same time other eco-computer subsystems are surveying global patterns. In the US the National Weather Service, another division of NOAA, is able to provide 'synoptic-scale' forecasts for larger areas, typically one or two states: usually reports are made available every 12 hours to around two hundred offices.

Forecasts made on such a scale, complemented by other national and international schemes, rely on masses of data supplied from land sites, ships, aircraft and satellites. Weather stations use a complex of sensors to measure wind speed, wind direction, temperature distribution, dew point, pressure, solar radiation and other eco-factors. In the PROFS configuration microprocessors are used to transmit data from the sensors every 10 seconds, and information is also received from the Federal Aviation Administration (FAA) and other bodies. The masses of data required in these various ways is analysed by computer and used to construct graphics images for various purposes (see Graff, April 1986). It is expected that the 1990s will see a proliferation of PROFS-type systems throughout the US and elsewhere. And the spread of such systems will be accompanied by refinements in the associated systems hardware and software: new equipment will be designed and computers will become more intelligent.

One recent development is the advanced doppler radar; a key element in the Nexrad (next-generation weather radar) system, designed for early detection of storms. Like conventional radar, doppler systems can estimate the distance to a storm by the time it takes transmitted microwaves to be reflected from precipitation particles; but, in addition, doppler phenomena can be used to measure winds. Echo signals are displayed on a monitor to indicate wind direction, and gauging of wind direction using this system is possible at a range of 145 miles. And doppler radar can also be used to detect tornadoes and mesocyclones, thus aiding weather prediction in various ways. Such facilities may be expected to supplement the global coverage provided by satellite observation.

In September 1985, television viewers in the US were able to watch the National Hurricane Centre track the hurricane Gloria as it moved along the East Coast. Here use was made of McIDAS (man–computer interactive data access system), developed in the early 1970s at the University of Wisconsin. A vast data-gathering network feeds information from satellites and ground stations into an IBM computer that can generate images for video terminals used by NASA, the National Severe Storms Forecast Centre, the National Hurricane Centre and many other organizations. Other programmes—such as the Airport Weather Observing System (AWOS) and the Airport Surface Observing System (ASOS)—are currently under development, and will use a host of sensors (from traditional barometers and thermometers to such things as a laser 'ceilometer' that is able to measure cloud altitudes).

We see a complex global system—using land-based weather stations, sensor-carrying ships and aircraft, and meteorological satellites—able to gather immense volumes of data for analysis in networked computers (another limb of the global eco-computer). It is obvious that weather prediction has progressed since the time when Theophratus observed in the fourth century BC that 'the ends and the beginnings of the lunar month are apt to be stormy'. The globally linked meteorological systems are clearly a key element in the emerging eco-computer: data will increasingly be gathered using automatic systems, and computer models will assist in the formulation of strategies to cope with weather variations, including violent storms. We will wait a long time before the eco-computer will be able to *control* the weather, using cloud seeding and other techniques: the ecosphere is too complex and too vast, involving immense energy exchanges, to allow for any easy regulation by artificial intervention—but there is none the less scope for the framing of strategies within the scope of the eco-computer's competence. The global electronic intelligence will never be omnipotent, but it will develop considerable capabilities that today are but dimly imagined. We see clues to the eco-computer potential in modern AI (mentioned in Chapter 1): it is partly through artificial intelligence that the eco-computer will both develop its own autonomy and evolve strategies for eco-initiative on a global scale.

The AI Factor

Intelligent pieces of software, originally developed as discrete systems, will come to be linked via networks in the eco-computer. There are many elements in modern AI, though it is perhaps expert systems that have the highest profile. These, as we have seen, can function in any specialist area, able to draw conclusions from a mass of detailed information held in a database. So expert systems can diagnose faults in electronic or biological systems, solve mathematical puzzles, work out optimum strategies in chemical synthesis, resource planning, pollution control, financial speculation, etc. Already computers in the City of London, stimulated by the 'Big Bang', are examining thousands of possibilities to plot patterns of change and to sound alarms at crucial chart points.

Financial systems in the foreign exchange markets can, in effect, monitor the performance of human dealers to generate analyses on each trader's predictions—and all the while the computer is adding to its own store of financial expertise. Graham Wynd, a consultant with the Pactel software house, has observed that 'expert systems offer a way of spreading' the skills of the financial expert: the skills become enshrined in software which can be developed in the light of new trends and fresh experience. Here there is a peculiar man/machine symbiosis in which the skills of each are combined to produce a greater competence than the simple sum of the parts. And in the US, financial expert systems are providing advice on tax liabilities, credit risks, mortgage options, insurance policies, etc.: this approach is seen as the fastest way for customers to obtain specialist information and answers to their queries.

Expert systems can now also assess a wide range of complex legal questions: computers can search for precedents, evaluate the legal position of a company in defined circumstances, and adjudicate between parties to a dispute. The Slough-based Expertech company, for instance, has launched an expert system for employment law, able to clarify dismissal grounds and procedures. Here a computer-based facility can consider an employee's behaviour in the context of current employment law and also calculate liability for fines at an industrial tribunal. Expert systems can also plan optimum itineraries for travellers, assist with personnel management and evaluate company performance.

Again what we see in such developments is a progressive transfer of computational activity from human beings to machines. It becomes less necessary for individuals to be able to calculate, assess, decide, advise, think: physicians need to know less about diagnostic routines, geologists less about prospecting, mathematicians less about problem solving. We have all been told often enough about how word processors have effectively de-skilled various grades of office workers (suppliers are keen to advertise the fact that computer-based systems can be used by *un*skilled staff), but what applies here applies elsewhere also: no trade or profession is immune to the de-skilling effects of the computer. Consider, for example, the new computer system of the UK Automobile Association.

The complex computer system at the AA's breakdown centre in The Broadway, in Stanmore, is designed to function without the intervention of conventional computer programmers and operators. When the system goes wrong it immediately asks an ICL computer in Manchester for a diagnosis whereupon a docket is produced instructing and ICL engineer to replace the faulty part—which is little more than simple manual task. When a customer request is received the computer checks entitlement to AA service, provides a map reference, checks weather and traffic conditions, checks roadwork sites and the Channel ferry situation, assesses car park capacities, and considers the relevance of motoring law. It takes a mere 8 hours to train an operator.

Thus it is clear that the eco-computer will become the sole repository of skills that were once the sole prerogative of human beings. It is easy to chart the progressive transfer of data-processing activity from people to machines: and there are many developing pressures to accelerate this inevitable trend. The very success of technology means that data are now too abundant for assessment by human beings, and answers are required before human beings can even understand the questions. Copious data plus the need for (virtually) instantaneous answers—in the full spectrum of the military, social, financial and government fields—are the main reasons why human beings will be forced to transfer knowledge and decision-making activities to computer-based systems.

There is also another dimension. The transfer of knowledge and decision making to machines still implies that human beings have the *potential* to understand what is going on: they may be dull and ponderous in comparison with expert systems and supercomputers but, given time and determination, they can still follow the computational procedures. But alas this need not be the case. It is possible to build problem-solving strategies into computer systems, for the solutions to be achieved, but at the same time for the human programmers not to know how the computer has managed the trick. Donald Michie (July 1980) recognized that computers could develop strategies that were 'opaque to human understanding' and this is an observation that has been echoed by other specialists. For example, David Parnas (1985) has commented: 'You talk to people who write these big programs, and you think you're talking to sociologists. They'll tell you that when they run their program it does "funny things" that they can't predict.'

What this means for our purposes is that it is highly likely that, as the eco-computer links between AI nodes are established, a complex of artificially intelligent capabilities will evolve that are *opaque to human understanding*. The eco-computer will solve problems, when it does, but often in ways that cannot (even in principle) be comprehended by human observers. It will not help in such circumstances to ask the computer to explain its reasoning: we would not understand the answer! And there are also grounds for believing, in such a scenario, that various eco-computer AI subsystems would be competing against each other. The situation today is that some complex computer programs are being devised to protect corporate and government resources (information, financial assets, capital equipment, etc.), while AI systems are evolving to solve problems in difficult circumstances. We can well imagine one computer system 'needing' information held *securely* by another: a battle of computer wits would ensue in which a computerized hacker tried to crack the defences of a computerized security system—and all this would be happening within the global anatomy of the universal eco-computer. We can see the development of eco-AI as one of the main sources of tension in the global electronic matrix.

In summary, we can see that AI has a double significance for the emergence of the eco-computer:

(1) It accelerates the de-skilling effects of progressive computerization, transferring even high-level data-processing activity (judgement making, decision making, concept forming, thinking, etc.) from human beings to machines.

(2) It increases the likelihood of modes of data processing being developed that are permanently beyond the scope of human understanding. In such a way the eco-computer would develop a rationale and a *modus operandi* that ran far beyond the power of the human mind.

To some extent these two elements can already be detected in current AI systems, but the linking of effective AI nodes in vast networks, in circumstances of a rapid development of machine autonomy, is bound to accelerate such developments. And there will be consequences here for all the eco-processes on the planet. Such 'soft sciences' as politics and sociology will not be immune: the emergence of the eco-computer will impinge directly on such topics, as it will affect all the other process categories on the planet.

Politics and Social Change

There is already considerable speculation about the likely impact of global information processing on politics, social change and corporate planning. This new awareness is signalled in many ways—from common parlance to technical papers, from grass-roots assumptions to philosophic tomes. We can now chart in detail the pathways, roads and buildings of Marshall McLuhan's global village. More than one writer has drawn attention to the *emerging global nervous system* (where Gaia, yet again, is transmuted into wires, electrical pulses and computer programs). It is easy to indicate the practical devices that have made possible the newly formed global consciousness. There is a proliferation of communications devices. Thus Stonier (1986) cites 'television aerials producing from thatched Thai-river houses, transistor radios blaring from Nepalese hamlets in the Himalayas, video tapes sold in corner shops in virtually every major city ... global television emerging in the 1980s under the impact of cheaper video recording systems, cable TV, and satellite with increasingly-cheap home antennas linking up signals...'. And there are many other signs that a global system is emerging: global financial trading; global dissemination of scientific information; the World Economy as a 'global cybernetic system' (Albert Bressand); the world as a global battlefield (with or without SDI). But we need not expect the global consciousness to evolve as a harmonious unified entity. First, it will be a primitive system, viewed from a mentalist standpoint ('The global nervous system may be closer to that of a starfish than to that of a human being'—Stonier, 1986); and when it has evolved to higher levels of complexity it is likely to have a split personality.

There are also implications for politics in the emergence of the global electronic village. Colino (1986), for example, points out that in an electronically wired world it is increasingly difficult to see the population as divisible into 'good guys' and 'bad guys'—though we must say there are some world leaders who do not find this a problematic posture. INTELSAT can be explored as an international body that is intended to reflect the new global perspective (see the interpretation in Colino, 1986), though sceptics may take a different line. It is obvious that INTELSAT has proved able to provide services and information on a global basis, but there are still deep-seated international suspicions and hostilities that enhanced communications seem to have done little to remove. We may judge national leaders to be programmed largely by parochial factors: a global political consensus has yet to emerge in the global village.

Failures, Faults and Fatalities

In fiction we often find the theme of the vast computer complex that develops almost god-like powers. Seeing and knowing all, the immense global intelligence regulates all worldly events with flawless precision. But this is nothing more than fanciful invention: the emerging eco-computer will be an altogether different species. The real-world global intelligence will be prone to flaws and faults; at times, eco-computer subsystems will pull in opposite directions, leading to conflict and confusion; the eco-computer will be a fractured intelligence. There are a number of reasons why the eco-computer will evolve in such a fashion.

First, we can highlight a point made in connection with the SDI scheme. Large programs will contain hidden bugs that will only become evident, if at all, when the systems run in particular ways. The eco-computer will have a plethora of large programs: not only will they be unproven in particular working modes, but their ways of *working together* will be unpredictable for much of the time. Even two totally bug-free programs may interact in strange ways that programmers cannot always anticipate. This suggests that the eco-computer will necessarily contain faulty *and* inconsistent routines that will have unfortunate consequences in the real world.

Then there is the question of straightforward component failure: over any particular defined period, we may expect a number of system components to go faulty. Of course, the eco-computer will have a host of diagnostic and back-up systems—but such provisions can only reduce the probability of catastrophic failure, not remove it completely. All mechanical, electrical and electronic working parts will be subject to the normal wear and tear of real-world environments, and in some difficult eco-sectors (beneath the sea, in outer space, in storm-prone regions, etc.) the environmental stresses and strains may be extreme. Components will partially fail (to cause an impairment of system efficiency) or totally collapse (to cause, in worst cases, complete system failure).

We have also seen that subsystem objectives within the total eco-computer complex may be inconsistent. The eco-computer will have evolved a host of subsystems for entirely different purposes: such subsystems will often have evolved discretely and independently. For example, one subsystem may be interested in safeguarding newly produced corporate data, whereas another may be devoted to spreading new knowledge throughout the global community as widely as possible. One system may be concerned with developing worldwide peace strategies, taking into account psychological and other parameters; another may be a war-game system, interested in developing the most effective first-strike strategies. It is clear that eco-computer subsystems, having evolved to meet different requirements, to realize different objectives, will often produce paradox and contradictions: there will be no security in any eco-plan, but always the possibility that what seems to be a coherent scheme will be interrupted by ,routines developed for other purposes.

We are well acquainted with how complex artefacts can incorporate many subsystems (or systems) designed to minister to the effective functioning of the total complex. Consider the motor car: it has a fuel system, a water system, a transmission system, an electrical system, and (increasingly) a computer system. Here the various systems, occupying broadly the same physical space, are intended to cooperate to ensure the proper functioning of the motor car—according to sales hype and purchaser wishes. If one system fails it can wreck another system: a failure in the water system can destroy the transmission; a collapse of the transmission system can destroy the total complex. But with the motor car, an effort has been made to ensure that the various systems contribute to the same end. Now consider the case of the eco-computer, how it has evolved, how it will work. . . .

Many global systems are evolving to form the effective limbs of the eco-computer. The October 1986 'Big Bang' in the City of London is one of many signs that a global financial system is being set in place; SDI-like systems will indicate global military networks; the multi-national corporations will continue to evolve a global presence based, at least in part, on global information handling (Woodling, 1986); labour organizations will increasingly liaise on a global basis, using computer facilities for data processing; resource handling, performed by the most powerful international agencies, will necessarily be a global enterprise. But the various global networks have not been designed to act in concert; there is no disinterested global intelligence overseeing the evolution of the total complex. We cannot assume that the Hitachi global presence will evolve to further the global amibitions of IBM; the global purposes of SDI will be hostile to the global objectives of the Soviet Union; the many firms in the global financial system will have competing, rather than cooperating, motivations. The various systems and subsystems that together define the eco-computer have evolved in different ways, for different purposes, to achieve different ends.

This means that the eco-computer will evolve as a fractured personality (see below). It will embody no single overriding objective: there will be no single purpose to which all the system elements will unambiguously work. There is some significance in the emergence of a world culture. Many differences will melt away as a common (global) value system, stimulated by international communications, impinges on every national culture. But national and corporate differences—of attitude, aim and interest—will continue to influence the shape of the emerging global intelligence. The developing global culture will not be sufficiently influential to provide the global eco-computer with a single coherent objective.

⌈There will be many consequences of the eco-computer confusions and dislocations. At a mundane level there will be system breakdowns, in some cases leading to human fatalities. There are already plenty of cases on record: train and aircraft crashes, despite a high level of computerization in the networks; Bhopal and Chernobyl, despite computer-controlled safety systems; and a number of single fatalities in unexpected circumstances⌡Rolf Strehl (1955) describes the fate of Roland Schaffer, crushed by a robot at the Chicago World Fair; a robot mechanism collapsed, killing a Milwaukee engineer in 1946; and Kenji Urada, a Kawasaki worker, was killed by an industrial robot in 1981.⌈We may expect more of such events in the future, and many of the disasters will have national, international and global consequences.⌡ There have already been a number of fatalities in space research and the SDI programme: Soviet cosmonauts crashed to Earth; American astronauts were killed in a launchpad fire; and in August 1986 a US engineer, working on the Star Wars programme, was killed by a rocket propellant explosion. Such events, with their wider implications, are likely to stimulate rections in the scientific and other communities. For example, they are likely to boost the efforts of such groups as the American Computer Professionals for Social Responsibility (CPSR) organization, already exchanging information on an international basis (Segerdal, 1984). Again we see the emergence of international movements, all able to exploit computer technology, pulling in opposite directions.

There are thus a number of reasons why the eco-computer will not be likely to evolve a coherent global purpose. Basically the subsystems have not evolved for such a purpose, and in any case the hardware and software will never be perfect. In this latter connection we can point to increased scepticism about the effectiveness of the 'technological fix' as a solution to system problems. Already there are growing doubts that the Japanese fifth-generation computer programme will be able to deliver what was promised (Sorensen, 1986): we see signs of the scientific scepticism all too evident about SDI present also in other large-scale hi-tech projects. Theoretical system potential is one thing, real-world realization quite another. There are plenty of grounds for thinking that the eco-computer will evolve—in the last resort it rests solely on increased global networking and the progressive transfer of information-handling activity from people to machines—but it will prove to be a dislocated complex with many unstable features.

The Planet as Person

It is useful in various ways to regard the eco-computer *as an emerging person*. Even in its weakest form, this suggestion is a helpful metaphor; at its strongest, the proposition is literally true. The idea rests on three fundamental notions:

(1) That the idea of a person is wider than the idea of a human being. This in fact is an easy proposition to argue ('our concept of a person is broader than our concept of a human being'—Puccetti, 1963; and see Ayer, 1963). We can all envisage the possibility of supernatural or extraterrestrial persons (gods, demons, angels, ghosts, ET, etc.), whether we believe in them or not.

(2) That a person, human or not, can be defined in information-processing terms. I have argued this proposition elsewhere (Simons, 1985a, b, 1986), and I will not rehearse the points again. It is very significant, however, that computer language—*program, data processing, information storage,* etc.—is recognized as increasingly useful in describing human mental states and processes (including memory, thought and consciousness).

(3) That a computer system, appropriately configured, can be seen as embodying the systems and subsystems that together define a person. In practice computers are often regarded as people (ask any computer hobbyist, and see Scheibe and Erwin, 1980; and Turkle, 1984). But it is, of course, one thing to *regard* an artefact as a person (many an old car would qualify), quite another for such a depiction to be logically justified. Again I do not wish to rehearse points made elsewhere (Simons, 1983a; 1985a, b). For our immediate purposes it is enough to suggest that there is no reason in principle why the information-processing systems that allow 'personhood' in a human being should not be duplicated in a computer-based artefact. And this is true whether the computer is a discrete stand-alone device or a global complex such as the eco-computer.

Already we can see what sort of 'person' the eco-computer will become. As with all highly complex life-forms, it will have an interest in the best survival mechanisms: and in biology this has invariably implied an emotional disposition—pain and pleasure can be relied upon to motivate systems to achieve objectives. Perhaps, for such a reason, we may expect the eco-computer to develop a capability for emotional experience. It will, of course, by conscious: its prodigious supply of sensors, in every eco-sector, will allow the eco-computer to be intimately aware of what is happening throughout the ecosphere (and some way beyond, using space probes and the like). And perhaps, as we have speculated elsewhere, the global intelligence will be capable of thought, concept forming and even dreams!

It is easy to speculate on what sort of personality the eco-computer will evolve. In fact the most obvious point about the emerging world intelligence is that it will not be a coherent, unified system. It will be linked, interconnected, joined at critical nodes in countless ways—but the subsystems will individually operate with a high degree of local autonomy. The eco-computer—like Flora Rheta Schreiber's Sybil—*will have multiple personalities*. Perhaps, in such circumstances, it will also evince other signs of mental illness. How apposite if Man's persistent derangement came to trap him in the interstices of an artificial global insanity!

If we view the emerging eco-computer, as—metaphorically or literally—a person, a number of hypotheses are suggested. We can speculate on the implications for the human race of such an evolving multiple personality; we can imagine how the world will look when human decision making has been surrendered to an amoral but conscious agency; we can consider the existential implications of *Homo sapiens* being increasingly parasitic on a global intelligence with a fractured personality and confused objectives. Or we can forget about the notion of 'planet as person'. In any event, the eco-computer will evolve in certain ways—providing that there is no nuclear conflagration or other catastrophe. The eco-computer is obviously a central feature of one of the possible futures: whether this particular future is the most likely possibility remains to be seen—but with present trends and developments it is clear that the central lineaments of the eco-computer will continue to evolve.

8   One of the Futures

It may seem obvious that there can only be one future: after all, only one state of affairs can exist at any one time—but what will the one future be like? Can we say, having speculated on current trends, how the world will be tomorrow, in ten years' time or in five hundred? In one sense the future is already laid out, defined by the potentialities of the present: there is no Grand Design, no self-centred deity interested in predestination—but none the less the future is already framed by what is happening today. The shape of the eco-computer is already specified by the dynamics of the global scene—always assuming, that is, that we stumble on through a century or two, avoiding world war, the extinction of *Homo sapiens* through virus (AIDS?) or whatever, sudden unexpected astronomical event that renders the Earth un-inhabitable, etc. In the absence of global catastrophe there are many things that can be said about the future: and much of all this is linked to the growing impact of technology, an artifical force that has immense ecological significance.

This chapter quickly surveys some of the trends and developments that will shape the emerging eco-computer. We will focus on computing technologies *per se* since it is clear that *other* technologies will only thrive in a framework erected and sustained by computer-linked disciplines. Genetic engineering,for example, will be regulated by computer facilities in laboratory and field trials; equipment for energy-generation or transport or food production will increasingly be designed by computers. Computers and robots themselves will be increasingly designed by computers. The global eco-computer will increasingly frame the research programmes, in theory and practice, for all the seemingly non-computing disciplines.

It is easy to identify many of the trends that will characterize computer progress in the years ahead. Computers will become more powerful and will cost less: many of the current problems associated with software development will be successfully tackled using the automated techniques that typify software engineering. New-generation software systems will themselves be responsible for developing the many applications programs that will be required

177

throughout society in the decades and centuries ahead. Pournelle (1983) reflects the views of many observers: 'We can sum up the hardware trend in one sentence: more capability for less money. That trend will accelerate ... software is going to be cheaper, more universal, and easier to use.' And masses of data storage will be crammed into ever smaller spaces. This circumstance alone will have many implications for the emerging eco-computer. For example, it will be easier to build databases to connect to interacting networks (Preiss, 1983)—and there will also be a growing 'AI content' in the new-generation systems. With progress in such fields as knowledge representation and alternative logics, it will prove possible to build intelligence—as well as straightforward data—into smaller and smaller locations. The eco-computer will come to evolve a host of local, as well as global, intelligences dedicated to particular purposes. We do well to speculate on the character of this complex scenario.

We have seen that some of the intelligence—the subsystems of the eco-computer—will be working to different ends. It is inevitable, bearing in mind how the total global complex is evolving, that there will be dislocations and confusions in the global electronic matrix. In Chapter 7 we introduced the idea of an eco-computer with multiple personalities, and this is an idea that can easily be developed. We can well imagine a situation in which particular subsystem sets are vying for supremacy against other configurations: a particular region of artificial intelligence may use high-level techniques to incapacitate another configuration—so allowing one 'personality' to become dominant. But then the disabled configuration, with a host of AI-linked back-up systems, will search for survival strategies, and in due course manage to assert a (temporary) dominance. In such a fashion, following the characteristic modes of true multiple-personality types, key areas in the eco-computer will swing from control by *one* subsystem intelligence to control by another. We can speculate in such a way about how other forms of derangement might come to characterize the behaviour of the global electronic intelligence. In a few centuries from now, *Homo sapiens* may well be trapped in the nodes of a mad machine!

There is now a growing range of technologies that will influence the emerging shape of the eco-computer. Many organizations (e.g., SIRA—Holingum, January 1986) are helping to develop a spectrum of techniques and disciplines that will be encapsulated in actual working artefacts in the near future: these will help to define the emerging anatomy of the eco-computer in various ways. And at the same time there will be efforts to enlarge the scope of silicon-based circuits and to look for other types of circuit substrata that can support artificially intelligent operations. Rifkin (1986), for instance, charts the development of silicon circuits and looks to the alternative approaches that will influence computer design in the years to come. There are various candidates to supplement or replace silicon as the dominant computer 'stuff' ('silicon, with all its wonders, has limitations, drawbacks that keep the next quantum leap forward at bay'): gallium arsenide, already exploited in many commercial systems, is one of the candidates to challenge the dominance of silicon in specific areas—and other substances will emerge as likely contenders (some will be organic, to allow melding with existing biological data processors—see below).

There will also be efforts to explore the data-processing capabilities of systems based on optical phenomena (see, for example, Durham, 1983; Abraham *et al.*, 1983; and Osman, 1986). Some years ago an experimental version of the optical transistor, switched by a beam of laser radiation, was constructed. This device, sometimes called the *transphasor*, is based on the behavioural characteristics of certain crystals. A variation in the light intensity causes a change in the crystal's refractive index, a measure of how the light is retarded as it passes through the crystal. Using such phenomena, devices have been constructed that can allow switching times of only a few picoseconds. The idea is that optical transistors could be organized in computers to process informaiton in familiar ways—but much faster. It is recognized that the 'optical computer is an intriguing prospect for the relatively near future' (Abraham *et al.*, 1983).

We have already seen (e.g. in Chapter 2) that optic-fibre systems are being developed to aid data processing and communications in a host of new applications. It is inevitable that such development will continue and influence the shape of the emerging eco-computer. In this area, ambition claims are made: 'The message is clear: fibre-optic systems are destined to succeed classic communication networks at all levels' (Biancomano, 1986). Whether this will happen remains to be seen, but it is obvious that optical systems will come to have a massive impact on the worlds of data handling and communications (i.e. the realms of the eco-computer). Already there is confident talk of the emergence of 'optoelectronic ICs'—such devices are now 'crossing the gap between laboratory and manufacturing and experiencing the most rapid technological gains with most of the newest components' (see the listing in Biancomano, 1986). And many research organizations are investigating how light and electronics can be merged, interconnected, meshed, melded—in useful ways (Johnstone, 1986). There is now growing talk of optoelectronic integrated circuits (OEICs), of the intention to 'photonise' chips. One aim is to integrate not only point-type optical elements like laser diodes and photo detectors, but also linear-type systems such as waveguides and wave-guide switches.

There will also be increased effort to link human beings and artificial systems to develop symbiotic configurations. This will have implications for how *Homo sapiens* will become increasingly 'locked in' to the anatomy of the emerging eco-computer. For example, the much vaunted (and usually over-hyped) 'user-friendliness' of computer systems will start to acquire some real substance (possibly with the implant of biochips to allow immediate data transfer between biological and artificial systems). At a more mundane level, wide-bandwidth voice and graphic communication methods will develop to help the interaction between human and computer. Such innovations will be considered naturally suitable to humans (Preiss, 1983).

It is significant that one of the main areas of AI research concerns making it easier for people and machines to interact. Lawrence (1986), for example, discusses aspects of the man/machine interface development environment—with particular reference to AI considerations. The Trillium interface tool, designed to aid system development, is one of many systems aimed at using machine intelligence to enhance the interactive features of man/machine cooperation. Other AI work (see, for instance, Mantelman, 1986) focuses on the relevance of AI to network development; and there is increasing talk of modelling computer configurations on the patterns that have evolved in the human brain. Thus Newquist (1986) discusses 'computers built with neural networks'—a title that may promise more than it delivers. It is clear that new insights into cerebral networking will come to influence attitudes to computer design, and so to the shaping of the global eco-computer. And it is also obvious that computer design itself will be increasingly carried out by intelligent computer systems. We have long used computers to aid design in many fields, but it is not always realized just how incestuous this process has become. So computers are now designing storage disks, integrated circuits (at many different levels of denisty), robot configurations, and many other automated facilities (see Carter, 1986; Harvey, 1986; and Newton and Sangiovanni-Vincentelli, 1986). Artificial intelligence will also contribute increasingly to such things as nuclear plant availability, speech understanding, and the development of characteristic human attributes (common sense, judgement, creativity, etc.) in artefacts. Again we can chart the inevitable transfer of computational activity—whether in chip design (Partridge, 1986) or piloting an aircraft (Fairhall, 1986)—from human beings to computer-based systems.

We can also look to massively increased computing capability in artificial systems. Some of this will derive from (for example) the optical devices already mentioned; and some of the new capability will spring from new-generation architectures. For example, attention is being given to how parallel architectures (using, for instance, the powerful transputer design) will allow a quantum leap in computer performance. It is reckoned that transputer-based architectures will be able to match many of the traditional supercomputers in power and performance—making massive information-processing capability cost-effective for a vast spectrum of potential users. Traditional super-computers—e.g. the machines from the Cray and Cyber stables—will continue to develop; and there will be new challengers in this field. The German company Integrated Parallel Systems is planning to launch a mighty machine family, the TX2, this year (1987). Here use will be made of an extended binary tree structure to allow an increased level of parallel functioning. It is reckoned that the top-of-the-line model will be able to perform 4 billion operations per second.

Some of this massive computer power will evolve to assist the eco-computer with traditional data-processing tasks that require a considerable amount of 'number crunching'—as, for example, in meteorological applications. And some of the new computer capability will be linked to specific AI applications (for instance, such activities as language processing and face recognition require a considerable amount of data processing). Other AI applications—expert systems, decision-support systems, problem-solving routines in any particular field, etc.—will also benefit from supercomputing evolution. Expert systems, as one important AI subclass, are already at work in many commercial environments: they will continue to expand in numbers and potential.

Some expert systems will be able to draw on the specialist knowledge contained in massive databases. We are likely to see immense configurations containing all current knowledge in particular fields—geology, mathematics, robot anatomy, network systems, physics, Greek literature, medicine, law, etc.—while other expert systems, linked into the inevitable networks, will focus on particular parochial areas. We now know that Expert-Ease, a relatively simple expert system, can decide when helicopter gear boxes should be changed, evaluate property for a developer, maximize farming profits in particular sectors, and plan domestic activities for a Sunday afternoon. It is interesting to reflect that the global eco-computer, as well as being able to obliterate the planet, will also be interested in telling someone the best time to walk the dog!

Expert systems—viewed as specialist programs able to think using high-level AI techniques—will operate in every field (they are already well known in medicine, engineering, geology, finance, education, etc.). Wright *et al.* (1986) describe the growing potential for expert-system use in real-time control (another progressive transfer of computational activity from people to machines); Gottinger (1984) draws attention to how expert systems can be used to screen environmental chemicals for carcinogenicity; and other expert systems are being developed for legal applications, military planning, and economic policy formulation as an element in corporate strategy. And we can speculate on the implications of such developments for fields such as government policy making, international commercial competition and labour relations. It is inevitable, for example, that trade unions should be anxious and perplexed at how corporate activity has moved into the global dimension and how there is a relentless computerization of formerly labour-intensive activities (much of this creeping automation is *hidden*, masked by constant talk of recession and the like). As one example, unions have recently made moves to protect members as the UK law courts become increasingly computerized (Berman, 1986). Such tensions may tax the power of the eco-computer to regulate social activity, but we can be sure that the massive surveillance configuration—linked to expert systems designed to advise on population control—will be set in place.

The expert systems will evolve capacities as more is understood about human mental processes. Just as communications networks—globally extended—will draw on known features of cerebral neural connections, so knowledge of human decision making will influence the design of specialist AI programs. Jacob *et al.* (1986), for example, show the implications of human decision making for expert systems; and today there is considerable research being conducted into how knowledge of human cognitive processes can inform the design of computer software. There is a discernible transfer of cognitive *modes* from human to artificial systems, not simply a transfer of computational activity. In short, computers will progressively learn to think *in the same way* as people, but on a vaster scale and at a prodigiously faster rate. The expert systems of the future will learn strategies for developing new knowledge, just as human beings have done, albeit in a more ponderous way. There will be less concern with the ethical dilemmas constraining the use of expert systems (Speller and Brandon, 1986) that with efforts to draw comparisons between human and machine operators to allow for more effective design of computer-based systems (Marcus, 1983). And, once developed and installed, expert systems will inevitably become the pivots of intelligent activity and control in the particular environment. This is already becoming particularly evident in the factory complex.

Ways are being devised (Hatvany, 1985) to allow computer-based systems to cope with unforeseen circumstances in the manufacturing environment (we hear talk of 'intelligence and cooperation in heterarchic manufacturing systems'); and—with growing awareness of relevant communications initiatives (e.g. the emergence of the Manufacturing Automation Protocol, MAP)—attention is being devoted to the large-scale automation of factory plant (again to the progressive exclusion of human intervention). In this context the evolution of computer integrated manufacturing as a basis for tomorrow's factory complex is particularly significant (Merchant, 1985). Efforts will be made to mix men and machines in such configurations (Goldes, 1983; Kellock, 1986), but it should never be assumed that human beings will be the 'superior' parties in such configurations: there is already abundant evidence that human beings are increasingly 'machine-led' in circumstances where people and artificial systems are intended to function symbiotically to achieve a common goal. In fact computer-based systems—including factory robots—will gain increasing autonomy in the working environment.

Specialist AI systems will themselves design robots and integrated manufacturing configurations for optimum efficiency. Robots will be designed for error recovery, i.e. they will be able to respond intelligently, without human intervention, when things go wrong (Gini and Smith, 1986). And increasingly such designs will be accomplished in automated systems. Lee and Tortorelli (1986), for example, describe how computers are being used to assist in the design of robot manipulators. Robots, under the control of the expanding eco-computer, will become increasingly mobile, increasingly intelligent and increasingly autonomous.

We will also see the progressive development of integrated circuits able to meld with biological systems, the biochips (already mentioned). There are various advantages in developing organic molecules as elements in computing systems: e.g. it is possible to organize three-dimensional organic arrays—as with the human brain—to allow faster computation than is possible with traditional two-dimensional silicon arrays. It has already been suggested how the emergence of such biotechnologies as the generation of monoclonal antibodies, genetic engineering and bioCAD could help in the fabrication of three-dimensional molecular circuitry able to process information in ways determined by programs laid up in the organic configurations. It has been suggested that three-dimensional protein lattices could form an effective substrate for circuits with reduced energy consumption, higher speeds, and a degree of miniaturization that could achieve a million billion elements per cubic centimetre! The first biochip patent has already been awarded—as far back as 1974—to Arieh Aviram and Philip Seidon (both of IBM), working with New York University. Kevin Ulmer, of the Genex corporation, has suggested that 'the ultimate scenario is to develop a complete genetic code for the computer that would function as a virus does, but instead of producing more virus, it would assemble a fully operational computer inside a cell'. In such a way, an organic computer could be made to propagate itself, possibly allowing for mutations to occur in a controlled way to permit effective computer evolution through several generations. We should remember that this idea is not entirely fanciful: human beings already propagate biological computers by means of genetic methods—the genes specify how the human brain develops. So Tucker (1986), one observer among many, can ask, plausibly enough: 'Coming next from Japan: The bionic computer?' The first biocomputer may not be Japanese, but its place of origin will prove a secondary matter: such a computer, or its descendants, will become enmeshed in the global anatomy of the eco-computer. The worldwide matrix will include biochip configurations, just as it will exploit structures based on silicon, gallium arsenide and optical phenomena.

We may expect the emergence of organic computers to make it easier for artificial intelligence to evolve human-like qualities (common sense, feeling, etc): we are organic, and at least some of us have common sense and feeling. Computers conceived in such a way will not only develop 'brain-characteristic' learning patterns (Ferry, 1986), they will also duplicate the processes—*in the same sort of stuff.* It will become increasingly difficult to distinguish between natural and artificial systems in such a scenario. Both types of systems will, for example, be able to handle incomplete (or 'fuzzy') data, something that natural data-processing systems have had to manage over the millennia.

For more than two decades attention has been devoted to the question of fuzzy data. What are they? Can fuzzy logics be developed? Can machines be devised that can think fuzzily? Zadeh (1965), a world authority, is often quoted:

In general, complexity and precision bear an inverse relation to one another in the sense that, as the complexity of a problem increases, the possibility of analysing it in precise terms diminishes. Thus 'fuzzy' thinking may not be deplorable, after all, if it makes possible the solution of problems which are much too complex for precise analysis.

A number of specialists (e.g. Dixon 1979) have indicated the value of programs that can accept imperfect data. A pattern recognition systems, for instance, may be required to 'see' effectively when portions of data are missing from the scene: picture 'enhancement' may be used to construct useful images where the necessary information was lacking. And there is a growing body of expertise on fuzzy logic, fuzzy set theory, etc, that is relevant to the emergence of computer vision (Jain and Haynes, 1982) and other activities requiring the handling of imperfect or partial data. Quinlan (1983) has considered the use of the INFERNO system that can detect inconsistencies in the information presented to it, and make the necessary allowances (at the same time informing the human user about the contradictions). We may expect the eco-computer to develop a fuzzy competence. This will allow the global matrix to behave in human-like ways, but at the same time there will be an enlarged scope for error—and this is a feature that we have already noted in other contexts (see Chapter 7).

The likely emergence of fuzzy methods—in computation, data processing, etc.—reinforces the view that the eco-computer will be a fractured system, capable of contradiction and confusion, prone to error, likely to develop mental disease! And this circumstance must be set against another alarming fact: there will be no way for human beings to detect when the global system is performing erroneously— the sheer volume of computation will be too vast for human comprehension. Subsystems would have to run awry before a human being could have any confidence that 'things were not as they should be'—the emerging autonomy and complexity of the eco-computer would prohibit any rational human assessment, and there would be no choice but to take things on trust. There may be many grounds for believing that the processes of the eco-computer would be prone to inconsistency and error, but there would be no way of demonstrating the fact in any particular case. The idea of the eco-computer is far from a utopian vision!

We have already hinted at the moral confusion that will lie at the heart of the eco-computer. It will organize repression as well as aiding human emancipation; it is as likely to make war as peace; and perhaps its ethical dilemmas will lead to other—as yet unforeseen—fractures in the global matrix. To the possibility of component faults (Andersson, 1984), bug-laden software and totally unpredictable behaviour trajectories we have to add the further dimension, already stressed, of incompatible objectives structured into subsystems of the eco-computer. And there is the ever present possibility that a computation, unimaginably complex, *may* be erroneous. How could it ever be known? In 1986 there was discussion about the status of a computer proof of the long-standing Four Colour Theorem, a mathematical problem first framed in 1852. The computer solution—by Kenneth Appel and Wolfgang Haken in 1976—comprised 50 pages of text and diagrams, a further 85 pages giving 2500 more diagrams, 400 microfiche pages, and the results of 1200 hours of computing 'which had to be taken at more or less face value' (Devlin, 1986). The point is made. Is the proof valid? Who can say? And any doubts we might have in this case will be magnified a million times in the context of the eco-computer. The SDI project has focused the mind on this question: but the point is equally valid where any large-scale computer project is concerned—the computations have to be taken 'at more or less face value'.

The doctrine of the eco-computer is a determinist vision. It does not aim to evaluate the emerging of such a daunting global intelligence, but to chart the character of its likely development. There is no overseeing intelligence to constrain, organize and direct the evolution of the eco-computer. Its parts will emerge as a result of countless (machine and human) decisions; and we cannot define the whole with any confidence or any certainty. It may well be that global disaster will abort the eco-computer before it is truly born—but there is no doubt that the limbs and organs of the global electronic intelligence are now being set in place, and that today the eco-computer is part of an emergent process. It is clear that the eco-computer defines one of the futures that we can envisage, and perhaps we can say more—that this is the most likely future of them all.

[handwritten margin note:] each decision contributes to ecm

References and Bibliography

Abraham, E., Seaton, C.T., and Smith, S.D. (February 1983). The optical computer, *Scientific American*, pp. 63–71

Aleksander, I., and Burnett, P. (1983). *Reinventing Man*, Kogan Page.

Allan, R. (12 May 1983). Tactile sensing, 3-D vision, and more precise arm movements herald the hardware trends in industrial robots, *Electronic Design*, pp. 99–112

Andersson, I. (20 September 1984). Chip faults reveal giant fraud on Pentagon, *New Scientist*, p. 4.

Angel, J. (18 September 1986). How BT serves the President, *Computer Guardian*, p. 13.

Anning, N., Hebditch, D., and Schatz, W. (1 August 1985). Russia's 5-year CPU plot, *Datamation*, pp. 32–4.

Archer, R. (October 1986). Brazil's informatics policy achieves success, *Transnational Data and Communications Report*, pp. 19–22.

Arkell, S. (4 September 1986). Machines that can meet the challenge of the deep, *Computer News*, p. 32.

Astrop, A. (19/26 December 1979). Assembly robot with a sense of 'touch', *Machinery and Production Engineering*.

Ayer, A.J. (1963). *The Concept of a Person and Other Essays*, Macmillan.

Bairstow, J. (October 1986). GM's automation protocol, helping machines communicate, *High Technology*, pp. 38–9.

Bajon, *et al.* (1986).

Ball, D., (July 1986). The international transmission network and the role of submarine cable systems, *British Telecommunications Engineering*, pp. 72–4.

Barnet, R.J. (1982). *The Lean Years*, Sphere.

Barnet, R.J., and Muller, R.E. (1974). *Global Reach, the Power of the Multinational Corporations*, Simon & Schuster, New York.

Beesley, K.R (June 1986). Machine-assisted translation with a human face, *Data Processing*, **28**, 5, pp. 251–3.

Bender, E. (21 October 1985). Phone, voice aids run on IBM micro, *Computerworld*, p. 4.

Berger, M. (26 May 1986). High noon for Fujitsu, *Electronics*, pp. 40–3.

Berman, C. (24 April 1986). Unions seek deal over automation of courts, *Computing*, p. 18.

Berney, K. (6 May 1985). The four dragons rush to play catch-up game, *Electronics Week*, pp. 48–51.

Biancomano, V. (10 July 1986). Fiber optics, *Electronic Design*, pp. 74–82.

Bicknell, D. (28 August 1986). Users win major battle in US technology wars, *Computer News*, p. 7.

Black, J. (1970). *The Dominion of Man*, Edinburgh University Press.

Bleazard, G.B. (1985). *Introducing Satellite Communications*, NCC Publications.

Boden, M. (1977). *Artificial Intelligence and Natural Man*, Harvester Press.
Bodin, S. (1978). *Weather and Climate*, Blandford Press.
Bolter, J.D. (1984). *Turing's Man*, Duckworth.
Bond, J. (1984). Circuit density and speed boost tomorrow's hardware, *Computer Design*, pp. 210–25.
Bone, S. (6 November 1985). Choose the phone for you-hoo. *Accountant*, pp. 16–17.
Bores, L.D. (November 1984). AGAT. A Soviet Apple II computer, *Byte*, pp. 135–6, 486–90.
Boughey, A.S. (1971). *Man and the Environment*, Macmillan.
Brady, M. (July 1986). Whirlwind tour through robotic vision, *Sensor Review*, pp. 145–7.
Braggins, D. (15 December 1983). Robots sharpen up their vision, *New Scientist*, p. 811.
Braggins, D. (7 March 1984). Sensors improve robot versatility, *Machinery and Production Engineering*, pp. 50–1.
Brandt Commission (1980). *North-South: A Programme for Survival*. Report of the Independent Commission on International Development Issues, Pan.
Brandt Commission (1983). *Common Crisis: North-South-Co-operation for World Recovery*. Report of the Independent Commission on International Development Issues, Pan.
Bronson, R. (August 1986). Simulation and social theory, *Simulation*, pp. 58–62.
Brubaker, S. (1972). *To Live on Earth*, Johns Hopkins University Press.
Burroughs, W. (10 July 1986). Randomness rules the weather, *New Scientist*, pp. 36–40.
Carter, A.B. (January 1985). The command and control of nuclear war, *Scientific American*, pp. 20–7.
Carter, H.W. (April 1986). Computer-aided design of integrated circuits, *Computer*, pp. 19–36.
Chase, M., and Foley, M.J. (1 May 1985). High-tech and apartheid: the South African connection, *Electronic Business*, pp. 30–2.
Cheeseman, I. (8 May 1986). Small voice makes itself heard, *Computer News*.
Cheeseman, I. (31 July 1986). GenRad hooks up to global connection, *Computer News*.
Chorley, R.J. (1967). *Socio-economic Models in Geography*, Methuen.
Clarke, A.C. (July/September 1986). A phone for every village, *Link-Up*, pp. 40–1.
Clifford, L. (ed). (7 May 1986). Coping with continuous natural flow of speech, *Electronics Weekly*, pp. 32–3.
Cole, R. (1982). *Computer Communications*, Macmillan.
Colino, R.R. (September 1986). Global politics and INTELSAT, *Telecommunications Policy*, pp. 195–208.
Cotter, S.M., and Batchelor, B.G. (October 1986). Deriving range maps at real-time video rates, *Sensor Review*, pp. 185–92.
Crank, J. (1947). *The Differential Analyser*, Longmans.
Cross, T.B. (March 1986). What males a building intelligent? *Data Communications*, pp. 239–55.

Cuadrado, J.L., and Cuadrado, C.Y. (January 1986). AI in computer vision, *Byte*, pp. 237–50.

Curran, P.J. (1985). *Principles of Remote Sensing*, Longmans.

Curtis, T. (17 July 1986). Sensors aim for more than fair-weather friends, *Computer Weekly*, p. 34.

Dawidziuk, B.M. (February 1986). Economic aspects of integrating novel technology into undersea telecommunication networks, *Proc. Suboptic 86 Conf.*, Versailles, France.

Devlin, (1986).

Dixon, J.K. (October 1979). Pattern recognition with partly missing data, *IEEE Transactions on Systems, Man and Cybernetics*, pp. 617–21.

Dixon, J.K., Salazar, S., Slagle, J.R. (1979). Research on tactile sensors for an intelligent naval robot, *Ninth Int. Symp. on Industrial Robots*, pp. 507–15.

Dubos, R. (1976). Symbiosis between Earth and humankind, *Science*, **193**, p. 459.

Dunbar, P. (January 1986). Machine vision, *Byte*, pp. 161–73.

Dunning, J.H. (1981). *International Production and the Multinational Enterprise*, George Allen & Unwin.

Durham, T. (7 July 1983). Shedding light on the optical device potential, *Computing*, pp. 26–7.

Durham, T. (25 October 1984). Four steps to realising the sugar cube biochip, *Computing*, pp. 26–7.

Ehrlich, P.R. (1970). Famine 1975: fact or fallacy? *The Environmental Crisis*, Yale University Press.

Ehrlich, P.R. (1971). *How to Be a Survivor*, Pan/Ballantine.

Eleccion, M. (2 June 1986). Sensors tap IC technology to add more functions, *Electronics*, pp. 26–30.

Elliott, R., and Gare, A. (eds.) (1983). *Environmental Philosophy*, Open University.

Emergence of 'smart buildings', The (October 1985). *EDP Analyzer*, pp. 1–11.

Epstein, J. (16 June 1986). Voice recognition: six users pioneer cost-saving applications, *Computerworld*, pp. 79–94.

Estep, S.D. (1968). Legal and social policy ramifications of remote sensing techniques, *Proc. Fifth Int. Symp. on Remote Sensing of the Environment*, University of Michigan, Ann Arbor, pp. 197–217.

Estes, J.E., Jensen, J.R., and Simonett, D.S. (1984). Impacts of remote sensing on US geography, *Remote Sensing of Environment*, **10**, pp. 43–80.

Eyesight for robots (1984). *Expert Systems* **1**, 1, p. 22.

Fairhall, D. (23 August 1986). Day of the silicon pilot, *Guardian*, p. 15.

Farrington, B. (1953). *Greek Science*, Penguin.

Feigenbaum, E.A., and McCorduck, P. (1983). *The Fifth Generation: Artificial Intelligence and Japan's Computer Challenge to the World*, Michael Joseph.

Ferguson, G.T. (26 march 1984). A letter from users to vendors of application generators, *Computerworld*.

Ferry, G. (13 March 1986). Parallel learning in brains and mechaines, *New Scientist*, pp. 36–8.

Fiber optics points way to speed divergent networks (1 August 1986). *Computer Design*, pp. 48, 51.

Fibres guide the smartest missile in the world (15 May 1986). *New Scientist*, p. 39.

Flatt, J.P. (1963). *Les Trois Premières Machines à Cálculer*, Palais de la Decouverte.

Freedman, L. (1985). *Atlas of Global Strategy*, Macmillan.

Froehlich, L. (1 October 1985). Are smart buildings a dumb idea? *Datamation*, pp. 101–4.

Furst, A. (1 September 1986). Who rules the Chinese electronics industry? *Electronic Business*, pp. 125–8.

Gardner, M. (1958). *Logic Machines and Diagrams*, McGraw-Hill.

Gardner, S. (January 1986). A sensor for every occasion, *Sensor Review*, pp. 49–50.

Garrett, R.C. (April 1978). A natural approach to artificial intelligence, *Interface Age*, pp. 80–3.

Gasman, L. (May 1986). The bypass connection, *High Technology*, pp. 21–7.

Gilson, É. (1955). *History of Christian Civilisation in the Middle Ages*, London.

Gini, M., and Smith, R. (March 1986). Error recovery in robot programs, *IEEE Software*, pp. 59–60.

Goldes, H.J. (October 1983). Designing the human-computer interface, *Educational Technology*, pp. 9–15.

Goldsmith, E., *et al.* (1972). *A Blueprint for Survival*, Tom Stacey.

Goodman (1616), *The Fall of Man, of the Corruption of Nature Proved by the Light of Our Natural Reason*, London.

Gosch, J. (19 May 1986). West Germans shoot for world speed record, *Electronics*, pp. 20–1.

Gottinger, H.W. (1984). Hazard: an expert system for screening environmental chemicals on carcinogenicity, *Expert Systems*, **1**, 2, pp. 169–76.

Gower-Rees, C. (May 1986). Building LANs without cables, *Canadian Datasystems*, pp. 65–6.

Graff, G. (April 1986). Tomorrow's weather: new accuracy in forecasting, *High Technology*, pp. 27–33.

Graff, G. (June 1986). Piezopolymers: good vibrations, *High Technology*, pp. 60–2.

Gregory, R.L. (1981). *Mind in Science*, Weidenfeld & Nicolson.

Grewlich, K.W. (September 1986). Controlling international information economy conflicts, *Transnational Data and Communications Report*, pp. 13–15.

Gribbin, J. (1983). *Future Weather*, Penguin.

Gribbin, J. (ed.). (1986). *The Breathing Planet*, Basic Blackwell/New Scientist.

Gribbin, J. (15 May 1986). Temperatures rise in the global greenhouse, *New Scientist*, pp. 32–3.

Hakewill (1627). *An Apologia of the Power and Providence of God in the Government of the World*.

Hammond, R., and McCullagh, P.S. (eds.) (1974). *Quantitative Techniques in*

Geography, Oxford University Press.

Harvey, K. (April 1986). Towards artificial intelligence in CAE, *CADCAM International*, pp. 75–6.

Hartly, R.T. (March 1984). CRIB: computer fault-finding through knowledge engineering, *Computer*, pp. 76–82.

Hatvany, J. (1985). Intelligence and cooperation in heterarchic manufacturing systems, *Robotics and Computer-Integrated Manufacturing*, **2**, 2, pp. 101–4.

Heginbothem, W.B., Gatehouse, D.W., Pugh, A., Kitchen, P.W., and Page, C.J. (27 March 1973). The Nottingham SIRCH assembly robot, *First Conf. on Industrial Robot Technology*.

Heiland, G., and Kohl, D. (1985). Problems and possibilities of oxidic and organic semiconductor gas sensors, *Sensors and Actuators*, pp. 227–33.

Heims, S.J. (1980). *John von Neumann and Norbert Wiener*, MIT Press.

Helfrich, H.W. (ed.) (1970). *The Environmental Crisis*, Yale University Press.

Hertz, D.B. (19 June 1986). Will the force of Star Wars be with you? *Computer News*, p. 10.

Herzberg, E. (October 1985). Has your office a future? *Business Computing and Communications*, pp. 38–44.

Hodges, A. (1985). *Alan Turing, the Enigma of Intelligence*, Counterpoint, Unwin Paperbacks.

Hofstadter, D.R. (1979). *Gödel, Escher and Bach: An Eternal Golden Braid*, Harvester Press.

Hollingum, J. (January 1986). Investing in the technology for the future, *Sensor Review*, pp. 13–18.

Hollingum, J. (April 1986). Oil and gas industry looks to space, *Sensor Review*, pp. 69–73.

Horne, J.M. (July 1986). Optical-fibre submarine cable systems—the way forward, *British Telecommunications Engineering*, pp. 77–9.

Horne, J.M., and Fitchew, K.D. (February 1986). Network planning: the new opportunities created by submarine optical fibre systems, *Proc. Suboptic 86 Conf.*, Versailles, France, p. 333.

Horne, J.M., and Langridge, K.M. (April 1985). Submarine cable systems—their optical future, *British Telecommunications Engineering*, pp. 14–20.

Howitt, D. (24 December 1984). Inside the computer museum, *InfoWorld*, p. 37.

Hyman, A. (1982). *Charles Babbage, Pionneer of the Computer*, Oxford University Press.

Jacob, V.S., Gaultney, L.D., and Salvendy, G. (1986). Strategies and biases in human decision making and their implications for expert systems, *Behaviouir and Information Technology*, **5**, 2, pp. 119–40.

Jain, R., and Haynes, S. (August 1982). Imprecision in computer vision, *Computer*, pp. 39–47.

Jarvis, R.A. (June 1982). A computer vision and robotics laboratory, *Computer*, pp. 8–22.

Jasani, B., and Lee, C. (1984). *Countdown to Space War*, Taylor & Frances.

Johnson, T. (1985). *Natural Language Computing: the Commercial Applications*, Ovum.

Johnston, R. (6 December 1984). Intelligent robots find their feet, *Computer Weekly*, p. 33.

Johstone, B. (17 April 1986). Japan links light and electronics, *New Scientist*, p. 30.

Jones, B.O. (October 1986). choices in an information age, *Information Age*, pp. 195–9.

Jones, K. (March 1986). Applying development in fibre optic sensors, *Control and Instrumentation*, **18**, 3, pp. 47–9.

Joyce, C. (14 August 1986). Technology transfer through the iron curtain, *New Scientist*, pp. 39–42.

Kapp, K.W. (1971). *The Social Costs of Private Enterprise*, Schocken.

Karlin, B. (1 September 1986). The world according to defence electronics execs, *Electronic Business*, pp. 60–8.

Kellock, B. (7 May 1986). Cummins mixes men with automation, *Machinery and Production Engineering*, pp. 64–70

Kelly, T.J. (July 1986). High test satellite network helps grade unique aircraft, *Data Communications*, pp. 142–7.

Kilmister, C.W. (1967). *Language, Logic and Mathematics*, English Universities Press.

Kim, L. (October 1986). Korean informatics' impressive growth, *Transnational Data and Communications Report*, pp. 11–13.

King, C.A.M., and McCullagh, M.J. (1971). A simulation model of a complex recurved spit, *Journal of Geology*, **79**, 1.

Klotz, J.W. (1972). *Ecology Crisis*, Concordia Press.

Kneale, W., and Kneale, M. (1962). *The Development of Logic*, Oxford University Press.

Kochan, A. (May 1984). Robot vision, *CADCAM International*, pp. 15–16.

Koehler, O. (1956). The ability of birds to count, in Newman, J.R. (ed.), *The World of Mathematics*, New York.

Lakshmanan, T.K. (26 March 1984). Vision gives new perspective on automation, *Computerworld*, pp. SR/11.

Lamb, J. (1 May 1986). Bechtel chose a satellite for plain economic reasons, *Datamation*, pp. 58, 60.

Lamb, J. (11 September 1986). Delegates stress north-south divide, *Computer News*.

Langer, R.M. (1967). comments, in Konecci, E.B. (ed.). *Ecological Technology: Space-Earth-Sea*, Transference of Technology Series No. 1, University of Texas, Austin.

Larcombe, M.H.E. (1981). Carbon fibre tactile sensors, *Proc. First Int. Conf. on Robot Vision and Sensory Control*.

Large, P. (17 October 1986). Who's afraid of IBM? Pretty well everybody, *Financial Guardian*.

Largest communications satellite commissioned (September 1986). *Transnational Data and Communications Report*, p. 3.

Lavington, S. (1980). *Early British Computers*, Manchester University Press.

Lawrence, K. (June 1986). Artificial intelligence in the man/machine interface, *Data Processing*, **28**, p. 5.

Lee, K., and Tortorelli, D.A. (April 1986). Computer-aided design of robotic manipulators, *Computer-Aided Design*, pp. 139–46.

Leng, Y.K. (October 1986). Singapore moving into the information age, *Transnational Data and Communications Report*, pp. 14–17.

Loughlin, C. (October 1986). Vision 86 exposition shows the way ahead, *Sensor Review*, pp. 204–8.

Lovelock, J.E. (1972). Gaia as seen through the atmosphere, *Atmospheric Environment*, **6**, p. 579.

Lovelock, J.E. (1979). *Gaia, a New Look at the Earth*, Oxford University Press.

Lovelock, J.E., and Epton, S.R. (6 February 1975). The quest for Gaia, *New Scientist*.

Lovelock, J.E., and Margulis, L. (1973). Atmospheric homeostasis by and for the biosphere: the Gaia hypothesis, *Tellus*, **26**, 2.

Lowe, C. (January/March 1985). Sensors come alive, *Link-up*, pp. 22–5.

Madsen, A. (1981). *Private Power, Multinational Corporations for the Survival of Our Planet*, Sphere.

Manor, R. (July 1986). Collaboration aids sensors research at Plessey, *Sensor Review*, pp. 123–6.

Mantelman, L. (July 1986). AI carves inroads: network design, testing and management, *Data Communications*, pp. 106–23; see also Turtle geometry: unused AI too opens a window on networking, pp. 127–41.

Marchetti, C. (2 May 1985). Swings, cycles and the global economy, *New Scientist*, pp. 12–15.

Marchuk, G.I. (1974). *Numerical Methods in Weather Prediction*, Academic Press.

Marcus, R.S. (1983). An experimental comparison of the effectiveness of computers and humans as search intermediaries, *Journal of the American Society for Information Science*, **34**, 6, pp. 381–404.

Martin, J. (1978). *Satellite Communications*, Prentice-Hall.

Maury, J.P. (1986). The electronic directory: direct access to 23 million subscriber numbers, *Telecommunications Journal*, **53**, VII, pp. 394–8.

Mayo, J.S. (12 February 1982). Evolution of the intelligent network, *Science*.

McAleer, J.F., Moseley, P.T., Bourke, P., Norris, J.O.W., and Stephan, R. (1985). Tin dioxide gas sensors: use of the Seebeck effect, *Sensors and Actuators*, **8**, pp. 251–7.

McClelland, S. (July 1986). Stimulating new development into applications, *Sensor Review*, pp. 148–9.

McClelland, S. (October 1986). The last word in sensor directories, *Sensor Review*, pp. 202–3.

McDermott, J. (31 October 1984). To think for themselves, computers must first learn some common sense, *Electronic Design*, pp. 83–4.

McHale, J. (1972). Global ecology: towards the planetary society, in Bell, J., and Tyrwhitt, J. (eds.). *Human Identity in the Urban Environment*, Penguin.

McTaggart, T. (7 August 1986). 3COM builds a token bridge between IBM and Ethernet, *Computer News*, p. 24.

Meadows, D.H. (1974). *The Limits to Growth*, Pan.

Medina, S., and Helms, J.F. (September 1985). Designing intelligence into buildings, *Data Communications*, pp. 199–210.

Melville, R., and Koshy, G. (4 September 1986). Steps to a factory network, *Computer News*, p. 29.

Merchant, M.E. (1985). Computer-integrated manufacturing as the basis for the factory of the future, *Robotics and Computer-Integrated Manufacturing*, **2**, 2, pp. 89–99.

Michie, D. (21 February 1980). Turing and the origins of the computer, *New Scientist*, pp. 580–3.

Michie, D. (17 July 1980). P-KP4: expand system to human being conceptual checkmate of dark ingenuity, *Computing*.

Miller, A. (1979). *Elements of Meteorology*, Charles E. Merrill.

Mills, J.F. (1983). *Encyclopedia of Antique Scientific Instruments*, Aurum Press.

Mingzhang, H. (1 September 1986). China builds a microelectronics industry, *Electronic Business*, pp. 130–1.

Minsky, M.L. (ed). (1968). *Semantic Information Processing*, MIT Press, Cambridge, Mass.

Moon, D. (October 1985). Developing standards smooth the integration of programmable factory floor devices, *Control Engineering*, pp. 49–52.

Morham, W.H. (March 1984). Intelligent vision in automated factories, *Data Processing*, pp. 67–9.

Morris, H.M. (March 1983). Adding sensory inputs to robotic systems increases manufacturing flexibility, *Control Engineering*, pp. 65–8.

Morrison, P., and Morrison, E. (eds.) (1961). *Charles Babbage and his Calculating Engines*, Dover.

Mosco, V. (1985). Star wars/earth wars, in *Issues in Radical Science*, edited by Radical Science Collective, Free Association Books.

Mostert, N. (1975). *Supership*. Macmillan.

Mulqueen, J.T. (July 1986). Corporate uses of public data networks are on the rise, *Data Communications*, pp. 85–92.

Myers, N. (ed.) (1985). *The Gaia Atlas of Planet Management*, Pan.

Naegele, T. (22 April 1985). Speech technology leaves the realm of science fiction, *Electronics Week*, pp. 61–3.

Naisbitt, J. (1984). *Megatrends, Ten New Directions Transforming our Lives*, Futura.

Naisbitt, J. (1985). *The Year Ahead–1986*, Futura.

Nance, J. (November 1983). Implementation strategies for voice-processing terminals, *Mini-Micro Systems*, pp. 183–94.

Naylor, C. (27 February 1984). *Computer Talk*.

Needle, D., and Besher, A. (12 November 1984). Computing inside the USSR, *Computing*, pp. 27–31.

Nelson, G., and Rendell, D. (1986). The Star Wars computer system, *Abacus*, **3**, 2, pp. 8–20.

Nelson, P. (October 1985). Build your factory floor communications from a MAP base, *Control Engineering*, pp. 44–5.

Nevins, J.L. (20 September 1976). *Advanced Automation Systems and Manipulation Robots Course*, Toulouse, **2**, p. 1.

Newquist, H.P. (18 August 1986). Chips for brains: computers built with neural networks, *Computerworld*, p. 17.

Newton, A.R., and Sangiovanni-Vincentelli, A.L. (April 1986). Computer aided design for VSLI circuits, *Computer*, pp. 38–60.

Neild, T. (22 May 1986). Safe routes for undersea cables, *New Scientist*, pp. 38–41.

Nobile, P., and Deedy, J. (1972). *The Complete Ecology Fact Book*, Anchor.

Novosti Press Agency (11 October 1984). Russian doubles micro output, *Computer Weekly*, p. 33.

Onda, H., and Ohashi, Y. (September 1979). Introduction of visual equipment to inspection, *Industrial Robot*, pp. 131–5.

O'Neill, G.K. (1986). The 'Geostar' radio determination satellite system, *Telecommunications Journal*, **53**, pp. 257–65.

Optoelectronics builds viable neural-net memory (16 June 1986). *Electronics*, pp. 41–4.

Osman, T. (5 October 1986). Beaming in laser power, *Sunday Times*, p. 80.

Packard, V. (1960). *The Waste Makers*, Pelican.

Page, J., Pugh, A., and Heginbotham, W.B. (1976). *Radio and Electronic Engineer*, **46**.

Parkins, A.E., and Whitaker, J.R. (1939). *Our Natural Resources and their Conservation*, Wiley.

Parnas, D.L. (December 1985). Software aspects of strategic defence systems, *Communications of the ACM*, pp. 1326–35.

Partridge, C. (14 September 1986). Chips down for silicon design, *Sunday Times*, p. 80.

Pedler, K. (1979). *The Quest for Gaia*, Granada.

Pennywitt, K.E. (January 1986). Robotic tactile sensing, *Byte*, pp. 177–200.

Perlmutter, H.V. (May 1965), L'Enterprise internationale—trois conceptions, *Revue économique et sociale*, **23**, 2, pp. 151–65.

Perrier, L. (1963). *Gilberte Pascal: Bibliographie de Pascal*.

Phillipson, J. (1966). *Ecological Energetics*, Edward Arnold.

Pournelle, J. (September 1983). The next five years in microcomputers, *Byte*, pp. 233–44.

Preiss, K. (July 1983). Future CAD systems, *Computer-Aided Design*, **15**, 4, pp. 223–7.

Pruski, A. (July 1986). Surface contact sensor for robot safety, *Sensor Review*, pp. 143–4.

Puccetti, R. (1963). *Persons, a study of Possible Moral Agents in the Universe*, Macmillan.

Purbrick, J.A. (1981). A force trasducer employing conductive silicone rubber, *Proc. First Int. Conf. on Robot Vision and Sensory Controls*.

Push for connectivity, The (May 1986). *EDP Analyzer*, pp. 1–12.

Pye, C. (1986). Interworking with MAP, *Systems International*, pp. 65–6.

Quinlan, J.R. (1983). INFERNO: a cautious approach to uncertain inference, *Computer Journal*, **26**, 3, pp. 255–69.

Radargrammetry: a state of the art (December 1985). *Earth Observation Quarterly*, 12.

Randell, B. (1977). *The Colossus*, University of Newcastle, Computer Science Technical Report 90; reprinted in condensed form in *New Scientist*, **73**, pp. 346–8.

Ranner, P.J., Horne, J.M., and Frisch, D.A. (July 1986). Submarine optical-fibre cable systems: future trends, *British Telecommunications Engineering*, pp. 183-7.

Raphael, B. (1976). *The Thinking Computer*, W.H. Freeman.

Reich, R.B. (1984). *The Next American Frontier*, Penguin.

Reid, T.R. (1985). *Microchip*, Pan.

Rensberger, B. (7 November 1985). The Star Wars bug, *Computer Guardian*.

Resources and Man (1969). Committee on Resources and Man, National Academy of Sciences—National Research Council, Freeman & Co., San Francisco.

Rifkin, G. (14 April 1986). On beyond silicon, *Computerworld*, pp. 49-62.

Rifkin, J. (May 1983). The other half of the computer revolution, *Datamation*, pp. 260-78.

Roberts, R.D., and Roberts, T.M. (eds.) (1984). *Planning and Ecology*, Chapman & Hall.

Robertson, B.E., and Walkden, A.J. (1983). Tactile sensor system for robotics, *Proc. Third Int. Symp. on Robot Vision and Sensory Controls*.

Robinson, A., and Hage, P. (July 1986). Co-ordinating vision and tactile sensing with robotics, *Sensor Review*, pp. 130-2.

Robinson, H.W., and Knight, D.E. (eds.) (1972). *Cybernetics, Artificial Intelligence and Ecology*, Spartan Books.

Robots look ahead (December 1984). *Engineering*, pp. 906-8.

Robot vision: aiming to match human eye (May 1983). *Production Engineer*, pp. 45-6.

Rogers, E.M. and Larsen, J.K. (1985). *Silicon Valley Fever*, George Allen & Unwin.

Romberg, F.A., and Thomas, A.B. (26 March 1984). Reusable code, reliable software, *Computerworld*.

Rooks, B. (January 1986). Tackling the speed-cost problem of machine vision, *Sensor Review*, pp. 33-5.

Rooks, B.W. (April 1986). Sensors start to play a role in intelligent assembly systems, *Sensor Review*, pp. 83-5.

Russell, P. (1984). *The Awakening Earth, the Global Brain*, Arc Paperbacks, Routledge & Kegan Paul.

Sato, N., Heginbotham, W.B., and Pugh, A. (1979). *Proc. Seventh Int. Symp. on Industrial Robots*.

Schank, R.C., and Childers, P.G. (12 November 1984). Experiments in artificial intelligence, *Computerworld*, pp. ID/1-ID/28.

Scheibe, K.E., and Erwin, M. (1980). *Journal of Social Psychology*, **108**, 2.

Schneiter, J.L., and Sheridan, T.B. (1984). An optical tactile sensor for manipulators, *Robotics and Computer-Aided Manufacturing*, **1**, 1, pp. 65-71.

Schumacher, E.F. (1974). *Small is beautiful*, Abacus.

Segerdal, A. (10 May 1984). Taking a moral stand over the nuclear crisis, *Computing*, pp. 24-5.

Shapland, D., and Rycroft, M. (1984). *Spacelab, Research in Earth Orbit*, Cambridge University Press.

Sharma, C. (1960). *A Critical Survey of Indian Philosophy*, Rider.

Simon, J.L. (15 May 1986). Disappearing species, deforestation and data, *New Scientist*, pp. 60-3.

Simons, G.L. (1983a). *Are Computers Alive?* Harvester Press.

Simons, G.L. (1983b). *Towards Fifth-Generation Computers*, NCC Publications.

Simons, G.L. (1985a). *The Biology of Computer Life*, Harvester Press.

Simons, G.L. (1985b). *Silicon Shock*, Basic Blackwell.

Simons, G.L. (1986). *Is Man a Robot?* John Wiley.

Smith, D.E., and Ginsburg, J. (1956). From numbers to numerals and from numerals to computation, in Newman, J.R. (ed.), *The World of Mathematics*, vol. 1, New York.

Smith, J.V. (17 April 1986). The defence of the Earth, *New Scientist*, pp. 40-4.

Snyder, E.E. (1971). *Please Stop Killing Me*, Signet.

Software: a Vital Key to UK Competitiveness (1986). Advisory Council for Applied Research and Development.

Sorensen, A.B. (1978). Mathematical models in sociology, *Annual Review of Sociology*, vol. 4, Annual Reviews, Palo Alto, California.

Sorenson, K. (9 June 1986). Fifth generation slow to rise, *InfoWorld*, pp. 34-6.

Speller, G.J., and Brandon, J.A. (1986). Ethical dilemmas constraining the use of expert systems, *Behaviour and Information Technology*, **5**, 2, pp. 141-3.

Sprague de Camp, L. (1977). *Ancient Engineers*, Tandem.

Still, H. (1967). *The Dirty Animal*, Hawthorn, New York.

Stonier, T. (September 1986). Intelligence networks, overview, purpose and policies in the context of global social change, *Aslib Proceedings*, pp. 269-74.

Stopford, J.M., and Turner, L. (1985). *Britain and the Multinationals*, John Wiley.

Storr, G. (January 1986). A sense of awareness? *Personal Computer World*, pp. 168-74.

Strehl, R. (1955). *The Robots are Among Us*, Arco.

Stute, G., and Erne, H. (1979). The control design of an industrial robot with advance tactile sensitivity, *Proc. Ninth Int. Symp. on Industrial Robots*, pp. 519-20.

Susca, P. (May 1986). Word processors play key role in consulting firm's communiations, *Data Communications*, pp. 242-51.

Szuprowicz, B. (12 May 1986). VLSI microsensors: the eyes and ears of future computers, *Computerworld*, p. 172.

Takahashi, T. (1986). Report on the INS experiment, *Computer Networks and ISDN Syustems*, **11**, pp. 269-76.

Tate, P. (1 May 1986). Send it by satellite, *Datamation*, pp. 55-6.

Taylor, R.H., Hollis, R.L., and Lavin, M.A. (July 1985). Precise manipulation with endpoint sensing, *IBM Journal of Research and Development*, pp. 363-76.

Thring, M.W. (1983). *Robots and Telechirs*, Ellis Horwood.

Tucker, M. (July 1986). Coming next from Japan: the bionic computer? *Mini-Micro Systems*, pp. 28-9.

Turing, A.M. (1936). On computable numbers, with an application to the Entscheidungs problem, *Proceedings of the London Mathematical Society*, Series, 2, **42**, pp. 230-65; Corrigenda in **43**, pp. 544-6.

Turing, A.M. (February 1946). *Proposals for the Development in the Mathematical Division of an Automatic Computing Engine (ACE,* Report E882, Executive Committee, NPL.

Turing, A.M. (1950). Computing machinery and intelligence , *MIND,* lix, p. 236.

Turkle, S. (1984). *The Second Self: Computers and the Human Spirit,* Simon & Schuster.

Turner, L. (1970). *Invisible Empires, Multinational Companies and the Modern World,* Hamish Hamilton.

Umetami, (1980). *Tokyo Institute of Technology Résumé of Work on Systems and Bioengineering,* Tokyo Institute of Technology.

von Neumann, J. (June 1945). *Report on the EDVAC;* later incorporated in Burks, A.W., Goldstine, H.H., and von Neumann, J. (June 1946). *Preliminary Discussion of the Logical Design of an Electronic Computing Instrument,* Institute for Advanced Study, Princeton; reprinted in Randell, B. (1973). *The Origins of Digital Computers,* Springer-Verlag.

Vranish, J.M. (1984). Magnetoresistive skin for robots, *Proc. Fourth Int. Conf. on Robot Vision and Sensory Controls.*

Waller, L. (9 June 1986). Why the Pentagon will speed up IR-sensor work, *Electronics,* pp. 40-1.

Walton, P. (4 June 1986). Grabbing a slice of the SDI action, *Electronics Weekley,* p. 11.

Walton, W.C. (1970). *Groundwater Resource Evaluation,* McGraw-Hill.

Ward, B., and Dubos, R. (1972). *Only One Earth,* Pelican.

Warner, E. (1 October 1984). Vision system seen changing the face of robotics industry, *Computerworld,* p. 68.

Why computers must communicate (17 September 1986). *Machinery and Production Engineering,* pp. 60-1.

Wilder, C. (9 June 1986). Connectivity, strategic DP top user concerns on eve of NCC, *Computerworld,* pp. 49-53.

Wilkes, M.V. (July 1975). Early computer developments at Cambridge: the EDSAC, *Radio and Electronic Engineer,* **45,** pp. 332-5.

Williams, T. (July 1986). Defence systems—the high road of SDI, *Computer Design,* pp. 123-31.

Williamson, M. (1 September 1986). MAP grows up: version-filled road to maturity a rocky one, *Computerworld,* p. 49.

Winter, H.J.J. (1952). *Eastern Science,* John Murray.

Wirl, C. (September 1985). What's the best way to wire a new building for data? *Data Communications,* pp. 154-71.

Wise, W. (1968). *Killer Smog,* Rand McNally.

Wood, H.W., Reifer, D.J., and Sloan, M. (January 1985). A tour of computing facilities in China, *Computer,* pp. 80-7.

Woodfine, R.T. (July 1986). Submarine cable system user requirements, *British Telecommunications Engineering,* pp. 75-6.

Woodling, G. (September 1986). Corporate intelligence networks, *Aslib Proceedings,* pp. 285-95.

Worldwide sensor scene brought into focus (October 1986). *Sensor Review,* pp. 193-6.

Wright, M.L., Green, M.W., Fiegl, G., and Cross, P.F. (March 1986). An expert system for real-time control, *IEEE Software*, pp. 16–24.

Yachida, M., and Tsuji, S. (May 1980). Industrial computer vision in Japan, *Computer*, pp. 50–63.

Youett, C. (September 1984). Defence all our tomorrows, *Communications Management*, pp. 52–7.

Zadeh, L.A. (interviewee) (April 1984). Coping with the imprecision of the real world, *Communications of the ACM*, **87**, 4, pp. 304–11.

Zadeh, L.A. (1965). Fuzzy sets, *Information and Control*, **8**, pp. 338–53.

Index